HERE ARE THE QUESTIONS . . .

°If the pyramids are supposed to be tombs for the pharaohs—why were no pharaohs ever buried in them?

°Who carved the Great Sphinx—five thousand years before the first Egyptian Kingdom came into being?

°How did the gigantic stones get to Stonehenge?

°What are huge underwater stone walls doing off the coast of the Bahamas . . . in the place seer Edgar Cayce said Atlantis once existed?

°What caused the "vanishings" in the Bermuda Triangle, including the loss of the *Sea Venture* in 1609 and the ghost ships of the 1800s?

°How did the primitive Easter Islanders move twenty-five-ton statues onto pedestals constructed *hundreds of years earlier*?

°What does modern pathology show about the man whose image appears on the Shroud of Turin?

°How did the surgeons of India learn to perform cataract surgery . . . *three thousand years ago*?

°What does recent evidence show about the most ancient mystery of all—life after death?

NOW DISCOVER THE SHOCKING ANSWERS IN
CHARLES E. SELLIER'S
MYSTERIES OF THE ANCIENT WORLD

MYSTERIES
OF THE
ANCIENT WORLD

Charles E. Sellier

A DELL BOOK

Published by
Dell Publishing
a division of
Bantam Doubleday Dell Publishing Group, Inc.
1540 Broadway
New York, New York 10036

ISBN: 0-440-21805-5

Printed in the United States of America

Published simultaneously in Canada

November 1995

10 9 8 7 6 5 4 3 2 1

OPM

To Patrick Frawley, Jr., who taught
me that the pursuit of a mystery is
an admirable trait

ACKNOWLEDGMENT

I want to express my deep appreciation to Joe Meier for his editorial assistance on this book. We wish the reader as much joy in reading about these discoveries as we had in researching them.

CONTENTS

1

A WORLD OF MYSTERIES

Mystery: 1. Something that is not or cannot be known, understood, or explained. 2. Any action, affair, or thing that arouses curiosity or suspense because it is not fully revealed. Obscurity or darkness: [something that has] baffling character or properties.[1]

[1] *Funk & Wagnalls*, Standard Encyclopedic Dictionary, p. 431.

As I BEGIN THIS BOOK IT ONLY SEEMS FAIR TO CON-fess that I have always been drawn to the mysteries of this world in which we live. Even as a student I found myself captivated by those events in history that could not be understood or explained. It is perhaps not too surprising then that my sense of curiosity has, over the past twenty-plus years, led me to try to find answers to some of these mysteries, to seek explanations where none seem to exist, and bring events hidden in obscurity out into the light, where they can be examined carefully and critically.

On second thought, it's probably something more than just a sense of curiosity that made me want to go into the Bermuda Triangle, for example. In this strange part of the world, sudden squalls erupt out of nowhere. Sometimes an almost explosive calm descends upon the ocean and seems to suck every sound out of the universe. The hair stands up on the back of your neck and your skin tingles as you realize that hundreds, even thousands of people have disappeared here without a trace.

No, it would have to be more than just curiosity. It is, in fact, a fascination with the mysteries of the world that has held my interest ever since I can remember. I am fascinated by the fact that some ancient people living on the earth left great monuments to something or other, and to this day we don't know precisely what. More important, we don't know how those monuments were built. Herodotus, the ancient Greek historian, stood in awe before the Great Pyramid of Cheops and tried to give us an explanation of how it came to be. The Great Pyramid, he wrote, was built in twenty years by work teams of a hundred thousand men who were rotated every three months. Egyptologists today blandly accept his supposed findings in spite of a growing body of evidence to the contrary.

Alexander the Great and Napoleon both sought the solution to the mystery of the Great Pyramid and both were unsuccessful. But modern archaeologists fare no better. They assure us the pyramids were built as burial tombs for the pharaohs even though no king or consort has ever been found in any pyramid. To the contrary, the tombs of the pharaohs appear to be in the Valley of the Kings, some three hundred miles from the nearest pyramid. But even if the pyramids are gigantic tombs built to venerate Egyptian god-kings, that doesn't begin to explain the remarkable mathematical precision or the astronomical, geometric, and geologic science employed in their construction. And it doesn't explain why, with all our modern technology—computers, lasers, satellites—we still can't figure out how the ancients did it.

What did they know that we don't? More to the point, where did they learn it?

There's another very basic question that needs to be asked as well: Why do we care? What difference can it possibly make to you or me if none of these mysteries is ever resolved? The answer to that question, of course, depends a great deal on the person doing the asking. But it seems to me that if there is in fact some verifiable connection between the Great Pyramid at Giza and the face that has been identified on the planet Mars, most of us will have to reexamine our view of the universe and our place in it.

A term I have run across a great many times in my travels through the realms of the mysterious is "scholarly consensus." I have been amazed at how frequently the "scholarly consensus" proves to be wrong. Throughout history scholars have charted a path for the rest of us to follow only to have us discover later on that it's the wrong one. Scholars insisted the world was flat until Columbus proved them wrong. Galileo paid a terrible price for pointing out to the scholars of his day that the Sun, not the Earth, was the center of the solar system. The medieval physician, Nostradamus, was shunned by the medical community for refusing to "bleed" his patients. Yet, each of these men, by solving one of the mysteries in his world, brought enlightenment to all humankind. We learned, we grew, we became more than we were because of these discoveries.

The mysteries that are left for us to solve could have a similarly dramatic impact on our lives. For example, there is a piece of ancient linen cloth held in veneration in a church in Turin, Italy. Armies have been raised to procure it. Knights were burned at the stake for refusing to reveal its whereabouts. Its long history includes stories of miraculous cures, earthquakes, fire, and conquest. The only thing that sets this piece of cloth apart from thousands of others discovered in burial tombs around the world is that this particular piece of cloth appears to have impressed upon it the image of the man who was buried in it. Could this be the burial shroud of Jesus Christ?

Today the scholarly consensus seems to be that the shroud is a medieval forgery. But within the past two decades a team of forty scientists has spent in excess of 150,000 man-hours studying and testing this piece of linen. The results of their findings are astonishing. Could we be on the verge of scientific proof of the Resurrection? What impact would the solution to this mystery have on civilization as we know it?

There are thousands of mysteries that might have been chosen for this work. Charles Berlitz, author of *The Bermuda Triangle* and several other books on strange occurrences, listed no less than 331 such events in just one of his books.[2] In addition, there are literally hundreds of authors and investigators devoting their entire lives and careers to events, both real and imagined, that make up the realm of the mysterious and unknown.

My own fascination with the mysteries of the world, coupled with a life-long career as an author and a movie maker, has given me the opportunity to investigate many of these strange and wonderful places and things first-hand. And the more I learn, the more I realize how exciting a new discovery can be and . . . how little we truly know about our world. So some care has been taken in the selection process for this book. I wanted to be sure the discussion would be enlightening as well as entertaining. As a consequence, some of the mysteries that have been chosen for inclusion you have probably heard about and—to this point at least—they are unsolvable by any modern means.

Perhaps the insights and information I have been able to gather over the years will put this beautiful but perplexing world in a little clearer light for readers who have not had the same opportunities to travel and explore.

[2] *Charles Berlitz*, World of Strange Phenomena, *1988.*

In addition to those mysteries already mentioned, we will be exploring several other unresolved puzzles and enigmas.

We like to think we have explored every nook and cranny of our home planet, but apparently we have not. Modern sonar equipment has tracked at least two very large, rapidly moving objects deep beneath the surface of Loch Ness in Scotland. Could it be that not all the dinosaurs died out? Descriptions and a number of photographs have been offered as evidence that the Loch Ness monster does in fact exist, and that it looks very much like a prehistoric amphibian. And if the Loch Ness monster survived whatever catastrophe destroyed the dinosaurs, isn't it possible that there could be other survivors yet to be discovered?

Modern man tends to look upon himself as being on the top rung of the evolutionary ladder. If that is true, why haven't we been able to figure out how a relatively small population of natives on an isolated Pacific island moved twenty- to thirty-ton statues over rocky terrain without scarring them, and then stood them upright and put a five- to ten-ton hat on top of each statue's head? How did they do that?

If we are so smart, how is it that in nearly two hundred years no one has been able to discover what lies buried in a concrete and oaken vault 180 feet beneath the surface of Oak Island in Nova Scotia? Thousands of man-hours and millions of dollars have been spent trying to solve a puzzle created by some nameless and long-forgotten engineer who devised an ingenious means of protecting his buried "treasure." To date there are only theories and an ongoing embarrassment for the world engineering community. What lies hidden in the money pit of Oak Island? Who put it there? And to paraphrase an old nursery rhyme, why can't all the king's horses and all the king's men figure out how to get their hands on it again?

Then there are some so-called mysteries whose origins are so completely lost in antiquity that it is impossible to discover whether or not the event involved ever happened or the people ever existed. Accepting the notion that there were six planets revolving around the Sun created an upheaval in religion and science that reverberated down through the centuries until it finally came to be accepted as fact. Of course, just in the last century we have discovered that there are nine planets in our solar system, a fact confirmed by telescopes of amazing power.

How could it possibly be, then, that ancient Sumerian texts, mankind's oldest written records, dating back ten thousand years, speak of twelve planets? The Sumerians counted the Moon and the Sun as planets, and they suggest there was yet another planet between Earth and Mars. And even more astonishing, how could they know that they should number the Earth as the "seventh" planet, which it is, if you are counting from the outside rim of the solar system in toward the Sun? Modern astronomers, of course, refer to the Earth as the "third" planet, counting from the Sun outward. Until this century the scholarly world didn't know those other planets were out there. Did the Sumerians have access to information we didn't? Or were they just lucky guessers? Maybe we . . . or they . . . just imagined the whole thing. It's going to be fun to find out.

In the past twenty-one years, I have been to the Bermuda Triangle, sought mysterious monsters the world over, looked at life beyond death's door, tried to find solutions to the mystery of possible evidence of aliens from outer space, and explored the world of psychic phenomena. I have found in people wherever I go a fascination for mysteries that stretch all the way from Sleepy Hollow to the top of Mount Ararat. In this book we attempt to discover, perhaps for the first time, some definitive answers to many of those mysteries.

Did a French physician living over 400 years ago actually predict the tragic loss of the space shuttle *Challenger*? Could the same man have also predicted the rise of Hitler and the assassination of both Kennedy brothers? The man's name is Nostradamus, and if he did make those amazing predictions, we had better start paying more attention to his writings because he has had some frightening things to say about events in our very near future.

Nostradamus is perhaps the most famous of all the seers outside the Bible, but he is by no means the only person to have the "gift" of foresight. This is another of the world's great mysteries we'll be examining in some detail. Is there such a thing as clairvoyance or ESP? Can certain people—or can all people—somehow tap into the cosmic hot line and listen in on the future?

Given the limits of space we won't be able to explore in this book all of the world's great enigmas, of course, but one we will be sure to investigate is a tiny speck of land lost in the vast reaches of the South Pacific that holds one of the world's most incredible mysteries: the great stone giants of Easter Island. This is one stop that we, along with Captain Cook and Thor Heyerdahl, simply have to make. Some of these mystifying statues are still lying in their mountain quarry, others are buried chest deep in the island sand, and still others are standing on pedestals and wearing huge stone topknots. So far these huge hand-carved monoliths have defied all attempts to determine how they got from their ancient bed in the mountain to the seashore, a distance of some twenty miles. How could these primitive island people, cut off from any other culture by literally thousands of miles of ocean, move these great stone carvings such a distance? How did they stand them up? On pedestals? And how did they get stone hats, or "topknots," situated securely on their heads?

All such mysteries appear to have one thing in common: They transcend the barrier of time no matter where they occur in the world. One of our modern enigmas, UFOs, or unidentified flying objects, may have had an exact counterpart in ancient times. Certain hieroglyphic and archaeological evidence from various parts of the world seems to suggest that very early civilizations were dealing with the same problem. Could the Bible, as some experts suggest, be a living record of outer-space aliens of some sort coming to Earth? And what of the huge land carvings that depict animals, spiders, and men but can be discerned only from great heights? Did ancient visitors, capable of flight, carve them? What earthly purpose could they have? All we really know is . . . they are there. That fact is indisputable. That they serve no *earthly* purpose we know of is likewise not arguable. Why, then, are they there? Who constructed, or supervised, their construction? Are extraterrestrials a part of our life history that we have as yet refused to accept? A great adventure lies just ahead in the chapter on aliens.

Speaking of aliens, there are those who attribute the legend of Atlantis to some alien culture. The theories are many and diverse and date back to antiquity, but all we know for sure is that the legend of Atlantis originated with the great Greek philosopher Plato. Some experts say he was merely translating much older

Egyptian hieroglyphics. If that's true, how did the ancient Egyptians find out about it?

According to Plato, Atlantis was an earthly paradise with a large and thriving population. Yet, in a single day and a night, this mighty empire disappeared into the sea. The mystery has been with us for some nine thousand years.[3] In spite of its antiquity, the story is still maintained by many with verve and imagination.

Edgar Cayce predicted that parts of Atlantis would be discovered sometime in the 1960s. And, indeed, it may have been. No one is quite sure what we are looking for, or precisely where to find it, but remnants of columns, foundations, and stone roadways have been found under the sea. Could they be portions of the lost city of Atlantis?

Not all of the world's mysteries have to do with places and events, however. Some of the most perplexing enigmas have to do with what can only be described as "things," or "creatures": The Loch Ness monster in the deep lakes of Scotland is only one of many. Others include Bigfoot, roaming the forests of the Pacific Northwest, the Abominable Snowman of the mountains of Tibet, and Ogopogo, a huge creature that inhabits Lake Okanagan in southern Canada. All of these creatures, and more, have fired the imagination of people the world over for generations. Yet, for all of the sightings, footprints, photographs, and/or film, no one can say for sure that any of them actually exist. Some insist they are all just hoaxes perpetrated on a gullible population eager to find monsters behind every bush or snowbank. That may be, but on closer examination we discover a broad base of scientific evidence beginning to emerge suggesting there is more to these

[3] *Charles Berlitz,* The Mystery of Atlantis, *p. 12.*

phenomena than the "scholarly consensus" might think. Much of this evidence has been made available in just the past decade or so. Some of it you may be reading about for the first time.

One thing we can be sure of: The facts as to what these creatures are and where they might have come from have proved to be as elusive as the creatures themselves. One of the few examples of concrete evidence was recently hauled in by Japanese fishermen. The decaying remains of a large and previously unknown sea creature has a general shape and dimensions that closely match the description given by those who claim to have seen "Nessy," the Loch Ness monster. Could it be that we still share this Earth with living beings from another age, or perhaps even another planet?

And there are still other mysteries we'll be delving into, mysteries that have the capacity to keep us humble. But then maybe it's good for us to be reminded occasionally that we are not the repository of all wisdom.

Most of us hear the term "modern medicine," and we just assume that our day and age is the beneficiary of medical miracles never before known to man. Yet ancient physicians used techniques today's doctors think they invented. In the third century B.C., Etruscan dentists were using gold in Etruscan mouths. Pre-Columbian, Peruvian surgeons performed brain surgery, apparently routinely. A passage in the Code of Hammurabi suggests that Babylonian physicians were familiar with cataract surgery twenty-six hundred years ago. And ancient Hindu surgeons invented a method of rebuilding noses that is still used in the twentieth century. How could these primitive practitioners have known what it has taken others three thousand years to learn? The question is fairly asked, even if we don't yet have the answer.

Then, of course, there is the most enduring of all mysteries, the great, unknowable, and much discussed mystery of life after life. What is the future beyond what we euphemistically call "this vale of tears"? What evidence do we have that there is anything beyond what we know and can see around us? Is the grave, indeed, a final resting place, or simply a portal to something beyond? Kings and commoners from the beginning of time have sought an answer to that question, and except for those who have made the journey, all of them, so far as we know, have been more or less unsuccessful in finding the answer. And perhaps it's better that way. If we knew for certain that something else, something far better, lay beyond the grave, how many of us would continue the struggle here?

There are places we can still go on this planet, things we can touch that for hundreds, even thousands of years have evoked the deepest sense of mystery and awe in all of us. Yet in spite of all our knowledge and technology we are no closer to understanding them than were our ancient forebears. With all our gathered wisdom we still cannot penetrate the veil of mystery that would tell us how Stonehenge was built or why the Great Pyramid is located precisely at the center of the earth's landmass. We have theories and guesses, but we don't know whether there is (or ever was) an "Atlantis," or if flying saucers visit us from outer space. The Bermuda Triangle intrigues, even frightens us and we're not sure why. Monsters may or may not roam the high mountains or slink through the icy waters of great inland lakes. Some claim to have seen them, but to this point at least, we can't be sure.

Or can we?

In the process of exploring these mysteries in the following pages, we will have the opportunity to uncover new facts and discover previously overlooked bits of evidence. Hidden away in the dark corners of ancient history are clues that can illuminate the future. Many of them have been discovered by modern scientists and investigators, and they can now be understood . . . and criticized as never before.

Oh yes, the critics will have their say. Virtually every mystery presents us with at least two points of view, and some of them offer many more. There have been over eighty translations of the Nostradamus quatrains, for example, in Europe *alone*! But then that's all part of the excitement of discovery. The man who gave up a lucrative job and a comfortable home in Florida to spend over twenty years digging in the freezing mud of Oak Island has earned the right to argue with those who say there is nothing there and never has been. The three scientists who conducted the carbon-14 tests on the shroud of Turin face off squarely with the forty other scientists who come to a completely different conclusion. On which side does the weight of the evidence fall? You get to decide.

Someone once said that everyone loves a mystery. I'm not sure the sentiment is entirely universal, but I certainly do. My goal is to share that love of mystery by taking you on a journey through the greatest mysteries of the ages. Open up your mind to *all* of the possibilities. It is a wondrous experience.

Our journey begins by candlelight. In a small room accessible only by a narrow wooden staircase, a man sits on a three-legged stool and stares into a brass bowl hung from a metal tripod and filled with some dark liquid. A single candle placed upon a crude writing desk behind the man struggles against the darkness but loses the battle before it reaches the rough stone walls.

There is a sharp intake of breath and the man sits upright, his eyes never leaving the brass bowl. In a moment his shoulders sag and he turns to the writing desk and picks up one of the sharpened quills lying next to a much used inkwell. With resignation he begins to place words on the page. He pauses only briefly as a tear splashes onto the rough parchment and he is forced to avoid that particular spot as he continues to write.

Hundreds of years later, in laboratories and libraries the world over, students and scholars alike will stand in awe of the mystery created by this one lonely man.

2

NOSTRADAMUS—PHYSICIAN, POET, SEER

"Sitting alone at night in a secret study; it is placed on the brass tripod.
A slight flame comes out of the emptiness and prophesies that which should not be believed in vain."

Nostradamus

THE VERY NAME OF NOSTRADAMUS CONJURES UP one of the most enduring mysteries of the ancient and the modern world.

From time immemorial there have been those who have claimed to be able to see into the future. And there have been those in every epoch of man's existence who have strenuously resisted the notion that anyone, by whatever name, can know what lies beyond what they can see, touch, and feel.

To these people, the ancient prophets of the biblical record were simply manipulating an unlearned and superstitious people. Indeed, the argument is much the same today. Either the charlatans have gotten more clever or people generally are still primitive and superstitious.

In biblical times the problem was easily resolved. If a prophet was wrong, that is to say if his prophecies failed to come true, he was simply stoned to death. And who can forget King Nebuchadnezzar ordering the death of *all* of his priests, magicians, and astrologers simply because none of them could tell him what he had dreamed the night before. Later on, magicians, astrologers, and other soothsayers who lacked or lost the patronage of the king or consort were likely to suffer a similar fate if their predictions proved to be less than sound. But the point is, there were kings, potentates, judges, and tyrants of every stripe who *believed* what their prophets or magicians told them.

Down through the ages kings did not lose their desire to know what the future would bring, nor did they lose their inclination to punish the "prophets" if the future did not turn out to be to their liking.

All of this did not prevent prophets from prophesying, nor did it change the fact that while many predictions proved to be wrong, a great many proved to be uncannily accurate. Which means the mystery and the unanswered question is still with us. Is it possible for someone to see into the future and truly know what the future will bring?

To those who have slipped the bonds of primitive superstition and found refuge in the comfortable realms of science, the answer is an instantaneous no! Science recognizes only matter and energy. The principles that apply to the physical, then, when they are duly applied to the nonphysical, even the spiritual, to no one's great surprise, just don't work. Therefore, anything that is not subject to the laws of matter and energy, according to scientific theory, simply cannot exist. Prescience, clairvoyance, prophecy, seership, even astrological calculations, which at the very least pretends to have a scientific base, are all summarily denied by those who ascribe to that theory.

The phenomenon of clairvoyance, by its various and sundry names, does exist and has existed for thousands of years. Such great thinkers as Plato, St. Augustine, Kant, and Schopenhauer did not doubt the existence of this power,[4] even though none of them could explain it.

---

[4] *Arthur Prieditis*, The Fate of the Nations, *p. x.*

Modern scientists also despair of explaining clairvoyance (though some have tried), and for that matter, so do the practitioners themselves. To them it is simply "a gift." If that is true, then Nostradamus was the most richly endowed of all recipients of this marvelous gift, either before or since his comparatively brief lifetime. What's more, both in terms of time and distance, his range seems to go far beyond that of any other practitioner of this lonely art.

For example, William Lilly, an English astrologer, was among the seers who foresaw the Great Fire of London and the plague that followed. In 1648, eighteen years before the event, his prophecies were published: "[I]t will be ominous to London, unto her merchants at sea, to her traffique on land, to her poor, to all sorts of people, inhabiting in her or to her liberties, by reason of sundry fires and a consuming plague."[5]

But a hundred and eleven years *earlier* Nostradamus had already written, "The blood of the just requires London to be burned with fire in sixty-six."[6]

The Great Fire of London did indeed reduce much of the city to ashes in 1666. From a small village in France, Nostradamus's remarkable gift of prophecy stretched across a century and a continent to watch the largest city in England go up in flames. It is precisely this remarkable reach into the future and into other lands and cultures that has fascinated Nostradamus researchers for centuries.

Still, by and large, mainstream science ignores what has come to be called the "occult sciences." To quote Arthur Prieditis, author of *The Fate of the Nations*, "They think it beneath them even to investigate such

---

[5] *Justine Glass,* They Foresaw the Future.
[6] *Ibid.*

phenomena. They believe only in science. And modern authorities have declared—have they not—prophecy and similar phenomena to be impossible."[7]

But then the "modern" science of almost any era has a habit of ridiculing what it does not understand. Benjamin Franklin was laughed off the world stage when he tried to explain the lightning conductor. Alexander Graham Bell was ridiculed, as was Pasteur, Diesel, and a host of others. It may, in fact, be a sign of considerable progress that so-called "psychic phenomena" are permitted use of the term "science," even if it is preceded by "occult."

To be fair, not all mainstream scientists are so quick to disparage things that are as far afield as even astrology. C. G. Jung, the great psychoanalyst, wrote, "Although half-educated people still sneer at astrology as a long-ago wound-up science, astrology again knocks at the doors of all universities." And the eminent physicist Albert Einstein wrote that he had occupied himself with astrology and had "found it extremely useful."[8]

It is impossible to delve very deeply into the history of the occult without coming across the name of Nostradamus. In many ways he seems to define this great mystery. Why? Who was this amazing man? And what did he do that has managed to captivate the imagination of the entire world for over four hundred and fifty years? A great many books have been written to try to answer those questions, and not all of them agree in all the particulars, but the following is probably as close as anyone can get to an accurate biography.

Michel de Nostredame was born on December 14, 1503 by the old Julian calendar, December 23 by the

---

[7] *Prieditis*, The Fate of the Nations, *introduction*.
[8] *Ibid., p. ix.*

Gregorian calendar. The world first heard his cry in St. Rémy de Provence, probably under rather ordinary circumstances. Some historians claim his family line proceeds from an illustrious line of Jewish doctors, but that appears to be at odds with the facts. Michel's grandfather, Peyrot or Pierre, was an established Jewish grain dealer who married a Gentile girl named Blanche. Their son, Michel's father, was Jaume or Jacques de Nostredame, who gave up the family business and became a successful notary public. Nostradamus's only connection with the practice of medicine seems to have come through his father, and it is a rather thin connection at that. Jacques married Reyniere de St. Rémy, who was the granddaughter of an ex-doctor turned tax collector.[9] It was this grandfather who, throughout Nostradamus's childhood, guided him in the rudiments of the classic languages and in Hebrew and astrology.

Some historians credit the family's "conversion" to Christianity to an edict of Louis XII, who, on September 25, 1501, gave all Jews the choice of changing to the Catholic faith and being baptized within a period of three months or leaving Provence.[10] Whether by edict or choice, the family converted.

Nostradamus never made any attempt to disguise his Christian piety, seeming to fully embrace Catholicism throughout his life. But by the same token, he did not deny his Jewish heritage, which some historians trace through his mother to the lost tribe of Issachar, the tribe that could read the moon and the stars and interpret the heavens. Whatever the truth of that, it is

[9] *Erika Cheetham,* The Further Prophecies of Nostradamus, *p. 60.*
[10] *Ibid.*

well known that even as a youngster, Michel de Nostredame was fascinated by the study of astrology.

When he was an adolescent, he was sent to Avignon, where he studied philosophy, and from there he went to the University of Montpellier. As a young man of nineteen, he began his studies to become a doctor and graduated in three years with a bachelor's degree.[11]

It is interesting to note that he received his license to practice medicine in 1525, the year of his graduation, an accomplishment not to be taken lightly. According to Erika Cheetham, "The process of getting a degree was far more arduous than in the present day, and lasted much longer. The examinations consisted of the following routine. From 8:00 A.M. until noon the pupil was given an oral examination in Latin, during which he was asked questions demanding complicated answers, having to avoid traps and prove his own learning in return. Once successful, the newly fledged doctor changed his black robes for the red ones of the learned doctor.

"But in the sixteenth century, to get one's degree did not qualify a candidate to practice. Far from it. Nostradamus now had to give five lectures chosen by the dean of the University over three months. Again in Latin. The lectures approved, Nostradamus had to pass three *per intentionem* examinations, which consisted of four different questions, each presented one day in advance and each of which had to be discussed for an hour, and the format varied. If you were unlucky, all four subjects had to be discussed on the same day, or otherwise, two on two consecutive days.

"That ordeal passed, the candidate was given a fur-

[11] *Henry C. Roberts,* The Complete Prophecies of Nostradamus, *p. xv.*

ther subject eight days later, and this was discussed extemporaneously in front of the chancellor of the University himself. To crown all this, Nostradamus would then be given an aphorism of Hippocrates on which he had to produce a thesis the next day. These last two tests were known as *les points rigoureux,* which they really were. A successful candidate was then given a license to practice by the bishop of Montpellier."[12]

For Michel de Nostredame (he was not yet using the Latinized version of his name) to have achieved all of this at the tender age of twenty-two speaks volumes, not only of his intelligence but of his dedication as well.

During this entire period of intense study his interest in astrology continued to grow. His fellow students referred to him goodnaturedly as "the little astrologer," and he upheld the Copernican theory that the world was round and revolved around the Sun a hundred years before Galileo was prosecuted for the same belief.[13]

The Black Plague was ravaging much of France during this period, and the young doctor soon became known as a great healer. He refused the "magic coat of seven colors" believed to protect doctors from the ravages of disease, and proceeded to use what were very unorthodox methods for the time. His methods angered some of his contemporaries, but they healed a great many people, and by the time he returned to Montpellier in October of 1529 to complete his doctorate, his reputation had preceded him. Many on the faculty were already his enemies solely on the basis of his reputation for using unorthodox healing methods.

Still, no one ever questioned his courage in facing

[12] *Cheetham,* The Further Prophecies of Nostradamus, *p. 14.*
[13] *Ibid., p. 62.*

disease, his humanity, or his kindness toward the sick. Prescriptions for his own cures, used with great success in the stricken towns he visited during this period, were published in a book called *Le Traité des Fardemens,* published in 1552.[14]

By 1532 Nostradamus had won the right to wear the black four-cornered cap of the D.Phil. (today's Ph.D.), which he wore proudly for the remainder of his life. And he was offered a teaching position at Montpellier. Nostradamus settled down to teach, for about a year, but he soon left teaching to resume his wanderings. For the next two years he traveled about, passing through Bordeaux, La Rochelle, and Toulouse.

It was while practicing in Toulouse that he received a letter from Julius Caesar Scaliger, a philosopher of international renown, whose Renaissance interests embraced mathematics, medicine, poetry, philosophy, and botany. Nostradamus replied, and the result was an invitation from Scaliger to stay at his home in Agen. Here, surrounded by physical and intellectual comfort, Nostradamus met and married a young girl of "high estate," whose name, unfortunately, we do not know. It is known, however, that he had a son and a daughter by her. Life, it seemed, was complete.[15]

But fate has a way of intervening in such happy circumstances. The plague, which Nostradamus had been so successful in fighting elsewhere, finally found its way to Agen. In spite of all he could do, his beautiful young wife and children were lost. Then a falling out with Scaliger turned a brilliant friendship into lifelong animosity, at least on the part of Scaliger, who never missed an opportunity after that to excoriate his former

[14] *Ibid,* p.62.
[15] *Ibid.*

companion. Nostradamus, for his part, and to his credit, continued to praise Scaliger for sharing his great intellect with him during his youth. The reason for the argument, alas, is unknown.

Devastated by the loss of his family, facing a lawsuit by his dead wife's family for the return of her dowry, and accused of heresy for a chance remark made to workmen casting a bronze statue of the Virgin Mary, Nostradamus began his wanderings once again, settling finally at Salon. Here he married again, this time a rather well-off widow, by whom he had six children, the eldest of which was named Caesar, and upon whose birth Nostradamus composed a most remarkable letter. A letter that may be said, in some respects, to be the beginning of his "prophetic" career. But more about that later.

One further note about Nostradamus, the man. By 1554 he had made his way to Marseilles. In November of that year Provence experienced the worst flood in its history. The plague, still rampant in France, now struck with even greater virulence, being spread by corpses floating in the polluted water. Nostradamus attacked the plague as a personal enemy. He was tireless in his efforts. While other doctors fled with those who had not yet contracted the disease, Nostradamus stayed and faced the "black death" virtually alone. According to contemporary records, Aix, the capital of Provence, was particularly hard-pressed, and officials there sent for Nostradamus. He arrived on May first, to a scene of complete hopelessness. Walking through the streets, almost silent with despair, he saw a woman sewing herself into her own shroud. There would be no one left to do it when she died, she told him.

Nostradamus went to work immediately. Upon entering a house, he would fling open the windows, letting sunlight into the dank interiors. If there was water in a basin or pitcher he poured it out, insisting on both fresh air and unpolluted water. These simple but unheard-of methods began to have an effect. He actually cured many who thought they were beyond help. It was a victory of sorts over the disease that had robbed him of his family, and his dedication would have far-reaching results. Once the community recovered, the city parliament at Aix voted him a lifetime pension.[16]

Nostradamus returned to Salon, having determined to settle there for the rest of his life, and except for occasional trips to various cities to cure diseases or meet with church officials or noblemen, that is where he spent the remainder of his days.

At this point in time, Nostradamus's fame, which was considerable, and his fortune, were due solely to his skill and courage as a physician. His ability to foresee events was not yet part of the mystique that would eventually surround him. A few stories were bandied about, but nothing serious. For example, there was the story, probably apocryphal, of Nostradamus's visit to a particular nobleman, who, having heard that the great physician could also tell of things to come, determined to test him. Pointing to two piglets, a black one and a white one, the nobleman asked Nostradamus if he could tell what was in their future.

"The white one," Nostradamus said, "will be eaten by a wolf. We will eat the black one."

The nobleman immediately instructed his cook to prepare the white one for dinner that evening, but a pet wolf cub, kept by one of the servants, made off with the meat. The cook, in a panic, killed and prepared the black one.

[16] *Ibid.*

That evening at dinner the nobleman chided Nostradamus for his failure to make a true prediction, assuring him they were eating the white pig. Nostradamus insisted they were in fact dining upon the black one.

"Bring in the cook," shouted the lord of the manor, "and we shall see whether our guest be a true prophet or not."

Nostradamus sat quietly as the trembling cook was brought before the assembled guests. As his host began to question the cook, Nostradamus caught his eye and smiled.

"I confess I was not able to carry out your instructions, muhlord," he stammered. "I did follow your instructions, and I prepared the white pig, but Pierre's wolf cub made off with it." The cook looked about the room nervously and added, "I did not dare risk your lordship's displeasure by having no meat prepared for your dinner, so I killed the black one"—he dropped his eyes to the floor—"which I trust you find acceptable."

A heavy silence hung in the air as the nobleman glared at his servant. At last he looked over at Nostradamus, who picked up his knife and said quietly, "My compliments to the chef."

His lordship roared with laughter and sent the cook scurrying back to the kitchen. "I must remember to consult you," he said to Nostradamus, "when it comes time to select a husband for my daughter."

It was upon such tales as this that Nostradamus's reputation as a prophet began to emerge.

It is unclear just when these stories started to circulate, but we do know the first official publication of any of Nostradamus's predictions came in 1550 when he published his first *Almanac,* a simple series of verses describing the weather, crop conditions, and the like. It was so successful that he published one almost every year until his death. It may also be fairly assumed that during this period Nostradamus began work on his *Centuries,* the volumes of poetic predictions that have come down to us today in any number of translations.

I say "assume" because it is impossible to pinpoint the exact day or time or even year when the mantle of prophecy first settled upon him. Whenever it was, Nostradamus kept it to himself for a number of years. According to one Jean-Aymes de Chavigny, a former mayor of Beaune who gave up his position to become a pupil of Nostradamus, "He set himself to write his *Centuries,* which he kept for a long time before publishing them, because he felt that the strangeness of the content could not fail to cause detractions, calumnies, and extremely venomous accusations."[17]

All of which turned out to be perfectly true. But as Nostradamus wrote in the letter to his newborn son Caesar,

> Although I have often foretold long before what has afterwards come to pass, and in particular regions, acknowledging all to have been done by divine virtue and inspiration, I was willing to hold my peace by reason of the injury—not only of the present time, but also of the future—because to put them in writing, the Kingdoms, Sects and Regions shall be so diametrically opposed, that if I should relate what shall happen hereafter, those of the present Reign, Sect, Religion and Faith, would find it so disagreeing with their fancies, that they would condemn that which future ages shall find and know to be true. Consider also the saying of our Savior, "*Such alone as are*

[17] *Ibid, p. 76.*

*inspired by the divine power can predict particular events
in a spirit of prophecy"* [emphasis added].

Nostradamus apparently knew, either through prescience or study, what the reaction of men would be
should his predictions not be to their liking. And as
surely as rain brings joy to some and discomfort to
others, there would always be those who would find his
forecasts "disagreeing with their fancies." In the sixteenth-century world, if that was the reaction of the
wrong king, nobleman, or sectarian or religious leader,
it could spell disaster for not only Nostradamus but his
entire family.

Interestingly, in matters pertaining to himself, Nostradamus was capable of clear and unambiguous forecasts, but in other matters his predictions are couched
in sometimes indecipherable enigmas. Still, it is clear
that he felt some responsibility or compulsion to di-
vulge in some manner the many fearsome visions he
had been given. Returning again to his letter to Caesar:

> For this reason, I have withheld my tongue from the
> vulgar and my pen from paper. But afterwards, I was
> willing for the common good to enlarge myself in dark
> and abstruse sentences, declaring the future events,
> chiefly the most urgent and those which I foresaw
> (whatever human mutation happened) would not offend
> the hearers, all under dark figures, more than prophetical.

Apparently knowing he would be taking some risks,
Nostradamus nevertheless committed himself to the
task of sharing his prophetic gift, for the sake of the
"common good." The literary device by which he
would accomplish this was a series of "quatrains"
grouped together in books called *Centuries*.

The quatrains of Nostradamus are individual prophecies set out in four-line poetic form. Before being published, the quatrains were assembled into groups of one hundred, hence the name *Centuries.*

Stop and consider for a moment what we are dealing with here: a man of enormous intelligence and supreme (for his day) medical skill. He has had settled upon him a lifetime pension, apparently sufficient for the care and keeping of his family, yet he is willing to put all of this at risk for what he deems to be the "common good." Whatever it was that compelled him to do so must have been powerful indeed.

Considering the fact that many, perhaps even most, of his predictions had to do with people and events far beyond either his country or his time, it seems curious that he would want to publish any of his predictions at all. Why bother to present his fantastic visions to a world incapable of understanding them, even if they had been presented in an unambiguous fashion? Who among his patients, or patrons for that matter, would care in the least if London burned in a hundred years?

Yet publish them he did, and the world has wondered at his amazing gift ever since.

Right here let's point out that not all of the *Centuries* contain precisely one hundred quatrains. The first book, for example, carried the letter to his infant son as a kind of "preface," and 354 quatrains. This book is called *The True Centuries.*[18] Thereafter the mathematics became somewhat more precise, though some of the later *Centuries* carry far fewer than one hundred quatrains. This "format," however, allowed him to do a number of things to make the predictions and their meaning more obscure. For example, quatrains written

[18] *Steward Robb*, Prophecies on World Events, *p. 9.*

in sequence and relating to a single event could be dropped randomly into other *Centuries*. Or, as some suggest, the number of a particular quatrain, or its position in one of the *Centuries* could be used to add significance or meaning. Or quatrains could be juxtaposed, putting the first part last and vice versa. All of these "devices," and many more, have been attributed to Nostradamus's attempt to make the meaning of his predictions as obscure as possible.

Was he successful? Historians, linguists, and philosophers are still struggling to untangle the web of prophecy he left spread across the face of the future. The prophecies he left all generations stretch literally from his own time to the end of the world. Today nearly a third of all his predictions remain undeciphered.

The next and perhaps more pertinent question is, has he been right? There are many researchers and translators who believe his record of accuracy is far too great to be attributable to mere chance. His ability to use names, places, and dates far into the future has proven to be not merely accurate, but astonishingly so.

All of that is well and good, but what does it have to do with you or me? Is the study of Nostradamus just an academic exercise? How could any of his predictions have meaning for us today? What could a sixteenth-century physician, even assuming he could see the multi-faceted problems of a twentieth-century world on the cusp of a new century, possibly have to say to us?

There are those who suggest his predictions concerning our day are some of the most volatile and the most useful of all time if we can only decipher them properly.

All the evidence seems to suggest that Nostradamus purposefully scrambled the quatrains to obscure their meanings. But did he leave us a key that will unlock the riddle? And can we find it? Modern linguistic experts and computer experts have tried. So far no such "key" has been found.

But given his record so far, and with so much still locked in obscurity, it is important to keep trying. It's a safe bet that this sixteenth-century seer still has much to tell us.

We can be certain of one thing: Nostradamus did not take the "gift" or the responsibility that comes with the gift lightly. He is quick to attribute his amazing faculties to divine sources and he approaches those sources with reverence, as evidenced by Quatrains 1 and 2 of the first *Centuries*.

> *Sitting alone at night in a secret study;*
> *it is placed on the brass tripod.*
> *A slight flame comes out of the emptiness*
> *and prophesies that which should not be*
> *believed in vain.*

The implication is clear that, whether he is ready or not, the inspiration will bring the prophecy to him. Then he must write it down:

> *The wand in the hand is placed in the middle*
> *of the legs of the tripod. He sprinkles both the hem*
> *And his foot with water. A voice: Fear: he trembles in his*
> *robes.*
> *Divine splendor. The God sits beside him.*

What a remarkable description of both the process and his feelings. Alone at night, Nostradamus, a pious and courageous man, launches himself on a journey of discovery that goes far beyond his own time. It is now up to us to see if we can follow him on that journey.

It may be a little bit frightening to discover what Nostradamus has already told us about our day and time, but can we afford to ignore him? Many researchers believe Nostradamus foresaw the end of the world. When is it coming? Is it inevitable, or can we forestall the awful consequences of his dire predictions?

You may never know, if you don't turn the page.

3

THE PROPHECIES—
FACT OR FRAUD?

---

*"Humane realm and angelic offspring
    causes lasting peace and unity.
War subdues under its control.
Peace is maintained."*

Quatrain 42, *Centuries,* X

SUPPORTERS OF THE NOSTRADAMUS PROPHECIES
(and there are many) point out that over four hundred
years ago this amazing man wrote of submarines and
air travel, of royal intrigues and presidential assassinations, the French Revolution (in astonishing detail), as
well as both world wars, Hitler, Mussolini, and the
many crises we of the twentieth century face in this
final decade leading up to the year 2000. None of these
things could have possibly been imagined in his own
day, but somehow Nostradamus wrote of them in considerable detail.

Is it possible to see into the future? A day? A year?
A hundred years? If it is, then is it something that can
be learned, or does the ability simply fall on whoever it
will? Are some people, such as the biblical prophets,
chosen? If so, how do we identify those whose gift can
be believed?

The questions are unending and have been asked
for centuries, but so far no one seems to have come up
with any satisfactory answers. Derek Partridge, writer,
journalist, TV news anchor, and host of a number of
television specials including "The Naked Truth," thinks
we should be cautious in accepting any such possibilities.

"In tens of thousands of scientifically controlled

tests," Partridge says, "precognizance, the ability to see events before they happen, has never been successfully scientifically proven." Partridge concedes that "there are some rare and singular exceptions, but even these are more likely cases of acute perception rather than genuine clairvoyance."

If Partridge is right, the evidence would seem to indicate that these "rare and singular exceptions" have been occurring with some regularity for thousands of years. Such great thinkers as Plato, St. Augustine, Kant, Spinoza, Newton, Freud, and Einstein had no doubt about the existence of clairvoyance.

Nostradamus himself, by the way, ranks right up there with those "great thinkers." He has been called a "celestial scientist," and in addition to his fame as a medical doctor he earned a wide reputation as an herbalist, a creator of cosmetics, and an expert in fruit preservatives. But it was his ability to foretell the future that made him such a truly unique and remarkable man. We begin to understand just how remarkable when we examine closely a 450-year-old prediction that some Nostradamus experts believe deals with the tragedy of the space shuttle *Challenger*.

> Nine will be set apart from the human flock, separated from judgment and counsel. Their fate to be determined on departure.
> The unripe fruit will be the source of great scandal.
> Great blame. To the other, great praise.

Mr. Jordan Maxwell, who has written and lectured extensively on religio-political philosophy for many years, and is coauthor of *The Book Your Church Doesn't Want You to Read,* believes the indicators are quite clear.

"There was a great scandal over sending civilians into space," Maxwell reminds us, "especially in an unproven vehicle. NASA was indeed the subject of 'great blame.' At the same time the Russian program was being greatly praised. His prediction aligns exactly with the tragic circumstances of the *Challenger* disaster."

Admittedly, the idea that anyone in the sixteenth century could predict a spaceship explosion staggers the mind. Dwayne Walker, the host of "Mars Hill," an inquisitive television show that examines new and old ideas and the effects those ideas have on our lives, is skeptical of the whole Nostradamus phenomenon.

Walker sums it up this way: "I believe that Nostradamus was playing a great practical joke on his peers as well as the royalty and nobility of the time. His quatrains are very simply nonsense verses of gibberish poetry. They make no sense at all. They might just as well be commercials for gasoline or breakfast food as predictions."

If Walker is right, then all of Nostradamus's writings about air travel, submarines, mechanized warfare, and the rise and fall of governments were just lucky guesses. The actual names he included in many of his predictions are the product of mere happenstance. For many people, myself included, that's harder to swallow than the predictions.

Still, it's obvious that Nostradamus went to great pains to make his visions difficult to understand. That, in and of itself, seems to have been a response to some sort of precognitive warning. He well knew, as evidenced by the letter to his infant son, that the leaders of "kingdoms, sects, religions, and faiths," would find his predictions contrary to what they would like to hear most of the time.

To those who have studied his life and works, there

seems to be no surprise at all in the fact that he waited years to actually publish his predictions in anything like the form we know them today.

Dr. Louis Turin, who, like Nostradamus, was born in Provence in southern France, and who has been called "Nostradamus reincarnated" by some of his clients, uses Nostradamus's unique "divine astrology" discipline in his own readings. According to Dr. Turin, "Kings ruled by divine right and Shakespeare had yet to write his first play when Nostradamus burst onto the scene. His study of astrology, then regarded as a science, was taken very seriously, and there can be no question that he was a talented writer. His books were penned in true poetic form and with great skill."

Nostradamus apparently used that skill to (1) satisfy whatever obligation he felt to the world and the source of his great gift and (2) to protect himself and his family from the wrath of those kings and clerics who would be offended or frightened by his predictions. Perhaps he was too skillful. Many of his quatrains are still unfathomable to even the most dedicated Nostradamus researcher.

But when he did publish his first quatrains, much to his surprise, he became the rage of the court. The queen, Catherine de Médicis, was one of his early and most loyal fans. Even though she learned to dread some of his prophecies, she was still a staunch supporter of Nostradamus and consulted him frequently on many matters.

The queen believed his predictions without reservation, but unfortunately her husband, King Henry II, did not share her fascination with Nostradamus. He did agree, however, that the "old lion" referred to in one of the prophet's more famous quatrains could refer to him and, upon hearing the dire prediction, promised the queen that he would avoid single combat.

The quatrain in question read,

The young lion will overcome the old one on the battlefield
   in single combat. In a cage of gold
   his eyes will be put out. Two wounds one.
Then to die a cruel death.

Nostradamus assured the queen this terrible fate for the king could be avoided with proper precautions. If he kept his promise to avoid single combat, he would surely escape the grisly fate Nostradamus had predicted.

But King Henry, three years later, at a festive gathering celebrating the wedding of his daughter and his sister in a huge double ceremony, insisted on a joust with the young Count de Montgomery. The queen protested to no avail. Even the young count, aware of the prophecy, tried to get the king to desist. Henry would not listen.

Everyone gathered at the lists to watch as Henry, not entirely unmindful of the Nostradamus warning, placed a gold helmet on his head and brought down a special visor that had been added to the helmet in order to protect the king's eyes. Surely he would be safe.

Seated in the place of honor, Queen Catherine emitted a small cry, and her hand clutched her breast. How like a "cage of gold" the king's helmet looks, she thought, but Henry was oblivious to her concern.

In the first charge Henry's lance caught Montgomery a glancing blow that nearly unhorsed him, but the "young lion" managed to stay in the saddle. Now full of confidence, the king gathered himself for the second charge. As the two riders thundered past one another, the king's shield deflected Montgomery's lance and sent it clattering to the ground. The next charge, Henry was confident, would prove to everyone that he was still master of the lists.

The groom quickly handed Montgomery another lance, and as the two warriors turned their battle mounts to face one another for the third time, Henry lifted his visor to let his opponent see the confidence in his eyes. There was only a moment's hesitation, then Henry slammed the visor closed and dug his spurs into the flanks of his charger. The horse bolted forward as Henry leveled his lance and leaned into his thrust, ready to strike the winning blow.

Montgomery braced his knees against his horse's sides and pointed the tip of his lance squarely at the center of the king's shield. If he was to be unhorsed, it would take a perfect hit. King or no king, he was a knight, and his pride was at stake. The two great horses quickly closed the gap between them and as Montgomery's lance found the king's shield, it suddenly splintered, sending the point through the opening in the king's golden visor. With a shriek of pain, King Henry fell from his horse and crashed heavily to the ground.

The queen and the physicians, Nostradamus perhaps among them, rushed to their fallen king, but there was nothing they could do. The splintered lance had pierced the king's eye and continued through, striking the brain. Truly two wounds in one. And in literal fulfillment of the prophecy, the king lay in cruel agony for ten days before he died.[19]

From this single event the fame of Nostradamus spread to every corner of Europe. Some feared him.

[19] *Cheetam,* The Further Prophecies of Nostradamus, *p. 83.*

On the night of the king's death an angry mob called upon the church inquisitors to burn him at the stake. He was, in fact, burned in effigy. The wisdom of concealing the true meaning of his predictions, if anyone ever doubted it, was now perfectly clear.

Dolores Cannon is the author of the trilogy *Conversations with Nostradamus*. Cannon describes herself as a "regressionist" and "psychic researcher" who records "lost" knowledge. According to Ms. Cannon, "The dreaded inquisition was at the height of its frenzy [at this time]. Just being denounced by the church was often enough for someone to be stripped of their property, jailed, tortured, and burned alive at the stake. The enemies of Nostradamus accused him of witchcraft, but lacking the skill to interpret his quatrains, their efforts were in vain.

"We should understand," Cannon says, "that these predictions are only a mystery to us because Nostradamus chose to make them so. The evidence suggests he saw future events with remarkable clarity."

One example that tends to support Cannon's thesis is evidenced in his almost offhanded salute to a young priest.

According to reports, Nostradamus, returning to Salon along a muddy path, stood aside to let a group of monks pass in the narrow road. As they came abreast of him, the venerable physician suddenly dropped to the ground and paid obeisance to the youngest of the group, Brother Felice Peretti, a monk of very low birth. Others in the group were taken aback and chided Nostradamus, thinking he was mocking them. They reminded him that Brother Peretti had only recently been rescued from tending a pigsty. Nostradamus replied that it was required that he yield and bend a knee before His Holiness.

The priests laughed and walked on. Forty years after the event and nineteen years after the death of Nostradamus, Brother Felice Peretti, the lowly born swineherder, became Pope Sixtus V.

According to Sean Morton, author of *The Millennium Factor,* "Nostradamus was very much a man of his own time. At least two hundred of the prophecies contained in his quatrains came true while he lived. But he was, beyond everything else, a man who saw tomorrow—and with incredible vividness.

"Consider the fact that during his lifetime every civilized nation in the world was ruled by an anointed king set upon the throne by divine right. Revolution and the execution of a king was unthinkable. Yet with the storming of the Bastille still two centuries away, Nostradamus wrote of events of that future time with uncanny accuracy."

In one of the many prophecies regarding the French Revolution, Nostradamus did in fact name names and identify locations.

> By night through the forest of Reims,
>   two partners by a roundabout route.
> The monk king dressed in gray at Varennes.
> The elected Capet causes tempest, fire and bloody slicing.

"Here," Morton says, "we have an opportunity to examine the prediction, line by line, against the actual events as they transpired. Louis XVI and his wife, Marie Antoinette, 'two partners,' escaped from the castle in Paris through a secret door. Their flight to Varennes took them through the forest of Reims, but they lost their way and, just as the quatrain predicted, they had to take a 'roundabout route.'

"The king, as a disguise, wore a plain gray monk's

cloak, fitting the quatrain perfectly, but it gets even more astonishing. Louis XVI was a Capet, the first *elected* king of France. Then, just as the last line states, he was both the 'cause and victim of the tempest.' And certainly no one can doubt the connection between the words 'bloody slicing' and the guillotine. Louis, and his queen, Marie Antoinette, as we all know, were both decapitated by this grisly device."

To the people of Nostradamus's day, two hundred years before the events would happen, it must have sounded like pure gibberish. Who in sixteenth-century France could have imagined an *elected* king—let alone entertain the idea of both him and his queen being executed by a guillotine?

But the amazing predictions of Nostradamus reach further into the future than that—much further. Nostradamus seems to have a firm grip on the future of France in its entirety. For instance, he was amazingly farsighted when it came to Napoleon, who wouldn't even be born for hundreds of years after the physician's death.

Nostradamus wrote,

An emperor will be born near Italy,
* one who will cost his empire dearly.*
They will say that with such people as rally round him,
* he will be found less prince than butcher.*

Once again, the remarkable, pinpoint accuracy of the prediction is truly amazing. Napoleon wasn't born in France, but on Corsica, an island "near Italy." The wars of Napoleon nearly bled France to death, both literally and financially, and he covered Europe and Asia, from the tip of the Italian boot to the gates of

Moscow with corpses—certainly more the mark of a butcher than a prince.

Experts seem to agree that seventeen of the quatrains spread through five of the *Centuries* are wholly and specifically applicable to Napoleon. But while the experts may be able to accept these findings with a certain degree of equanimity, it is still difficult for the average person to comprehend the fantastic ability that Nostradamus consistently demonstrates.

Imagine, if you will, someone from the *Mayflower* landing on Plymouth Rock and proclaiming that in the future there would be a great city in this new land, and in this city there would be a theatrical performance during which someone would be killed. And suppose this pilgrim tossed in the names of Lincoln and Booth just for good measure. Such a person, in all likelihood, would be hailed today as a remarkably gifted prophet.

Yet Nostradamus, who seems to accomplish precisely that kind of thing with astonishing regularity, still suffers the slings and arrows of a number of skeptics. For example, Father Leo Booth, author, international lecturer, and Episcopal priest, believes the so-called prophecies of Nostradamus can be easily explained.

"Fortune telling," according to Father Booth, "is based on generalities and probabilities. The problems of love, health, money, death, sickness, et cetera, are always with us. The probabilities never change. 'You will go on a journey and meet someone who will change your thinking' is not really fortune-telling; it is only a statement of generality and probability."

Generalities? Simple statements of probability? Does that account for the fact that Nostradamus seems to be able to name names right into the modern era with apparent ease. Consider his comment about the Spanish Civil War of 1936.

From Castille, Franco will bring out the assembly.
The ambassadors will not agree and cause a schism.
The people of the Riviera will be in the crowd.
The great man will be denied entrance to the gulf.

According to Dolores Cannon, "This is another of Nostradamus's incredible name couplings. Primo de Rivera was the dictator of Spain, and Franco exposed him. Franco was exiled to Morocco, thus being denied access to the Gulf. It couldn't be more precise. That hardly seems the stuff generalities are made of."

It is that kind of precision that has forced even the stubbornest of critics to a grudging admiration of Nostradamus's abilities to use proper names in the prophecies. Here is another eye-popping example:

The lost thing is discovered.
Pasteur will be celebrated almost as a god.
This when the moon completes her great cycle.
But he will be dishonored by other rumors.

Louis Pasteur's contribution to medical science is beyond calculation. Among other things he was the discoverer of vaccines and the first to use them to prevent the spread of disease. As a result, there was a movement in France to propose him for sainthood. But, still, certain factions in the French Academy of Science attacked him viciously in an attempt to ridicule the use of vaccines. The prediction couldn't be more precise. But it gets even better. In astrological terms, the great cycle of the moon ran from 1535, in Nostradamus's lifetime, to 1889, the year the Pasteur Institute was founded.

Once again, somehow peering over three hundred and fifty years into the future, Nostradamus seems to have precisely described a particular series of events.

And it doesn't end there. According to Dr. Louis Turin, "Perhaps the single most impressive group of his modern predictions are those having to do with Hitler and the Second World War. There are twenty quatrains that unmistakably refer to Adolf Hitler. Three in which he is mentioned by the name 'Hister.'"

Consider this quatrain:

> *From the deepest part of Western Europe, a child will be born*
> *of a poor family who will entice many with his oratory.*
> *His reputation will grow even greater*
> *in the kingdom of the East.*

Hitler was born in the Austrian Alps, the deepest part of Western Europe. His father had a low-level civil service job and could barely make ends meet. Hitler was certainly a child "born of a poor family." And there can be no denying that Hitler was a fiery and rousing orator, "enticing many." In the kingdom of the East, the USSR, Stalin considered Hitler his greatest single threat long before the rest of the world started taking the German dictator seriously. His reputation, such as it was, did indeed grow even "greater" among the Communists.

Perhaps the world might have taken Hitler more seriously if we had taken Nostradamus more seriously. Shouldn't we be asking ourselves if maybe there isn't a lesson to be learned in all of this? And if there is, have we learned it?

In some forty quatrains that have been expertly interpreted, Nostradamus foresaw not only aircraft, but battles in the sky, the bombing of cities, and paratroopers. His remarkable vision led him to write of submarines and the mining of shipping lanes. He saw tanks, rockets, and the people of London seeking shelter from bombs in subway tunnels. And while he did not name Mussolini precisely, he did say that his name was "lowly." Mussolini means "muslin maker," a craft regarded by Italian tradesmen as the lowest of the low.

All of this was available to world leaders long before Napoleon, Hitler, or Mussolini ever appeared on the scene. Why, then, was the world so surprised at their coming? Has Nostradamus told us what surprises are yet to come in *our* future?

As we proceed further through the quatrains and approach our own time, Nostradamus shows no signs of being less enigmatic or less accurate.

> *Pestilences extinguished, the world becomes small.*
> *For a long time the lands will be inhabited by peace.*
> *People will travel safely by air, over land, seas and wave.*
> *Then wars will start again.*

That certainly sounds like a description of the post–World War II era. Advances in medical science eradicated or brought under control many killer diseases. The jet age, along with communications advances undreamed of even by our own grandparents, did indeed make the world small. We have, in fact, become a global village. But still there is that note of warning.

The question is, even if we knew what was in store, would we do anything differently? Or would we, like King Henry, ignore the counsel and stubbornly ride to the joust? Jordan Maxwell thinks we have our modern counterpart.

"Of all the prophecies of Nostradamus dealing with our own time," Maxwell tells us, "I think the quatrains predicting the assassination of John F. Kennedy and his brother Robert are the most impressive."

Which of us, having seen the Zapruder film of those awful moments, can deny the veracity of the first lines of this quatrain:

The great man will be struck down in the daytime by a thunderbolt.

It was also widely reported that modern psychic Jeane Dixon sent a warning to John Kennedy imploring him not to go to Dallas. The quatrain continues:

An evil deed foretold by the bearer of a petition.

Then, just a few years later, Robert Kennedy was gunned down following a late-night speech in Los Angeles. According to the quatrain,

Another is struck at night.

The quatrain concludes with a sense of the shock and confusion the assassinations left in their wake in capitals around the world.

Conflict in Reims, London, and pestilence in Tuscany.

Maxwell asks: "What other way would a sixteenth-century man have of describing the striking force of a modern high-powered rifle? Jeane Dixon not only warned JFK, she sent a plea, asking him to avoid going to Texas. And Robert Kennedy was, indeed, struck at night. It is interesting to contemplate what the world might be like today had the Kennedys heeded the warnings of Nostradamus.

"Twelve of the Nostradamus quatrains deal with Kennedys," Maxwell reminds us, "not only the assassinations of JFK and Robert but the smear of Ted Kennedy arising from the Chappaquiddick incident as well."

The list goes on and on. Names, dates, and places appear far too often to just be written off as coincidence or as generalities. Unfortunately, we can only scratch the surface of the Nostradamus prophecies here in this chapter. He did, after all, leave us nearly a thousand quatrains, and most experts feel less than half of them have been fulfilled to date. Still, his predictions reach even further into our own century. Let's take a brief but closer look at how accurate Nostradamus is when it comes to just the past decade.

Ten years ago even the most optimistic political analyst would not have predicted the end of the Cold War and the collapse of the Berlin Wall, but four hundred and fifty years ago, Nostradamus wrote,

> *One day the great powers will be friends.*
> *Their power will be seen to increase*
> *The new land will be*
>   *at the height of its power*

In his prophecies Nostradamus frequently referred to America as the "new land." Many experts also believe numerous quatrains were numbered to correspond with the year of the predicted event. This particular quatrain is number 89 and it was indeed, 1989 when the United States and the USSR began to be seen as "friends."

Sometimes one gets the eerie feeling that over four centuries ago Nostradamus was somehow reading the headlines in today's paper. For example:

Many people will want to come to terms
   with the great world leaders who will bring war upon
them.
The political leaders will not want to hear anything of
their message.
Alas, if God does not send peace to Earth.

How many times has the world seen, not just in the last few years, but even in the last few months, political leaders reject the plea of people who "want to come to terms," and put an end to the wars that are "brought upon them"? At this writing, the war in Bosnia-Herzegovina has been going on over the objections of the people of the world, and even the people of the nations involved, for over a decade. But the leaders will not hear their plea. The last line of the quatrain seems to suggest that only God can save us from ourselves.

Doug Webber, a computer scientist, software expert, and Nostradamus researcher, believes that Nostradamus saw the problems of our modern world with at least as much clarity and perception as he saw his own.

"Time and time again," Webber tells us, "we have seen how his quatrains have been uncannily accurate. Doesn't it just make good sense then that we should pay considerable attention to what he has to say about the nineties, and our future beyond this quickly closing century?

"For example, Nostradamus tells us the alliance between the superpowers does not last:

The two will not remain allied for long.
Within 13 years they surrender to Barbare and Persian
leaders.

"Obviously, he is talking here about the Middle East, where Russia and its allies will support the Arab position as we continue to support the Israelis—a simple border conflict that could escalate into World War III. Again, quoting Nostradamus,

When weapons and plans are enclosed in a fish,
  out of it will come a man who will then make war.
His fleet will have traveled far across the sea
  to appear at the Italian shore.

"Not long ago the launching of a major attack with submarines would not have been believed. But a fleet of nuclear subs, which both the Russians and the United States possess, armed with nuclear warheads, could destroy half the planet in a matter of minutes."

Dire predictions indeed. But Nostradamus himself said his "predictions" were based on conditions, and these conditions could be changed. In other words, as the Bible teaches, we are the architects of our own destiny.

But are we?

Quatrain 42 of *Centuries* X states,

Humane realm and angelic offspring
  causes lasting peace and unity.
War subdues under its control.
Peace is maintained.

This is a particularly interesting quatrain in view of some current occult beliefs. Some "UFOlogists," for example, speculate that the "sons of God" mentioned in the Bible are the ancient astronauts who "seeded" this planet and that their return is imminent. These are the "angelic offspring" who will combine with the "humane realm" to unify all the races and peoples of this planet and eliminate war forever. This is certainly not a mainstream concept, but, then, Nostradamus is hardly a "mainstream" kind of prophet. The truth is, mainstream leaders, whether religious, political, or academic, have steadfastly refused to pay any attention to Nostradamus at all. On the other hand, recent conventions of UFO investigators and researchers have featured full sessions devoted exclusively to his prophecies.

So we have a sixteenth-century physician predicting both a horrendous future for us, and a future of incredible bliss. The legacy of his remarkable quatrains seems to be, if you choose the evil road, so shall your future be evil. Equally, the good road leads to a beautiful future for all the generations yet to be born.

If we are willing to make decisions based on his forecasts for us, we must ask the question one more time: Was Nostradamus really a great and true prophet? Could he, for example, see his own future? Consider the following:

On June 30, 1566, Nostradamus made arrangements for his fortune, estimated at 3,444 crowns (including 300 crowns just settled upon him by the king) to be distributed to his wife and children. He went to his beloved study, which for convenience' sake had also been fitted with his bed, and began to write:

> *On his return from the embassy, the king's gift put in place,*
> *He will do nothing more. He will be gone to God.*
> *Close relatives, friends, brothers by blood will find him*
> *   completely dead near the bed and bench.*

The following morning, when his family and a few friends came to visit, his assistant led them cautiously up the stairs. There they found Nostradamus, dead, slumped over on his writing bench, which was, in fact, right near his bed. A prophet to the very last, Nostradamus added yet one more prophecy by which the power of his gift can be measured. This, his last prophecy, reached out from the grave.

Two hundred and twenty-five years following the death of Nostradamus, the French Revolution was under way, just as he predicted. One humid spring night in 1791 a marauding band of partisan rebels were roaming the streets of Salon. Three of them, for some unknown reason, decided to desecrate the ancient grave of the great Nostradamus.

No one will ever know for certain, but it may have been an old legend that brought them to the graveside in the dark of night. The legend said that whoever drank from the skull of Nostradamus would inherit his great powers of prophecy. But in their haste, or perhaps their drunkenness, the marauders forgot the second part of the legend—that whosoever disturbed his grave would quickly die.

Feverishly, they dug away the earth until a shovel clanked against the wooden coffin. With an exultant shout, they cleared away the remaining dirt and pulled away the rotting boards that formed the lid of the prophet's resting place. One of them grabbed a lantern and cast its light into the open coffin. Suddenly they froze. There, on the chest of Nostradamus, still held in place by bony fingers, was a brass plaque, buried with him two hundred and five years earlier. It bore the simple legend "May 1791," correctly identifying the month and year his grave would be defiled.

Casting fear aside, one of the men reached into the grave and retrieved the skull. With only a moment's hesitation, he filled it with wine, then, laughing, he raised the skull to his lips and drained it. A deathly silence filled the graveyard as he turned to his two un-believing friends, perhaps to gloat, but before a word could escape his lips, a random shot fired by an un-known member of one of the prowling mobs struck him down. With a groan of anguish and surprise, the would-be successor to Nostradamus fell dead at the feet of the other grave-robbers.

The prediction of the legend had also been fulfilled —exactly.

Was Nostradamus a great prophet? Each of us will have to answer that question in our own way as the future becomes the present and more of the Nostrada-mus quatrains are deciphered. It is interesting to note, however, that Albert Einstein belonged to a school of great scholars who believed life and the universe were one unified time-continuum—an endless entwining of happenings and nonhappenings in which "reality" is only a mere subatomic particle. If this theory is true, then perhaps there are people who can glimpse the future, frozen in time, like two trains passing, caught in a stroboscopic moment.

Could it be that Nostradamus found a way to ride the tail of some time-continuum comet?

Ah, but that is another mystery.

For the time being there is mystery enough in the undeciphered and yet to be fulfilled prophecies of Nos-tradamus. These prophecies should be sufficient to oc-cupy us until at least the thirty-sixth century, when, according to the great man's writings, we will see . . . the end of the world.

4

THE SHROUD OF TURIN

"He saw the linen wrappings lying, and the napkin which had been over his head, not lying with the wrappings but rolled together in a place by itself."

John 20:6

THE SHROUD OF TURIN, IF IT IS AUTHENTIC, IS THE most valuable relic of Christianity, perhaps of any culture or precept, ancient or modern, in the history of the world. The implications of this ordinary piece of linen cloth go far beyond any other artifact because it seeks, by its very existence, to prove nothing less than the resurrection of Jesus Christ.

IF . . . it is authentic.

For at least six centuries millions of people have clung steadfastly to the belief that the shroud of Turin is, in fact, the burial cloth of Christ. There is, however, a considerable body of scholarly opinion that insists this cloth is nothing more than an elaborate medieval fraud.

This mystery is unquestionably the most sensitive, controversial, and emotional enigma in the world today. And perhaps it is the most bitterly fought, since the arguments are powerful and persuasive—on both sides.

The question is easily put: Is the shroud of Turin the burial cloth that covered Jesus Christ when his crucified body was laid in the tomb? The answer, at least a definitive answer, seems to be virtually impossible to come by. But perhaps we are getting closer.

And there is another question: If the shroud is not what its supporters say it is, then what is it? Because by any standard of measurement, religious, historical, or scientific, it is unique.

For those who may be unfamiliar with the argument and/or the relic, let's take just a moment and describe exactly what it is that has created such a furor in the religious and scientific worlds. It is important to know what we are dealing with here, because as the arguments continue and grow more strident, the general population at large is beginning to weigh in on one side or the other. And well they might. The implications of the shroud are enormous for everyone who lives or ever has lived on the Earth.

The shroud of Turin is a piece of linen cloth fourteen feet, three inches long and three feet, seven inches wide, and it is accepted without argument that it has existed since at least A.D. 1353. The cloth is made in a single piece of hand-loomed linen except for a strip three and one-half inches wide running the entire length of the left side and joined by a single, hand-stitched seam. It was nearly destroyed by fire in 1532, and molten silver is known to have dripped on it during that fire. The resulting series of burn marks down both sides of the shroud's entire length are similar to the paper cutouts we all made as children, and strongly suggest the cloth was neatly folded at the time of the fire.

For many years this strip of linen could be seen only in black-and-white photographs, but on November 22, 1973, in the former royal palace of Turin, a select group of people, including clergymen, scientists, and journalists, were invited to view the relic first-hand and up close. Ian Wilson, author of *The Shroud of Turin—Burial Cloth of Jesus Christ?*, was in that group and describes the event.

"The great frescoed Hall of the Swiss, a former

audience chamber, was ablaze with light. It had been converted into a television studio for the purposes of the RAI-TV exposition the next day, and the powerful lamps required for color cameras were full on. There, set against a huge ocher-colored screen, was the shroud.

"It was suspended in a plain, light oak frame, fastened at the top by a batten. Its fourteen-foot length hung loosely down. . . . Amazingly, the shroud was not protected by any glass."

Wilson's description of the cloth itself, as he saw it and touched it on this particular day, disputes some others who have described it as "coarse." According to Wilson, "The linen, though ivory colored with age, was still surprisingly clean looking, even to the extent of a damask-like surface sheen. It was possible to study closely the herringbone weave of the linen. In the areas untouched by the ravages of history it was in remarkably good condition. Even when examined under a magnifying glass, the fiber showed no signs of disintegration. The texture . . . was light and almost silky to the touch."[20]

It is not, however, the cloth itself that has generated such controversy. It is rather the faint, almost imperceptible, full-length image of a man, apparently dead and laid out for burial, that is imprinted on the cloth. This is what has aroused worldwide veneration— and scorn.

I should perhaps point out here, that my personal interest in this mystery is simply that it is . . . a mystery. I am not a scientist of any sort, and my life bears no particular religious trademark. But as a movie maker and author, I have, from my earliest beginnings,

[20] *Ian Wilson,* The Shroud of Turin—Burial Cloth of Jesus Christ? *p. 9.*

been fascinated with the unexplainable, the mysterious, and the seemingly impossible things and events that crowd in upon us. These are, after all, the things that challenge our comfortable notions of what is and what is not. On an almost daily basis, some new discovery forces us to change the way we perceive the world around us, but hardly ever is that change accomplished without a mighty struggle.

The shroud of Turin captured my attention many years ago because it appeared that just such a struggle was building up between the religious and scientific communities. And indeed it has. Both sides claim their only goal is the truth, pure and unvarnished. Yet in pursuit of that truth, both sides (at least some of the principle combatants) seem to have become polarized. Argument has turned into accusation, and in some cases just good old-fashioned name-calling.

It has always been my goal, whether in movies, television, or books, to present both sides of an argument as clearly as possible and let the readers or viewers decide the issue for themselves. Certainly that is the premise of this book and the television program that is based upon it. But it would be disingenuous of me to suggest that in dealing with the thousands of hours of research that go into the creation of something like this, I don't draw some conclusions of my own. It is fair to say that in some situations conclusions are virtually thrust upon you.

That is not, however, the case with the controversy surrounding the shroud of Turin. As we said earlier, the arguments on both sides are so powerful and so persuasive that with only the information now at hand, it is all but impossible to decide which "truth" is "truth." We will attempt, nonetheless, to distill the most pertinent aspects of the various arguments and put them before you. The judgment is yours to make, but be fore-warned: This is not a mystery that can be taken lightly. While it is true that your judgment may not affect the way the scientific or religious worlds view the shroud, the judgment you make may well, in all likelihood, change your life.

Let's get back to the shroud itself.

This obscure artifact, tucked away in what was once the place of private worship for the dukes of Savoy, onetime rulers of Italy, had gone largely unnoticed by the world generally for centuries. But for some long-forgotten reason, someone decided to allow photographs to be taken of the shroud.

To say it is tucked away is not an exaggeration. The *Santa Sandmen,* or "Holy Shroud," as it is known to the Italians, is kept at the Turin Cathedral of St. John the Baptist. A visitor must traverse the length of the cathedral and go up a flight of stairs by the side of the main altar. There he will enter a baroque chamber lined with white marble tombs and a soaring cupola. In the center is an ornate black marble altar set on a stepped platform. This altar is surmounted by a second altar, and it is here, in a locked cavity behind iron grilles, that the shroud is kept.[21]

According to Ian Wilson, "It lies rolled around a velvet staff and wrapped in red silk within a four-foot-long wooden casket ornamented in silver with the emblems of the Passion. The casket is kept within an iron chest wrapped in asbestos and sealed by no fewer than three locks, for each of which a separate key is required."[22]

But even kept far from the general view, and dis-

---

[21] *Ibid., introduction.*
[22] *Ibid.*

played very infrequently (less than a dozen times in over four centuries), the shroud managed to generate controversy.

The known history of the shroud begins in a small wooden church in the provincial town of Lirey, France, in 1357. The shroud's owner, Geoffrey de Charny, had been killed by the English the year before at the battle of Pouters, and his widow, nearly destitute, sought to earn a little money by displaying the burial garment of the Savior in the church of Lirey for whatever offerings the faithful might bring.[23]

According to a document that has recently become central to the shroud controversy, the bishop of Pouters, the local ordinary, ordered the exhibition stopped. The de Charny family kept the shroud, however. No one, it seems, ever bothered to ask, and the de Charnys never bothered to explain how an obscure French nobleman could have come into possession of such a fabulous relic. Only since the controversy erupted worldwide has a plausible explanation been offered. But we're getting ahead of our story.

Some twenty-five years later the shroud was once again put on display. This time, according to some historians, it was a Bishop Pierre D'Arcis, Bishop Henry's successor, who branded the shroud a forgery and wrote a much discussed "memorandum" to Pope Clement VII, demanding he stop the display. It should be noted that the D'Arcis memorandum is the only source for both his own and Bishop Henry's concern about the shroud. And as we shall see later on, this memorandum itself is highly controversial.

Be that as it may, the shroud later came into the hands of the powerful Savoy family and it was here,

[23] *Stevenson and Habermas,* Verdict on the Shroud, *p. 14.*

under the protection of the ruling house, that it was first accepted as the true burial shroud of Christ.[24] (I use the term "accepted" with reservations. In fact the Roman Catholic Church has never claimed the shroud is genuine.) But by no stretch of the imagination can it be said that the shroud was ever on "public" display. Rarely, and then only on very special occasions and for very brief periods of time, were the people permitted to view the shroud. Still, within certain circles the controversy raged, and finally, in 1898 what might be called the "modern" investigation—and controversy— over the shroud began.

A gifted Italian amateur photographer, Pia Segundo, was given a wholly unprecedented opportunity to take photographs of the shroud. Segundo packed up his gear and went to the cathedral filled with anticipation, but when the cloth was unfolded for display, his hopes fell. The image on the cloth could hardly be seen. In fact, if one was too close or too far away, the image simply disappeared. Still, he had come to photograph the shroud, and photograph it he did. What Segundo captured on his two glass photographic plates was to stun the world.

The faint, almost ghostlike images on the shroud now appeared in reverse on his negative, making them a *positive* image. For the first time in history the likeness on the cloth could be seen in full, majestic detail.

It is easy to imagine Segundo starring down at his negatives as the bruised features began to take shape before his very eyes. Surely he knew the Savoys venerated the shroud. Surely he knew why. If he agreed with them, the realization that he was the first to look upon

[24] *Ibid.*

the face of Christ in nearly two thousand years must have been overwhelming.

Dr. Albert Driesbach, Jr., director of the Atlanta Shroud Center, describes the photograph taken by Segundo: "It shows the double image, front and back, of a nude dead man," says Dr. Driesbach. "There appears to be markings of wounds that would indicate the man had something with many sharp points pressed onto his head. . . . A right shoulder that is badly bruised as though from carrying something heavy . . . the marks of a vicious flogging from the neck to the calves of the legs . . . nail wounds through the wrists and feet and a distension of the thorax . . . all of which would seem to indicate death by crucifixion . . . exactly as the Gospels describe the suffering and death of Jesus Christ."

No one argues with that description, but Joe Nickell, a professor of English and author of *The Shroud of Turin* and *Inquest on the Shroud of Turin,* is highly skeptical of the shroud's authenticity. According to Nickell, "There are two simple reasons why we can disregard the shroud as being the burial cloth of Christ. First, there is no historical chain of possession before the year 1353, and secondly, recent carbon-14 tests have confirmed that the shroud was, in fact, produced somewhere between A.D. 1260 and 1390. It may be an interesting artifact, but it is certainly not the burial shroud of Jesus Christ."

In response, Ian Wilson, whom we quoted earlier, introduces one of the most interesting aspects of the debate: science versus science. "Whatever else it may be," says Wilson, "the shroud of Turin is most definitely not a fraud. Many of today's most distinguished scientists, from dozens of different specialties and scientific fields are convinced that the shroud is genuine.

These scientists not only believe in its authenticity but also believe that the weight of scientific proof supports their beliefs."

Both men are quite correct in their assertions. Many scientists have, through their own work, become convinced of the shroud's authenticity. And recent carbon-14 tests do appear to pinpoint a medieval origin. But if the shroud is a fake, it is probably the most astonishing fake of all time. If it is genuine, then it is arguably the first tangible proof of the Resurrection. (Although a German writer, Kurt Berna, suggests just the opposite. According to Berna, the shroud "proves" Christ did not die on the cross, but rather, "the resurrection was merely a revival in the tomb."[25])

Some of the most critical opinions regarding the shroud's authenticity, however, have come from Christian churchmen, both past and present. Most prominent among them the Bishop D'Arcis of medieval France, in the "memorandum" cited earlier.

Bishop D'Arcis's now famous "Scandal at Lirey" letter, or "memorandum," as it has come to be called, was written in 1389. Since it is critical to the discussion from this point on, we will reproduce a translation that appears side by side with the original in the March 1991 publication of *The Catholic Counter-Reformation in the XXth Century*. The entire issue is devoted to the shroud of Turin.

> Most Holy Father, some time since in the diocese of Troyes, the Dean of a certain collegiate church, that of Lirey, falsely and deceitfully, being consumed with the passion of avarice, and not from any motive of devotion

[25] *Wilson*, The Shroud of Turin—Burial Cloth of Jesus Christ? *introduction*.

but only of gain, procured for his church a certain cloth cunningly painted, upon which by clever sleight of hand was depicted the twofold image of one man, that is to say, the back and front, he falsely declaring that and pretending that this was the actual shroud in which our Savior Jesus Christ was enfolded in the tomb, and upon which the whole likeness of the Savior had remained thus impressed together with the wounds which he bore. This was put about not only in the kingdom of France, but, so to speak, throughout the whole world, so that from all parts people came to view it, and further to attract the multitude so that money might cunningly be wrung from them, pretended miracles were worked, certain men being hired to represent themselves as healed at the moment of the exhibition of the shroud, which all believed to be the shroud of our Lord. The Lord Henry of Pouters, of pious memory, then Bishop of Troyes, becoming aware of this, and urged by many prudent persons to take action, as indeed was his duty in the exercise of his ordinary jurisdiction, set himself earnestly to work to fathom the truth of the matter. For many theologians and other wise persons declared that this could not be the real shroud of our Lord having the Savior's likeness thus imprinted upon it, since the holy Gospel made no mention of any such imprint, while, if it had been true, it was quite unlikely that the holy Evangelists would have omitted to record it, or that the fact should have remained hidden until the present time. Eventually, after diligent enquiry and examination, he discovered the fraud and how the said cloth had been the object of an artistic reproduction, as proved moreover by the artist who reproduced (or depicted) it, and who attested it was the work of human skill and not miraculously wrought or bestowed. Accordingly, after taking mature counsel with wise theologians and men of the law, seeing that neither ought

nor could allow the matter to pass, he began to institute
formal proceedings against the said Dean and his
accomplices in order to root out this false persuasion.
They, seeing their wickedness discovered, hid away the
said cloth so that the Ordinary could not find it, and they
kept it hidden afterwards for thirty-four years or
thereabouts down to the present year."[26]

So it is a fake, after all. Or is it?

According to the same publication from which we
took this translation, the editor states flatly, "No fair
copy of this document and no record of its having been
sent [to the Vatican] is to be found in the official
archives of the Chancellery."

Ian Wilson echoes that sentiment. "The reputed
Bishop D'Arcis's letter," Wilson states, "has never been
proved genuine. It is, in fact, somewhat questionable in
itself. The handwriting, for one thing, is definitely not
that of Bishop D'Arcis. And there is also no proof that
the pope ever saw it, or that it was delivered to him.
Neither has the slightest substantiating documentation
ever been found to support these allegations, nor has
any trace, or hint of identity ever been found of the
'artist' who, if he ever existed, would have been infi-
nitely superior to Michelangelo, Da Vinci, or Raphael.

"In addition," Wilson continues, "if the purported
letter were actually written by Bishop D'Arcis, the allegations were things that he only heard of . . . some
thirty-four years later. We have all witnessed enough
courtroom dramas on television to know that 'hearsay'
is not admissible in a court of law. Could there have

---

[26] *R. P. Georges de Nantes, ed.*, The Catholic Counter-Reformation in
the XXth Century, *March 1991*.

been perhaps a darker reason behind the purported Scandal at Lirey letter?"

But what of the other point made by Nickell and other critics who cite the fact that there is no historical trail by which the shroud can be traced prior to 1353. If that is true, there is a void of some thirteen hundred years from the time it was supposedly wrapped around the body of Christ to its appearance in the church at Lirey, France. Where was it all those years? Did it even exist during that period?

Dr. Albert Driesbach not only believes such an historic trail exists, he is convinced it goes back to the very day of the crucifixion. "The skeptics are completely wrong," says Driesbach, "when they insist that the trail of the shroud goes back only to the middle 1300s. It does, in fact, go back to the Bible itself, in the book of St. John, Chapter 20. Verse 6 states that when Peter entered the tomb of Jesus on Sunday morning he found the shroud. He saw strips of linen lying there. So we know that, whatever happened to the body, the shroud was left behind in the sepulcher. Surely the followers of Christ would have retrieved it and treated it with great reverence."

Anticipating the next question, Driesbach asks it himself: "But is there any evidence that the shroud wasn't simply lost? It is an important question if we are to believe that the shroud of Turin is indeed, the piece of linen cloth Peter saw in the Savior's tomb."

In an abstract titled "Did Peter See More Than an Empty Shroud?" published in 1991, Dr. Driesbach makes an effort to establish the existence of a knowledge of the shroud in the primitive church. In attesting to Peter's awareness of the image(s) on the shroud, and to make a case for Peter's having seen the image(s), Driesbach quotes from "The Gospel of the Hebrews," as saying, "When the Lord had given the linen cloth to *the servant of the priest,* he went to James and appeared to him."

In this same publication Dr. Driesbach quotes J. T. Dodd, writing in *The Commonwealth,* in October of 1931: "The original reading was Simon (Peter) instead of servant . . ." And Dodd goes on to say, "It was more likely that the original did state that Jesus gave the Shroud to Peter, because Paul . . . states that 'he was first seen of Cephas.' "

Driesbach also quotes Alberto Vacarri, who observed, "The Gospel of the Hebrews, not only confirms John's (20:2–10) account of the discovery of the shroud by Peter and John, it goes one step further by indicating its possession by Peter himself."

That such was the belief in the early church is further confirmed by Driesbach in a quotation from *The Life of St. Nino.* On her deathbed in A.D. 338, Saint Nino gave an account of what she had been taught in Jerusalem as a young girl.

> And they found linen early in Christ's tomb, whither
> Pilate and his wife came. . . . Now they did not find the
> Shroud (Sudari) but it is said to have been *found by Peter
> who took it and kept it* [italics added], but we do not
> know if it has ever been discovered.

There is, then, evidence that the early church believed and taught that the shroud was not only retrieved by Peter but was also in his possession for some indeterminate period of time. That the early Christians would have taken precautions to protect this holy relic is only common sense—particularly in view of the fact that they were severely persecuted and in constant fear for their lives. Hiding or protecting any relic would have been essential in order to protect themselves. What those protective measures might have been, however, is pure conjecture.

A reference to something that some sindonologists (*sindon* is the Greek term for shroud, the study of which has now become an independent discipline called "sindonology") believe could be the shroud appears in a fourth-century Syriac manuscript. According to Dr. Driesbach, the manuscript "tells us the king of Edessa, a man called Abgar, was cured of leprosy when he received a *cloth* from a group of Christians that had upon it the *image of Jesus' face.* We can reasonably assume then," Driesbach concludes, "that an early Christian band carried the precious shroud to Edessa for safekeeping."

That is an assumption that doesn't stretch credulity too far, but where did it go from there? Driesbach believes he has an answer. "Probably for protection," he tells us, "the shroud was placed in a specially made box of gold latticework. When [it was] folded upon itself four times, only the image of the head would be seen. And again, for the sake of protection, the caretakers of the shroud did one other thing: They began to refer to it as the *Mandylion,* a Greek term meaning simply 'towel.' "

Barrie Schwortz, an expert in still photography and electronic imaging, and a former faculty member at the Brooks Institute of Photography, believes the creation of the Mandylion is a most important event. "Up to the time of its [the Mandylion's] exhibition in Edessa, there were no realistic pictorial representations of Jesus Christ." According to Schwortz, "With the appearance of the Mandylion the pictorial concept of Christ changed drastically, from a beardless youth, like the Greek god Apollo, to what has become the universally accepted version today. There is no doubt among experts that what is known as the *Mandylion of Edessa* was the prototype for all the pictorializations of Christ from that day to this."

It is perhaps one of the more surprising aspects of Christian literature that nowhere in the Gospels is there even the slightest hint of what Christ might have looked like. None of his contemporaries tell us whether he was tall or short, fat or thin, bearded or clean-shaven. We have only Isaiah's prophecy that he would be "without beauty, without majesty . . . no looks to attract our eyes, a thing despised and rejected by men . . . a man to make people screen their faces; he was despised and we took no account of him" (Is. 53: 2,3). Or the Psalmist's assurance that "of all men you are the most handsome" (Ps. 45:2). The spectrum is as broad as man's imagination. Why, then, do all of the current depictions of Jesus of Nazareth bear such a startling resemblance to one another? And why, fourteen centuries after his death, were so many people willing to accept the image on the shroud as being a reliable representation?

If we go back from the point in time that the shroud is known to exist (middle fourteenth century) to the time of St. Augustine, we find that venerable saint complaining that the portraits of Jesus in his time (early fifth century) were "innumerable in concept and design [for] we do not know of his external appearance, nor that of his mother."

How is it, then, that at one given point, sometime in the sixth century, the features of Christ seem to have been brought into focus? The hair became long and parted in the center, the beard established and decidedly forked, the nose longer and more pronounced than in earlier depictions. Art historians suggest the phenomenon is due to the Byzantine tendency to set rigid standards for all generations to follow. If that is true, it is a remarkable coincidence that the likeness of the shroud was followed so precisely.[27]

There are those critics and skeptics who say it was the other way around. The forger of the image on the shroud simply copied the long-accepted Byzantine image, modifying it as necessary to the medium of linen cloth. The answer to which came first, the shroud or Byzantine imagination, will be determined only by establishing whether or not the shroud is genuine.

So far the shroud, or Mandylion, as it was then called, made its way from Jerusalem, north to Edessa where it was apparently lost, or hidden away and forgotten, until an earthquake broke the city gates of Edessa. The box containing the Mandylion, complete with its gold latticework, was found in the rubble. It was quickly returned to a place of veneration, and there it remained until 944, when the Byzantine emperor, having heard of its existence, sent an army to bring it to Constantinople.

It is interesting to note that historians, theologians, and archaeologists do not seem to question the validity of accounts pertaining to what is classically known as the Mandylion. The controversy occurs when various members of these disciplines question whether or not the Mandylion is, in fact, the shroud that Peter took from the tomb of Christ. But if it did not have some special religious significance, why would the emperor send an army to retrieve it? What great interest of the state could there be in just a "towel" in a gold box?

According to Dr. Driesbach, "We know that a great

[27] *Wilson*, The Shroud of Turin—Burial Cloth of Jesus Christ? *p. 83.*

holiday and parade accompanied its [the Mandylion's] entry into Constantinople, and we know it was once again revered as the true and miraculous image of Christ. But we are still a long way from the church of Lirey."

Dr. Daniel C. Scavone, professor of history at the University of Southern Indiana, sits on the board of directors of the American Shroud of Turin Association. Dr. Scavone has given more than 375 slide lectures on the shroud of Turin, and he believes that from Constantinople the shroud followed a very definable route.

"The Christian European knights of the Fourth Crusade stormed and sacked the Christian city of Constantinople," Dr. Scavone tells us, "and a French knight, Robert de Clari, kept a careful record of what he had seen. Constantinople was stripped of its treasury of art and relics, and the shroud disappeared at this same time. Many historians believe it was given into the safekeeping of the Knights Templar, then the most powerful organization in Europe. It is here that the final connection is made.

"A leading knight of the order at that time was Geoffrey de Charnay. It is believed the shroud was given to him for safekeeping, and even though de Charnay was burned at the stake, he went to his grave without ever revealing its whereabouts." According to some historians, de Charnay was accused of idol worship, because he venerated and would not recant his belief in the sacredness of some object or relic in his possession. If it is true that de Charnay was the knight to whom the shroud was given for safekeeping, it may well have been the object of his veneration. If so, he sealed his convictions with his death.

Interestingly enough, the undisputed historical chain of possession of the shroud at Turin begins with another Geoffrey. Could the young Geoffrey de Charny be the grandson of the old knight? The genealogy is not clearly delineated, but since they both come from the same area of France and since the names are virtually the same (only the letter "a" is missing from the younger de Geoffrey's name), it seems likely.

From this point on, the historical trail of the shroud becomes very easy to follow and is largely unarguable. According to Ian Wilson, "Geoffrey de Charny endowed the collegiate church of Lirey and gave into its keeping the artifact we now call the shroud of Turin. But for some reason, forty years later, de Charny reclaimed the shroud, and for another eighty years, Marguerite, de Charny's granddaughter, refused to return it to the church, even under the threat of excommunication.

"Finally, and probably for financial reasons, Marguerite transferred ownership of the shroud to the regal and wealthy Savoy family in 1452. Subsequently, in 1532 a fire in the Savoy Cathedral at Chambéry, France, damaged the shroud (leaving the diamond-shaped scorch marks down both sides of the cloth). Then in 1578 the Savoys moved to the city of Turin. Duke Louis Savoy was a pious man, and he had a special basilica built onto the Cathedral of St. John, and a vault of marble and iron, to house his most prized possession. And there it remains to this day. But after 1580 the shroud was rarely exhibited, and then only for short periods, some eleven times in four hundred years."

What we have described so far is the historic and religious shroud. When those startling photographs taken by Pia Segundo appeared in 1898, it brought into reality yet another shroud: the scientific shroud.

Can modern pathology confirm the method by which the man whose image is on the shroud died?

What has today's photographic technology added to the image first seen by Pia Segundo? Is there any scientific way to trace where the shroud has been? Finally, and perhaps most significantly, is the shroud of Turin simply the latest battleground in the war between science and religion?

In many ways the scientific shroud is the most fascinating of all.

5

THE SCIENTIFIC SHROUD

*"Until further and better evidence emerges,
the only explanation we can offer is that the
agency that produced the image was
supernatural."*

Donald J. Lynn, nuclear engineer

BEFORE WE BEGIN A DISCUSSION OF THE VARIOUS scientific examinations and tests that have been conducted on the shroud, it might be well to enumerate the various hypotheses of fraud that have been advanced. There can be no doubt that an image exists on this particular piece of cloth, and long before we get to the question of whose image that is, there is the question of how the image was transferred to the cloth in the first place.

Those who support one or more of the various fraud theories, beginning with the Bishop D'Arcis, have been more than willing to suggest methods by which the image got onto the cloth.

Perhaps the most prevalent theory is that the image was created by the application of paint, dye, powder, or other foreign substance. One critic, Walter McCrone, has suggested that iron oxide was used to touch up or create the shroud image.[28] Another, Joe Nickell, advances various ideas that ink or powder application produced the shroud image.[29] Addition of an acid or other chemical to the cloth to produce the image has also been suggested.

[28] *Stevenson and Habermas*, The Shroud and the Controversy, *p. 216.*
[29] *Ibid., p. 217.*

Other theories assert that the shroud image was created by the diffusion of gases upward onto the burial cloth from such sources as sweat, ammonia, blood, and burial spices, or that the shroud image occurred from contact with a body or due to fakery of some kind.[30]

Two things are certain: (1) of the hundreds of burial shrouds that have been recovered, only the shroud of Turin bears such an imprint, and (2) in point of fact, nobody knows for certain how the image was transferred to the cloth. Most investigators, critics and supporters alike, would probably agree that if we could determine precisely how the image got on the cloth, everything else would become quite clear. For over twenty years now a concerted scientific effort has been under way to make that determination.

Beginning in the early 1970s the shroud was made available for scientific study, and since that time various scientific disciplines have been employed to try and solve the problem. While none of the sciences have told us what caused the image to be impressed upon the cloth, they have been able to tell us some of the things that most assuredly did not create the image.

In assembling the data for this chapter, we endorse the statement by the Abbé Georges de Nantes in his opening remarks to a group of Catholics who had assembled to hear a series of lectures on the shroud given in Paris on Sunday, the 25th of November 1990.[31]

"Ours is the truth, whatever the cost," said the

[30] *Ibid.*, pp. *218–219.*
[31] R. P. *Georges de Nantes, ed., "The Holy Shroud" in* The Catholic Counter-Reformation in the XXth Century, *March 1991.*

abbé. "There is no halfway between the first and the fourteenth centuries, between authenticity and fraud. The image and blood of this cloth are either a divine miracle or a human imposture. They are either the work of a villainous and blasphemous lie motivated by lucre, or else they are the extraordinary result of a number of scientifically discernible causes."

What is, or is not, scientifically discernible with regard to the shroud of Turin has been largely determined by a team of forty scientists who established their effort under the name "Shroud of Turin Research Project." The name was a bit unwieldy for most reporters, and it was soon reduced to the acronym STURP. We will so refer to the project from here on. In terms of organization, the scientific investigations were carried out by the various team members, mostly on their own. They were scattered across America and abroad, and much of the work took place in individual laboratories where only the investigators directly involved were privy to the day-to-day work.[32]

According to John Heller, a member of STURP, and a biophysicist who "has an M.D. tucked far away" in his background, the team began to come together very informally in 1973. In the prologue to his book,[33] which is a comprehensive if not complete review of the work of STURP, he states that his interest was first stirred by the report of the deputy coroner and forensic pathologist of Los Angeles County, Dr. Robert Bucklin, with Dr. Joseph Gambescia, a pathologist in Pennsylvania concurring in the findings. Dr. Heller translates the pathology report as saying:

[32] *John Heller,* Report on the Shroud of Turin.
[33] *Ibid.*

Irrespective of how the images were made, there is adequate information here to state that they are anatomically correct. There is no problem in diagnosing what happened to this individual. The pathology and physiology are unquestionable and represent medical knowledge unknown 150 years ago.[34]

But how could all of this have come from the faint impressions of an image at least 600 years old and possibly 1,973 years old? Actually, as we shall soon see, the photographs of the shroud provide considerable more detail than Pia Segundo or any of the shroud investigators ever dreamed possible.

For example, one of the most puzzling and amazing aspects of the shroud investigation comes from the realm of photographic science. Not only is the image on the shroud actually a negative, it also provides three-dimensional information. According to an article in the scientific journal *Science,* certain investigating scientists, the initial STURP group, have actually produced a three-dimensional re-creation of the man in the shroud. The scientists mentioned in the article were from the image-enhancement team at the Jet Propulsion Laboratory. Consider for a moment the implications of that. Here you have a two-dimensional reproduction of what is essentially (to the human eye) a two-dimensional object. Yet, under the very latest technical analysis, the photographs yield perfect three-dimensional information. Other photographs under the same analysis provide only highly distorted information. Yet so perfect is the three-dimensional information on the shroud photographs that researchers were

[34] *Ibid.*

able to construct a perfectly proportioned statue from the data.

There was another amazing discovery in the photographs. This same team, according to the article, while processing the photographic image, found that it had a "wide range of spatial frequencies." This meant that however the image was applied to the cloth, it was completely random. Which further meant that the images could not have been formed by a human hand. It would simply be impossible. No method of applying anything by hand can be directionless.[35]

The leader of the team discussed in the *Science* article was Dr. John Jackson of the Air Force Academy, and the article ended by saying that Jackson's team would probably be permitted to examine the shroud itself in several months. The article concluded that a confrontation between religion and science could virtually be guaranteed.[36]

The business of deriving a three-dimensional image from a two-dimensional photograph, particularly a photograph of what is essentially a two-dimensional object, is surprising and so far unexplained. But when a photo of the man in the shroud is placed in a VP-8 image analyzer, a three-dimensional image of a scourged, crucified man appears on the screen. Furthermore, the VP-8's three-dimensional image is as different from the photograph as a statue is from a painting. Every detail appears in sharp relief. The hair, the beard and mustache, even the expression of the face, slam into one's consciousness. Dr. Jackson and Bill Mottern, a Sandia physicist, were the first to see this image, and they just

[35] *Ibid.*
[36] *Ibid.*

stared in disbelief. It was impossible, but it was there before them.

The VP-8 image analyzer is a computer that is programmed in such a way that "darker" is interpreted as further away. Normally the shadows of a photograph result only in distortion. It is only when actual depth is shown that the VP-8 can produce a three-dimensional picture. That there is three-dimensional information on the shroud is now indisputable. How it got there is the mystery.[37]

Earlier, and on a completely different front, another scientist had been pursuing his own course. "In 1973," according to Dr. Kenneth Stevenson, "the shroud was brought out for a brief examination by a group of European scientists. Among them was the late Dr. Max Frei, a Swiss criminologist and one of the greatest experts in dust and pollen in the world. Dr. Frei almost singlehandedly developed the techniques for determining where criminals had been by samples of dust and pollen from their clothing. This technique is now used universally in police work and forensic testimony.

"At first Dr. Frei's objective was simple," Dr. Stevenson writes. "If the shroud was forged in France of the fourteenth century, then only French and/or Italian pollens would be found in the cloth. But his exhaustive analysis found some fifty-eight specific pollens, many of them indigenous to the Holy Land and southern Turkey, the site of Edessa—and nowhere else in the world. That meant the shroud had been in these places at one time or another.

"Even without the place names, the trail of indigenous plants that have left their identities in the shroud

[37] *Ibid.*, pp. 38–39.

trace the origin from the Red Sea area through Palestine and then onward for its journey of thirteen and a half centuries to the church of Lirey."

Some detractors have suggested that the pollens were carried by winds from the Holy Land to Europe after the shroud was manufactured. Given that it was so infrequently shown and thus out in the open where winds carrying dust and pollen over twenty-five hundred miles could reach it, this suggestion seems a little far-fetched. It would require these serendipitous winds to have been blowing in the right direction at very precise times. And this fortuitous circumstance would have to have occurred several times.

But while we're on the subject of dust and pollen in the fabric, there is the matter of the fabric itself. A great many shroud skeptics allege that the type of linen, the distinctive herringbone weave, was very rare in the Palestine area, but that it was very common after the twelfth century in Europe. Dr. Stevenson says this is not true.

"At the beginning of this century, two of the first truly scientific examiners of the shroud, Professor Yves Delage of the Sorbonne and Professor Paul Vignon, did very comprehensive tests in this area. Under magnification it is easy to see the three-to-one weft that produces the distinctive herringbone pattern. This same pattern is identical to mummy wrappings that go back as far as 2000 B.C. Also, the threads appear to be *handspun* . . . a very ancient technique. By A.D. 1200 the spinning wheel was common in Europe. If the shroud were from that era, the fabric would clearly show it.

"Joseph of Arimathaea," Dr. Stevenson reminds us, "was a wealthy man, and a textile merchant. It is not unlikely that when he gave his tomb for the burial of

Christ, he also donated expensive Egyptian linen grave-cloths that were perhaps intended for his own burial."

Assuming for the moment that the shroud is trace-able to the time of Christ, the question still remains, is it an image of Christ, or a painting by a very clever artist as first claimed by our old friend, Bishop D'Arcis and later by several modern-day scholars?

Joe Nickell, who numbers being a private detective and stage magician among his other accomplishments, has produced negative images similar to those under discussion. His technique is embarrassingly simple and might possibly be the way the images were produced on the shroud.

According to Nickell, "The shroud's image was formed by means of red-colored powder, not liquid paint. The most probable powder was jeweler's rouge, which was certainly available in the fourteenth century when the faked shroud was produced.

"I took a statue of Christ," Nickell said, "and cov-ered the face with a wet linen cloth similar to the linen shroud. Then I pressed it to the statue's face, using a pointed instrument to press the cloth into corners and the details of the face, such as the smile lines around the mouth. Then I dusted on jeweler's rouge very lightly with a powder puff. I carefully removed the still damp cloth from the statue's face and flattened it. The result was a shroudlike face which resembles the mark-ings on the Turin shroud."

Dr. John L. Brown, principal research scientist in the Energy and Materials Sciences Laboratory at the Georgia Institute of Technology, disputes these asser-tions. According to Dr. Brown, "There is a major flaw in Nickell's experiment. Although the blood on the shroud has seeped right through the cloth, as liquid should do, the human image on the shroud is remarkable in that it is only on the surface fibers of the cloth. Nowhere does the image penetrate between the fibers to the back of the linen. But when Nickell's technique is tried on a linen cloth, the surface below is red with jeweler's rouge that has filtered through the cloth."

There is another test now available that was unknown prior to 1978. If the actual photo of the shroud can be processed through the VP-8, so can images created by other experts attempting to demonstrate how the shroud image was faked.

Dr. Brown submitted Nickell's imitation of the shroud to the VP-8 test.

"Interestingly enough," Dr. Brown told us, "when we looked at Nickell's imitation of the shroud, parts of the face which had too much colored powder jut out like mountain peaks. There is great distortion. A fourteenth-century artist/forger could not have gotten the color distribution perfect for sophisticated twentieth-century analysis devices. This is the flaw in Nickell's theory. The shroud of Turin has perfect 3-D information in it. Nickell's image does not."

A particularly sensitive point of discussion with scientists on both sides of the issue centers around what appears to be those bloodstains alluded to by Dr. Brown. The question is: Are the stains actually blood? And if they are, how did they get there?

Dr. Scavone's research into this aspect of the controversy has yielded some interesting results. According to Scavone, "In 1973, when Dr. Georgio Feache at the University of Modena in Italy tested bloodstained threads from the shroud in a chemical solution of benzidine, the test failed to prove the stains were blood. This raised the controversy to new heights. Actually, nothing about the shroud has been more elaborately tested than the purported 'bloodstains.' The stains are separate from the image and are of a reddish-brown color. They range from the puncture wounds in the head and scalp to the numerous marks of flagellation, to the wounds in the wrist and feet—wounds that flow from the right side. The question is, however, are they blood, or could they be paint?"

"Paint," Scavone assures us, "when X-rayed, shows up quite unequivocally. But X rays of the shroud do not show 'blood spots,' which means that the 'blood' could not be paint—at least not any paint that has ever been known. But among the literally thousands of tests that have been performed, one has provided a formidable proof. Test samples of the bloodstained shroud were taken to Yale University for study. Dr. Heller [whom we met at the beginning of this chapter] and his associate, a Dr. Adler, not only determined that the markings on the shroud were indeed blood, but blood and sera, highly loaded with bilirubin. Bilirubin is a bile pigment that would show up only if the dead man had been jaundiced, or . . . *severely and horribly beaten* [emphasis added].

"Meanwhile, on the other side of the ocean, and working completely independent of Heller and Adler, the noted pathologist Pier Baime Ballone came to the further conclusion that the blood spots on the shroud were human and were type AB.

"Of course, the spurious and alleged forger of the shroud could have used human blood, obtained from someone who had been brutally tortured, but that then brings up the question, how would he have known to do that?"

An excellent question, and one that might be asked about several of the alleged methods of forgery. How could a fourteenth-century artist, no matter how skillful, anticipate all of the modern high-tech analysis to which his work would be subjected? Even fifty years ago much of the science now being applied to the shroud was unknown.

But even if it can be proven that the image is not a forgery, and that the blood is indeed real, is that proof that this particular linen cloth is the burial shroud of Jesus Christ? Critics and skeptics don't think so. But there are other tests.

Earlier we mentioned the findings of Dr. Robert Bucklin, former coroner and forensic pathologist for Los Angeles County. Dr. Bucklin, you will remember, indicated there was no difficulty at all in determining what happened to the individual who had been covered with the shroud. If that is true, his findings should relate to what we know about the way Christ died.

Dr. Bucklin, using only the information on the shroud, gave the following analysis:

"This is a five-foot, eleven-inch male Caucasian weighing about 178 pounds. The lesions are as follows: beginning at the head, there are blood flows from numerous puncture wounds on the top and back of the scalp and forehead. The man has been beaten about the face, there is swelling over one cheek, and he undoubtedly has a black eye. His nose tip is abraded, as would occur from a fall, and it appears that the nasal cartilage may have separated from the bone.

"There is a wound in the left wrist, the right one being covered by the left hand. This is the typical lesion of a crucifixion. The classical portrayal of a crucifixion with nails through the palms of the hands is incorrect. The structures in the hand are too fragile to hold the live weight of a man, particularly of this size.

"There is a stream of blood down both arms. This indicates injuries to the wrists. Gravity would cause the blood to flow down the arms. On the back and on the front there are lesions which appear to be scourge marks. Historians have indicated that Romans used a whip called a flagrum. This whip had two or three thongs, and at the ends there were pieces of metal or bone which look like small dumbbells. Here [on the photographs of the shroud] you can see that the thongs and metal end-pieces from a Roman flagrum fit precisely into the anterior and posterior scourge lesions on the body. The victim was whipped from both sides by two men, one of whom was taller than the other. There is a swelling in both shoulders and abrasions, indicating that something heavy and rough had been carried across the man's shoulders within hours of death.

"On the right flank, a long narrow blade of some type entered in an upward direction, piercing the thoracic cavity through the lung and into the heart. This was a postmortem event, because separate components of red blood cells and clear serum drained from the lesion.

"Later, after the corpse was laid out horizontally and face up on the cloth, blood dribbled out of the side wound and puddled along the small of the back. There is no evidence of either leg being fractured. There is an abrasion of one knee, commensurate with a fall, as is the abraded nose tip. Finally, a spike has been driven through both feet, and blood has leaked from both wounds onto the cloth. The evidence of a scourged man who was crucified and died from cardiopulmonary failure, typical of crucifixion, is clear-cut."

Dr. Firpo Carr, an author and expert in Semitic languages who currently teaches computer science at UCLA Extension, tells us, "The coroner's report fits every recorded detail in the Bible account regarding the beating of Christ by the Romans, his wearing of the crown of thorns, his abrasions resulting from having to carry his own crucifixion cross and from falling on the cobblestone roadway en route to crucifixion, and finally the results of the Roman soldier driving a spear into his right side to make sure he was dead. It matches perfectly with everything we know from the Bible about the death of Jesus Christ."

There is other historic evidence that supports the biblical description and appears to be supported by Dr. Bucklin's analysis as well. We know, for example, that the victims of crucifixion died from suffocation when the weight of the body collapsed the lungs. Trying to avoid the inevitable, and in spite of the excruciating pain, pushing up against the nails in the feet would give the victim momentary relief and allow him a quick gasp of air. In order to hasten death, the Roman soldiers broke the victim's legs. In fact, virtually all crucifixion victims discovered to date have the bones in both legs broken. The Bible, of course, specifically states that no bones would be broken in the body of Christ.

Taken as a whole, the evidence is impressive indeed that the shroud of Turin could be the actual burial cloth of Christ. But advocates of that position received a serious setback in 1988. It had been ten years since the shroud had been exhibited, and then for only the fourth time in this century, but in an attempt to throw more light on the shroud controversy, the cloth was opened up to carbon-14 testing. Instead of illuminating the problem, the schism was only deepened, but this time it was scientist versus scientist.

In 1978 the STURP team had been invited, as promised by the Turin authorities, to do testing on the actual shroud rather than trying to seek answers just from photographs. Using the latest high-tech equipment, members of the STURP team examined the shroud for five intensive days. The data they recovered, including shroud samples, resulted in seven years of exhaustive study and over 150,000 man-hours of testing and interpreting the information derived from the shroud, making it one of the most intensively studied artifacts in history. Several of the results of these tests we have already discussed.

Then, in 1988 three independent laboratories took part in a carbon-14 dating analysis authorized by the Turin commission and supervised by the British Museum. The results proved disappointing to supporters of the shroud's authenticity and raised the controversy to a new level of charges and counter-charges that still rage to this day.

On the 14th of October 1988, a press conference was held at the British Museum, where the shroud was declared to be a hoax by Dr. Michael Tite, at that time director of the British Museum research laboratory. He was accompanied by Professor Edward Hall, then director of the Research Laboratory for Archaeology and History of Art of Oxford University, and by physicist Robert Hedges.

According to Dr. Tite, "Carbon-14 dating analysis conducted on the shroud of Turin at three separate laboratories in the United States, England and Switzerland, produced radiocarbon dates ranging from 1260 A.D. to 1340, about thirteen hundred years shy of being the possible burial cloth of Christ."

The reaction was immediate. According to Dr. Kenneth Stevenson, "The news conference resulted in an outpouring of articles saying that the shroud was obviously a forgery." But, Dr. Stevenson insists, "Nothing could be further from the truth. Even if the dating had not been fraught with scientific procedure problems, the shroud had been demonstrated to be a genuine burial garment and not a human endeavor. The mood of the day seemed to be to accept the dating without question and to leap to unwarranted conclusions."

Scientists involved with carbon-14 dating procedures now found themselves in direct opposition to scientists of virtually every other scientific discipline, with Doctors Tite and Hall at the very center of the storm. Accusations of scientific "fraud" were leveled, including a suggestion that the shroud sample had been switched with the sample from a mummy.[38]

Doctors Tite and Hall were invited to attend a Catholic symposium in Paris, scheduled for November of 1990, to hear the charges and respond to them. Their replies are indicative of the level of acrimony that has been reached over the carbon-14 test results. Dr. Hall's reply read,

> Dear Sir, I do not waste my time discussing serious matters with people who are bigoted. I will not be coming to Paris in November at which time you are welcome to make these sentiments known. As far as I am concerned the matter is closed. Yours sincerely for E. T. Hall [signature illegible].[39]

Dr. Tite's response was more civil, but expresses the same disdain for any suggestion that the carbon-14 tests were not decisive.

> Dear Brother Bruno, In response to your letter of 13 October I write to confirm that I remain fully convinced that the radiocarbon dates of the shroud of Turin as

---

[38] R. P. Georges de Nantes, ed., "The Evidence of a Scientific Forger" in The Catholic Counter-Reformation in the XXth Century, March 1991, pp. 1–9.
[39] Ibid., p. 3.

presented in the February 1989 issue of *Nature* are valid. Yours sincerely, M.S. Tite.[40]

We should point out that arguments questioning the validity of Dr. Tite's conclusions do not all come from theologians by any means. Russell Breault, a shroud researcher, lecturer, and author of a summary of the June 1993 International Scientific Symposium on the Shroud of Turin, says pointedly that "carbon-14 dating is far from an exact science. Freshly killed mollusks show they have been dead for three thousand years while bristle cone pine, the oldest trees on earth, always date too young by two thousand to three thousand years."

Dr. Scavone reports, "Recent carbon dating of a Nixon campaign button found along the berm of the Pennsylvania turnpike revealed its age as between one hundred and one hundred and twenty *million* years. We know, of course," Scavone is quick to add, "the reason for this was that the dating was reading the fossil-fuel age of the gasoline emissions. But the point remains that carbon dating is not always a dependable test, and certainly not in the case of the shroud."

Scavone may have hit upon a crucial point—that is, what is the effect of outside influences on an object being subjected to carbon-14 testing?

Breault's summary of the 1993 scientific symposium refers to the findings of Dr. Dimitri A. Kouznetsov, a specialist in physical-chemical research at the Moscow State Center for Sanitation and Ecology Studies. According to Breault, Kouznetsov dropped "the bombshell" of the conference.

"It is known," writes Breault, "that the shroud was

[40] *Ibid.*

nearly destroyed in a fire which occurred in 1532. The shroud was kept in a silver casket of which the top melted and burned through the shroud. Silver melts at nine hundred degrees centigrade. By simulating the environment of the fire, which would have been rich in carbon dioxide and carbon monoxide, Kouznetsov was able to show that linen will absorb up to forty percent more carbon 14 from the surrounding carbon-rich gases. This is referred to as 'isotopic exchange.' Kouznetsov sharply criticized the carbon labs involved in the 1988 test for not doing similiar experiments to see what altering effects the fire may have had.

"Kouznetsov claims that recalculating the results of the 1988 carbon-dating tests, taking account of . . . these variables would establish an age of the shroud at no less than nineteen hundred years, or first century."

Dr. Stevenson also investigated the investigators with some surprising results. "Three labs were selected to perform the carbon-14 tests," Stevenson told us. "They were given three samples to test. One sample was a piece of the bull mummy linen, the oldest of the samples and already known to be from 3000 B.C.! The three lab results on this piece of cloth varied from 3440 to 4517 B.C., a variance of 1100 years. On the other samples the range of error was from 439 to 1500 years.

"The testers defend the errors," Stevenson says, "as due to contamination of the samples. But after extensive retesting the oldest sample was still some one thousand years off—on the young side."

Stevenson concludes, "Carbon-14 testing is far from exact. There are simply too many variables that can affect the test sample, as in the case of the Nixon campaign button."

Interestingly, in comments on the British Museum's involvement in carbon-dating the Turin shroud,

William Meacham points out that "no testing or physical measurements were conducted on the site [from which the samples were taken] in question to ascertain if it had been damaged or altered in any way by the fire in 1532. This criterion for the C-14 samples to be tested was recommended unanimously by the Turin Commission on Carbon Dating. This condition was ignored, and the samples were taken from a scorched area."

And so the controversy rages. Science, it seems, rather than solving the mystery, has only added more fuel to the fire (so to speak).

So where does all of this leave us?

Dr. Scavone thinks we are still a few steps further down the road than we were before STURP and before the carbon-14 tests. "If, as the skeptics insist," he writes, "the shroud of Turin is a medieval fraud, then it was executed by an incredible genius with knowledge in several fields of the arts and sciences, from medicine and anatomy to photography, chemistry, and, of course, painting. A genius who anticipated the discovery of the microscope, spectrographs, photography and all the space-age technologies: A unique forger who found an ancient linen in Palestine and carried it on an incredible odyssey to give it the character ascribed and produced the dual images on it that not all the Michelangelos and Da Vincis of the Renaissance could have brought off in a hundred lifetimes."

Of the extensive and objective scientific tests that have been performed on the shroud, the preponderance favor authenticity. Indeed, only the carbon-14 dating tests, which the scientific world agrees are undependable and error-prone, point to the relic as a medieval fake. The shroud of Turin appears to be a genuine burial cloth from the time of Christ. But is it the burial cloth *of* Christ?

It is from the images on this cloth that the final judgment will have to be made. What, precisely, are they? How did they get on the cloth and remain visible and measurable after two thousand years?

Donald J. Lynn, a nuclear engineer at the University of California at Los Angeles, and an independent consultant, believes some process we have yet to discover may be the answer.

"The scientific team which examined the shroud in 1978," Lynn reminds us, "calculated that the longest period the body would have been in contact with the shroud was twenty-four to thirty-six hours. Then, in a mere millisecond of time, something happened that affected only the topmost fibers of the shroud. The concept of an unknown force of energy forming the image is implicit from the manner in which the image seems to have been created with a strict up-and-down direction, and with no apparent diffusion. There is no imprint either on the sides of the body or the top of the head. Until further and better evidence emerges, the only explanation we can offer is that the agency that produced the image was *supernatural*."

The shroud of Turin, at the present time at least, continues to be one of the great mysteries of the modern world. If it is authentic, it is the greatest, most wondrous relic of all time. If it is not, it is equally the greatest, most wondrous *fraud* of all time. As the Abbé Georges de Nantes said, "There is no halfway between . . . authenticity and fraud." It is one or the other.

That is precisely what makes the investigation of the shroud of Turin worth all of the effort that has gone into it thus far. Whatever else it takes to discover the truth will also be "worth it." We can only hope the authorities in Turin will continue to open this remarkable relic to study and examination. Obviously the carbon-14 tests need to be redone, taking into account some of the suggestions made by the critics of the last series of tests. It seems inconceivable that such explicit scientific studies could result in such diverse conclusions.

We are all, along with the abbé, waiting for the final truth.

6

THE OAK ISLAND TREASURE

"Forty feet below, two million pounds are buried."

Translation of an inscription on a stone found buried at the hundred-foot level.

JUST OFF THE COAST OF NOVA SCOTIA, IN ONE OF many indentations along the irregular line of the southern shore, called Mahone Bay, sits a tiny blip of land called Oak Island. It would be hard to find a more nondescript piece of real estate.

Oak Island is one of some three hundred and fifty islands scattered throughout Mahone Bay on the Atlantic coast, about forty miles southwest of Halifax. It draws its name from the large umbrella-domed red oaks that at one time proliferated on the island. Today only a few remain to remind us of the origins of the name, which dates back to sometime prior to 1776.

The island is about a mile long and less than half a mile wide at its broadest point and is in roughly the shape of a peanut, squeezing down to less than four hundred yards at its narrowest point. Its two ends rise to barely thirty-five feet above sea level. Since 1965 the western end of the island has been connected to the mainland by a causeway that was built to transport the heavy digging and pumping equipment that all but covers the eastern end of the island.

A few hundred yards from shore, lies "The Money Pit,"[41] a rather strange name for a hole in the ground

[41] *D'Arcy O'Connor,* The Money Pit.

that has not produced so much as a nickel in almost two hundred years. Of course, the name is very appropriate if what you really mean is a pit into which great sums of money are thrown.

There are other names for this tiny blip of land poking out of the North Atlantic. It has also been referred to as "Treasure Island," which, given the strange nature of this particular mystery, is also a massive misnomer. Perhaps a more accurate name is the one that appeared in the *Smithsonian* magazine in June of 1988 —"Death Trap"[42]—since to date this infamous pit has claimed six lives.

The mystery begins on a summer day in 1795. Daniel McGinnis, a teenager, was wandering through the densely wooded eastern end of the island when he wandered into an area that by all appearances had been worked in the past. Aged oak stumps were visible, but the thing that caught his eye was a distinct depression beneath one of the trees. This by itself might not have attracted his attention, but as he looked about he also noticed that the depression was directly beneath a large, thick limb about fifteen feet up that had been cut off several feet away from the trunk. The depression was shallow and saucer-shaped, and it seemed obvious to the boy that the ground had "settled" directly beneath this cut-off limb.

McGinnis had heard the stories about pirates and privateers that once roamed the waters of Nova Scotia, and the idea that maybe that depression meant someone had been digging there fired his imagination.

In fact at least one of the legends has it that the notorious pirate Captain William Kidd buried an enormous treasure somewhere on the coast of Nova Scotia.

[42] *Douglas Preston*, Death Trap Defies Tresure Seekers.

Oak Island was close enough to the mainland to be considered the coast, and someone had certainly disturbed the ground under that limb. It was, he noted carefully, sturdy enough to have been used to bring dirt up and perhaps let great treasure chests down.

One can only imagine what dreams of riches went through the boy's head as he raced back to the mainland to tell his friends of his discovery. The next day, McGinnis and two friends, John Smith, aged nineteen, and Anthony Vaughn, aged sixteen, returned to the tree with spades and pickaxes. They began digging and quickly discovered that their shovels easily penetrated the relatively loose soil of the depression. Two feet down they discovered a layer of carefully laid flagstones. When they cleared away the soil to remove the stones, they discovered they were working in a circular shaft with a diameter of roughly twelve feet that had obviously been refilled at some point in the past.[43]

The boys continued to dig and noticed that pick marks were clearly visible along the hard clay walls. Someone had done a lot of work in preparing this hole, but they couldn't have even begun to imagine how much.

At the ten-foot level they suddenly struck a tier of tightly fitted oak logs that completely covered the pit and was anchored in the walls. They removed the logs with some effort and continued digging, only to encounter the same log platform at the twenty-foot level and again at the thirty-foot level. By this time the three young men realized they were, both literally and figuratively, in over their heads.

All of this digging had produced nothing except the certainty that someone else had been digging in this pit

[43] *O'Conner*, The Money Pit.

before them, and from the look of the oak logs they removed, it had been a good long time before. They were also convinced that there must be something very valuable down there. What other reason could there possibly be for the kind of complicated workings they encountered.

Nevertheless, the three young men abandoned the project and apparently little else was done for at least seven years (accounts differ). The three boys, all of whom lived into the mid 1800s, never did find out just how "deep" this mystery really was, but all three—McGinnis, Smith and Vaughn—were recruited by a syndicate called the Onslow Company that was put together in 1802 to excavate the pit and find whatever it was that was buried there.

As part of that crew, they did discover that the pit extended down at least ninety feet, with the same oak platforms at each ten-foot level. Even more of a puzzle was the layers of charcoal, putty, and a fibrous material that turned out to be coconut husks covering some of the wood. (Unbeknownst to anyone at the time there were tons of these coconut husks on the island, but even if the diggers had known that, they wouldn't have been able to explain how the husks got there. The nearest coconut tree was at least fifteen hundred miles to the south.)

Setting aside for the moment any embellishments that might have crept into the accounts, everyone agrees that the pit was discovered by Daniel McGinnis in 1795 and that he and two friends, Smith and Vaughn, excavated it to a depth of about thirty feet. At that point they abandoned the work, without ever finding so much as a rusty nail. But, according to D'Arcy O'Connor, they had "launched the world's longest and most expensive treasure hunt."

It is a treasure hunt that has attracted not only gold seekers but many of the already rich and about to be famous. In 1909 a young law clerk named Franklin Delano Roosevelt came to Oak Island to test the idea of a treasure hunt. Reports have it that he arrived with a pick, shovel, and high hopes. Admiral Richard Byrd, Errol Flynn, and Vincent Astor likewise had heard of the Oak Island Treasure and developed an interest in the prospects as well.[44]

While working for the Onslow Company, the boys discovered yet another mystery, perhaps the most enigmatic of all. Just prior to reaching the ninety-foot level, they uncovered a large, flat stone. On the bottom of the stone two lines of strange and indecipherable geometric symbols were discovered. An inverted triangle followed by an inverted triangle with two diagonal lines through it, followed by a slash with tiny circles above and below the line, followed by a circle with a slash through it, another triangle, and a downward-pointing arrow . . . and so on. The inscription was neatly carved and certainly looked as if it were intended to serve some instructional or communication purpose. But whatever that purpose was, it was neatly concealed.[45] The workers could make no sense of it at all, and the stone eventually wound up in John Smith's house as a part of his fireplace.

At this point we'll leave the efforts of the Onslow Company and follow the journey of this "inscription stone," since it figured prominently in efforts to put together another syndicate to seek the treasure of the Money Pit.

A man by the name of A. O. Creighton, who was

---

[44] *Preston*, Death Trap Defies Treasure Seekers.
[45] *Ibid.*

trying to put together yet another treasure-hunting team, years after the Onslow Company gave up, came into possession of the stone somehow and brought it to Halifax in an attempt to attract investors. While it was there, a language professor at Halifax University claimed to have translated the inscription on the stone. According to the professor, it read, "Forty feet below, two million pounds are buried." But this heady translation was discounted by most people, since it seemed to serve Creighton's recruiting efforts far too neatly.

Reproductions of that inscription have come through an unidentified schoolteacher who claimed to have copied the characters for a brief narrative he was writing about Oak Island. He later sent his manuscript to the Reverend Mr. A. T. Kempton of Cambridge, Massachusetts, who, some forty years later, showed the inscription to Edward Rowe Snow. Snow included it in a book called *Mysteries and Adventures along the Atlantic Coast.*

Then, in 1987 Joseph R. Judge, retired senior editor of the *National Geographic* magazine, made an identical translation to the one provided by the Halifax University language professor. In explaining his deciphering system, Judge said, "I simply applied Poe's system from *The Gold Bug* in which he gives the most fundamental of all decipherment rules, that the symbol appearing most frequently will be an 'E' since it is the most frequently occurring letter in English. The most frequent symbol here is one of two dots stacked vertically, thus the second word is blank-E-E-blank. In a buried-treasure inscription that can only be FEET, and once that is known the ballgame is over. You have the F and T of FORTY, which then gives you O, R, and Y. And FORTY FEET blank-E-blank-O-blank can be guessed as BELOW at once. The rest is just working from known letters as they become known."[46]

That would seem to put a capper on it except for one thing: Judge went on to say that he believed the inscription as it has come down to us today is a hoax. "Two million of anything," according to Judge, "is of a modern scale." His presumption seems to be that anyone who had the intelligence to design the pit would devise a much more sophisticated message. All the records of the Onslow Company, did, however, mention the stone and some sort of inscription,[47] though no member of that company ever had the slightest inkling of its meaning.

So much for the inscription stone. Now let's get back to the Onslow Company and the original three treasure hunters. They were, after all, the ones to literally "spring the trap."

The Onslow crew had dug down to the ninety-foot level and were continuing on to what they fully expected to be another oak platform at one hundred feet. The stone they had found with an inscription on it, even though undecipherable, was further indication that their efforts were bound to meet with success.

At about ninety-eight feet the ground beneath them began growing mushy and easier to dig. To McGinnis, Smith, and Vaughn, it must have seemed that they were on the verge of claiming their prize. Shoving a crowbar through the now muddy bottom of the pit, they encountered something solid. Another wood floor perhaps—or a chest? They left the digging that night, prepared to return the next morning and finally discover the treasure they were certain was there.

---

[46] *William S. Crooker*, Oak Island Gold.
[47] *Ibid.*

But the next morning the diggers returned to the pit only to discover that some ancient engineer had created an enormous surprise for anyone penetrating the workings of his pit. The shaft, which up until the night before had been basically dry, was now filled with sixty feet of water. How could that be? The Atlantic Ocean was just a few hundred yards away, it was true, but the hard clay of Oak Island had held it at bay for eons. Why would the island now suddenly spring a leak?

Undaunted, the workers grabbed buckets and began to bail, but it didn't take them long to realize they were having no effect whatsoever on the water level. Discouraged, and up against "haying time," they discontinued the effort for the summer. The diggers, all local men, turned their attention to the matter of gathering in their crops. Members of the digging crew would check the pit from time to time, and were surprised to see that the water level remained constant. Later, in the fall of the year, the company hired a mechanic and a pump to drain the pit, but when the pump was lowered to the bottom of the pit and turned on, it burst before any water reached the surface. They might as well have been trying to pump the Atlantic dry. Which, in fact, they were, but no one knew it at the time.

Then someone noticed that the level of the water in the pit went up and down with the tide. The realization finally struck them; somehow the entire bay was being let into the pit.

The Onslow Company shut down until the following spring when it was shrewdly suggested they come back with a different plan. Even faced with the daunting task of putting the plug back in the ocean, the treasure seekers were not ready to give up. If anything, they were more convinced than ever that the most glorious treasure ever hidden away was somewhere down in that pit. It would have to be. No one would have gone to all that trouble just to hide a few hundred pieces of eight and a pot of jewels. There must be a mountain of gold down there.

The next year they were back, convinced the treasure was just below the ninety-eight-foot level they had reached the summer before. The new plan was to sink a parallel shaft some fifteen feet southeast of the Money Pit, as it was now called, then tunnel over. The new shaft was sunk a hundred and ten feet, and the tunneling began without incident. They bored to within two feet of the original shaft, assuming they were ten feet below the water line. Then the earth barrier gave way. First a trickle, then a stream, then the diggers were running for their lives. Within minutes the second shaft was filled to a depth of sixty-five feet.[48]

Bailing they now knew would be futile, and they were out of ideas. The Onslow Company's Oak Island expedition came to an end. It would be another forty-five years before anyone would again make a serious attempt to solve the riddle of the Money Pit.

Without knowing it, the Onslow Company, in its efforts to "get to the bottom" of the puzzle, had broken a very old but very effective hydraulic seal. When they removed the tightly fitted oak platforms, especially the platform just below the stone with the undecipherable legend, some unknown mechanism let the Atlantic Ocean in. Others would later discover that it had been planned that way, and with considerable genius.

In 1849 a new group called the Truro Company was

[48] *O'Connor*, The Money Pit.

put together to try to solve the problem. The lure of the treasure, if anything, had grown with the passage of time and the retelling of how much effort had gone into the construction of the pit.

McGinnis had died by this time, but Smith and Vaughn could still point out the location of the original shaft. This group dug down to eighty-six feet before the water came pouring in once again and the work was suspended. Later in the summer the Truro Company came back, and this time the workers brought with them a hand-operated pod auger like that used for prospecting for coal.

According to records kept by the company, the second hole bored struck the platform Smith and Vaughn had told them about precisely at the ninety-eight-foot level. After going through this platform, which was five inches thick and made of spruce, the auger dropped twelve inches, hit another four inches of oak, and then went through twenty-two inches of loose metal. The auger continued down into another four inches of oak and six inches of spruce. Something was definitely there between ninety-eight and a hundred and five feet. From there down to a hundred and twelve feet the auger encountered only clay.[49]

Eagerly retrieving the auger, the drillers expected to see some traces of the treasure, perhaps even some certain sign of gold coin or bars. What they were able to bring up was three small chain links resembling those on a watch chain. Whatever else might be there, that was all that was clinging to the auger. But they were made of gold and they now had the first tangible

[49] *Crooker*, Oak Island Gold.

evidence that something of value was in the pit below the ninety-eight-foot level.[50]

The Truro Company determined from its drilling that there appeared to be at least two large oaken chests or boxes, filled with something metallic and lying one on top of the other. If indeed they were right, the chests are still there to this day. But not for lack of an effort to remove them.

The Truro Company came back the next year with a new old plan: Dig another shaft, this time ten feet northwest of the original pit, and tunnel over. Same solution, same result. At a depth of a hundred and ten feet, in a perfectly dry hole, the workers began tunneling over to the Money Pit. Suddenly, as they approached the point of connection, water burst in and sent the workers once again scurrying for their lives. This time it took only twenty minutes for the new shaft to fill up to forty-five feet with seawater. Obviously, a huge volume of water was somehow engineered to enter the Money Pit at about the hundred-foot level. But how? They had encountered no feeder lines leading to the ocean or the bay. And the island didn't float, so how could the water be coming in from below?

Then someone noticed that at low tide in Smith's Cove, approximately five hundred feet east of the Money Pit, a small stream of saltwater trickled *out* toward the ocean at low tide. This was indeed a strange turn of events. Could the pit be draining back into the ocean? The men brought their picks and shovels and began tearing away at the beach. To their complete astonishment, they discovered that the entire beach was artificial.

Now braced for just about anything, they began

[50] *Ibid.*

digging into the sand. In a matter of minutes they were uncovering the same brown, fibrous material encountered in the pit (coconut husks), but here there were *tons* of it. Below that there was a layer of decaying eel grass, and underneath that a bed of tightly packed beach rocks. Immediately the Truro Company began building a coffer dam to hold back the tides. When it was completed several weeks later, and the area was water-free, the workers discovered the clay sea bottom under the artificial beach had been dug away and replaced with five well-constructed box drains. Stretched across the width of the false beach like the fingers on a hand, these catch basins sloped downward as the drainage system approached the shore.

The company of men were sure they had discovered the secret of the flooded Money Pit. But as luck would have it, an Atlantic gale came up suddenly and destroyed the coffer dam. Lacking the time and resources to rebuild it, the company decided to sink a shaft about a hundred feet in from Smith's Cove to intersect and plug the flood tunnel. A reasonable solution—but the men of the Truro Company hadn't even begun to understand the complexity of the task before them.

A new shaft was dug, the fourth so far, but at seventy-five feet they decided they had missed the flood tunnel and moved about twelve feet south. Shaft number five was begun, and this time, at a depth of thirty-five feet, they struck a boulder. When they tried prying it out, they were met with a rush of water. They had found the tunnel.

With confidence at an all-time high, they partially refilled the shaft and drove wooden pilings into its bottom. Surely that would shut off the flow of water and let them get at whatever it was they had been working for.

It was not to be. The flow slackened but didn't stop. One of the workers, McCully, considered the possibility of another drain, but even he was only beginning to comprehend the magnitude of the problem.

In the fall of 1850 the Truro group made one more attempt. They sunk a shaft, the sixth, west of the Money Pit and a hundred and twelve feet deep and tried to connect once again with a tunnel. This shaft was also quickly flooded and the Truro Company gave up.[51]

Someone had designed Smith's Cove as a enormous feeder system capable of dumping the Atlantic Ocean into the Money Pit at a rate of roughly six hundred gallons per minute through a system of stone-walled tunnels four feet high and two and a half feet wide, sloping downhill at a grade of twenty-two percent. The fiber was definitely identified as the fibrous husks that surround a coconut. The Smithsonian Institution, asked to examine the material, pointed out that it was especially resistant to seawater and might have been there in Smith's Cove for several hundred years. This particular kind of fiber, while not often thought of as a filtering agent, was commonly used from the sixteenth to the nineteenth century in the cargo hold of sailing ships to protect casks and crates from breaking and to protect cargo decks from water damage.

A complex system of tunnels, drains, and filters had been constructed that worked on the same principle as putting your thumb over the top of a drinking straw and inserting it into a glass of water. No water will enter the straw until you remove your thumb; when

[51] *Ibid.*

you do, the water in the straw rises to the level in the glass.

But since we know all of that, the mystery was solved and the treasure recovered, right?

Well, not yet. After all, we've only had a little more than a hundred and forty years to work on it.

One of the most bizzare incidents coming out of the Oak Island treasure hunt is the story of the severed hand. By the 1960s so many holes had been dug that the treasure seekers somehow lost track of the real Money Pit and began referring to the various shafts by number. In 1971 a man by the name of Dan Blankenship had enlarged borehole number ten to the point that an underwater video camera could be dropped down into it. He was monitoring the screen while other crew members manned the camera. Everything seemed to be going smoothly when all of a sudden there was an excited yell from Blankenship.

"I called each man," Blankenship recalls. "I didn't say anything, just pointed to the screen. Each man said, 'Damn, that's a hand.' "

A severed human hand seemed to be floating in perfect equilibrium in the murky water and was clearly visible. "I don't say, I *think* I saw a human hand," Blankenship insists. "I *saw* a hand. There's no question about it."[52]

Prior to 1965 Dan Blankenship had been happily and successfully engaged as a building contractor in Miami, Florida. Then one day he read an article about the mystery of Oak Island and decided he was the man to solve the problem. It proved to be a fateful decision. In 1992 Blankenship was still on Oak Island. He had given up his business, sold his home in Miami, and for

[52] Preston, Death Trap Defies Treasure Seekers.

twenty-seven years he and his wife Jeanie have been struggling with the puzzle of Oak Island.[53]

Treasure hunters have continued to return to Oak Island at varying intervals over the years, and while some pieces of the puzzle seem to have fallen in place, no one has yet been able to reach the "treasure," whatever it is. Divers have managed to go down as deep as 235 feet into a vast chamber beneath the area of the Money Pit. They reported V-shaped gouges extending upward, and while they couldn't see the bottom, they could stand on it.[54]

Several treasure seekers, beginning with those of the Truro Company, believe they encountered a cement vault containing a wooden box of some kind, and inside that, soft metal and small metal pieces, such as coins. One auger even brought up a piece of material that was later identified as sheepskin parchment with some kind of writing on it. This concrete vault, if it exists, is believed to be between 154 and 161 feet down, with an iron plate that cannot be penetrated some ten feet below the concrete bottom of the vault.

But who could've built this astonishing masterwork? And what treasure could justify such lengthy and difficult efforts to hide it? Gold? Jewels? Money? What else could it be?

Henry L. Bowdoin, an American engineer and adventurer, upon hearing of all the unsuccessful attempts to gain the treasure of Oak Island, determined that by using divers and heavy machinery he could overcome the water trap. Bowdoin bored twenty-eight holes between 155 and 171 feet deep. The drills encountered

---

[53] *Crooker*, Oak Island Gold.
[54] *Rupert Furneaux*, The Money Pit Mystery.

coarse gravel, sand, and cement, but—overconfident and undercapitalized—the attempt proved fruitless.

Not one to give his reputation up lightly, Bowdoin wrote an article for *Collier's* magazine in August of 1911 declaring flatly that there was no treasure at Oak Island and never had been. You would think that would have had some impact on others who might be thinking of risking their lives and fortunes on the unknown and seemingly unknowable treasure. It didn't.

Bowdoin's assertions went completely unheeded, at least by Gilbert Hedden of Chatham, New Jersey. The wealthy son of a steel-fabricating pioneer, Hedden decided to indulge an old ambition to go to Nova Scotia and solve the problem of Oak Island. When his father's business was sold to Bethlehem Steel, he found himself with the means and the opportunity to do just that. In 1935 Hedden purchased the east end of Oak Island for $5,000.00. He now owned the Money Pit. On one occasion, Hedden, a former mayor of Chatham, wrote to President Franklin Roosevelt advising him of his progress and explaining some of the legend of Captain Kidd, who Hedden believed to have buried the treasure in the first place.

FDR's cordial reply made reference to his earlier Oak Island adventures. Thanking Hedden for the information, he wrote, "It vividly recalls to my mind our semi-serious, semi-pleasurable efforts at Oak Island nearly thirty years ago. I can visualize the theories on which you were working. As I remember it, we also talked of sinking a new shaft on our main runout."

Hedden ultimately had to abandon the actual search when the Internal Revenue Service sued him for back taxes on the sale of his father's business in 1931. By 1942 he was virtually bankrupt, but he managed to retain ownership of the Oak Island property,

and his interest in discovering the secret of the Money
Pit never flagged. He continued his research and answered all of the thousands of letters that were sent to
him over the years concerning Oak Island. He also
learned what it might be that was worth more than
gold.

One of the most extraordinary suggestions Hedden
received stated that the original manuscripts of William
Shakespeare, as authored by Francis Bacon, lay beneath Oak Island.

Burrell Ruth, a professor of chemical engineering
at Iowa State and an avid subscriber to the Baconian
theory of authorship, upon reading of Hedden's search,
the complexity of the works at Oak Island, and the fact
that a piece of parchment had been brought out of the
pit, concluded that this must be the repository for
which Baconian scholars had been searching for centuries. Oak Island, he suspected, was nothing less than
the repository for the horde of original manuscripts
that would prove once and for all that Shakespeare was
really just a name and Sir Francis Bacon was the author
of his many plays and sonnets.

We are tempted to just write this one off, but a
couple of nagging coincidences crop up to keep everyone guessing. For example, Bacon was known to have
written on several occasions about the peculiar properties of mercury for indefinitely storing and protecting
almost anything of value. Such things as manuscripts,
he said, might be preserved for generations using mercury. He also hinted in many of his writings that only
future generations would know who he really was.

Ruth wrote to Hedden predicting he would find
mercury in the Money Pit. In his reply Hedden ac-
knowledged that one of the most widespread and persistent legends about the Money Pit was the curious

belief that it contained mercury. He also told Ruth that an old dump on the island contained thousands of broken pottery flasks (that might have held mercury?). What's more, an old coin and an ivory boatswain's whistle found nearby was dated back to the Elizabethan period.

Ruth's theory was that Francis Bacon himself, before his death in 1626, left instructions on where and how to conceal his original "Shakespearean" and other manuscripts. The complex workings on Oak Island according to Ruth, were designed by Francis Bacon himself.

The theory does appear to explain at least one part of the mystery. Many researchers and investigators have insisted that whoever buried whatever was there never intended to retrieve it. Could it be that Francis Bacon designed an unretrievable treasure chest? In point of fact, Hedden, in his later years, accepted the Baconian theory as one of the more "probable" explanations of the mysterious workings at Oak Island.

In September of 1974, forty years after beginning his search, Gilbert Hedden died without ever learning the answer to the riddle he had lived and struggled with most of his life.

To this point in time nearly two hundred years has been devoted to the mystery of Oak Island. As one group gives up the quest, another is waiting in the wings to take it up. Solving the problem has now become as important as retrieving any treasure that might still be there, whether it's gold or manuscripts. More than that, it has become a challenge to twentieth-century engineers. Can they outthink the mastermind who designed and built the puzzle several hundred years ago? The Canadian magazine *Consulting Engineer* is not quite sure. In an article written in 1973, the editors complained that the island has "emerged as a threat to the reputation of the engineering society as a whole."

A new company has taken up the challenge, however. In 1988 Trition Alliance Ltd., a group of Canadian and American investors, mounted the biggest assault yet on the Money Pit. They began digging a huge shaft two hundred feet into the very heart of the island. Trition's intent is to find the treasure, whatever it is, and perhaps uncover an important archaeological site as well. Or dump another ten million dollars into an empty hole.[55] (It can hardly be called "dry.")

D'Arcy O'Connor, a Montreal journalist who has written dozens of articles and two books about Oak Island said, "This is going to solve it. If this doesn't, nothing will." O'Connor was quoted in *Maclean's* in March of 1989. According to O'Connor, the plan called for "Trition to dam the flood tunnels and block them with cement grouting. It will then pump any remaining water out of the pit."[56]

Assuming they are eventually successful, the two great questions will still remain: Where did whatever might be buried in the pit come from? And who put it there? It's hard to imagine a pirate having the skill to create such a masterwork, let alone having enough booty to make it worth it. Moreover, most pirates planned on retrieving their buried treasure, at least in their lifetime. And the Baconian theory is still very much in doubt. What could be down there that would make it worth all the effort that was put into protecting it?

In one of history's little known and less regarded

[55] *Preston*, Death Trap Defies Treasure Seekers.
[56] *John Daly with John DeMont, "Solving Old Mysteries,"* Maclean's, *March 20, 1989.*

conquests, a British expedition captured Havana on
August 12, 1762. Two days later they officially took possession of the city's public monies, city warehouses
with their contents, public records, military equipment,
and a dozen warships. The British occupied Havana for
slightly less than a year, after which it was traded back
to Spain in exchange for the Floridas. During this term
of rule the British plundered Havana of its vast riches
and extracted huge quantities of gold and silver from
the Roman Catholic Church and the many noblemen
who lived in the city.[57]

What happened to all that wealth? Did the admirals
simply return to England and turn it over to the treasury? Or did they manage to divert a boatload or two
for their own use? Thomas H. Raddall's history of Halifax tells of a "wild visitation from the south" in 1762.
Apparently the British fleet and the army that had
plundered Havana arrived in Halifax and began an unbelievable spending spree. Raddall describes a "satur-
nalia as this rabble of gaunt, sunburned adventurers
. . . flung their pistareens, pieces of eight, and dou-
bloons over the tavern bar and into the laps of prosti-
tutes."[58] They came, it seems, "with enormous loot."

The suggestion here is that it was the British army
and navy, looking for a place to hide the untold wealth
plundered from Havana, who conceived and dug the
Money Pit with its diabolical water trap. Certainly they
had the manpower to do it, and under the strict command of hard-bitten, professional officers, a task of the
magnitude involved in the creation of the Money Pit
might well have been accomplished. And by any measure, the amount of plunder that could be buried

[57] *Crocker,* Oak Island Gold.
[58] *Ibid.*

there, if in fact it came from the spoils of Havana, would make it worth the effort. Still, there is nothing to confirm that British soldiers ever left the brothels of Halifax in order to go dig pits and tunnels on Oak Island.

Or is there?

In the late 1930s a four-year-old girl named Peggy Adams, who lived on the island with her parents, claimed to have seen something very strange. One cold winter day Peggy came running home to tell her mother she had seen "many men wearing red coats and hats that looked like firemen's helmets." Her mother, we may assume, was skeptical but went with her excited daughter to the place among the oak trees where she said she had seen these men. Peggy seemed to be describing a large number of them, but there were no footprints in the snow, no sign of anyone, let alone "many" men. Still, Peggy continued to insist that she had seen them.

Some years later, on a trip to Halifax, Peggy's mother took her to visit the citadel there, which includes a museum. Wandering through its many exhibits, Peggy suddenly stopped and pointed excitedly at the effigy of a British soldier dressed in the uniform of the period from 1754 to 1783. The uniform on the statue was red and the hat was not unlike a fireman's helmet. "Those are the men I saw," she exclaimed.[59] For Peggy, at least, the matter was settled.

Could it be that a youngster of four, innocent of greed or avarice, was witness to the ghostly watch that returns from time to time to see if their plundered treasure still lies safely at the bottom of the Money Pit?

Be that as it may, there are still two persistent leg-

[59] *Furneaux,* The Money Pit Mystery.

ends concerning the preconditions under which Oak Island's secret will finally be disclosed: One states that all of the island's large red oak trees must first die; the other is that the search will end after it has taken seven lives.

So far as we know, there are still a few red oaks remaining on the island, though the number is dwindling fast to make room for more and more men and heavy equipment. And as of this writing, six men have lost their lives seeking the treasure.

The search, and the mystery of Oak Island, still goes on, and we must move on to yet another mystery. This one perhaps the most perplexing of all.

Imagine yourself standing in the cold light of a gray dawn on the edge of the Giza plateau. The sounds of the ancient city of Cairo are swallowed up by the silent sand as you gaze eagerly out across the Gulf of Suez toward the great Sinai Desert somewhere to the east. You are one of a small group of people shivering in the cold as your eyes strain to catch a glimpse of the skyline. Slowly a pink cast begins to chase away the lingering darkness. A whisp of a cloud hangs just above the horizon, glittering orange and gold as the light of the sun begins to dance across its lonely face.

Suddenly there is a collective gasp and you are almost embarrassed to realize you were part of it. But it is unavoidable. There before you a stark stone giant thrusts itself upward as if to block the morning light. On the very top the few casing stones that still remain catch the sun's first rays and reflect a ghostly shade of white, a brief reminder that as great as it is, it was once even greater.

This is the Great Pyramid of Giza, a marvel of astronomical and mathematical information. As an engineering masterpiece it stands unparalleled in all the world. Thousands of people for thousands of years have marveled at this great stone structure. By all the known standards of mathematics, engineering, and construction, it simply cannot be. Yet there it is, confounding science and logic by the sheer fact of its existence.

The chill is suddenly gone from your bones as you struggle with the fact of it, and whisper to yourself, "I don't believe it." No description—nor even pictures—can prepare you for what now looms before your very eyes.

Nothing on the face of the Earth generates a more intense and genuine sense of awe in all those who see it. To look upon the Great Pyramid is to define wonder. Who built it? How did they do it? Why was it built? In over five thousand years none of these questions (the scholarly consensus notwithstanding) have been satisfactorily answered.

7

THE PYRAMIDS

"Everything fears time, but time fears the pyramids."

Ancient Egyptian proverb

THAT SAYING WAS OLD BEFORE MOSES LED THE IS-raelites out of bondage. Those eight words express the awe with which even the ancient Egyptians viewed the pyramids. Indeed, there are some who say the pyramids were old before the first Egyptian crossed the Nile. They are the last of the "seven wonders of the world" to remain standing, and they are still the oldest, and the largest constructions ever made by humans. Even the word "pyramid" is a mystery. Believe it or not, no one knows where it came from. There are no roots for the word in any language on earth.

Still, the idea that the pyramids are anything more than just gigantic construction projects to venerate dead kings is ludicrous to some experts. Dr. Barbara Mertz, Egyptologist and mystery writer, is confident that she and her colleagues have solved any puzzles that may have existed.

"There were some seven hundred pyramids built over five centuries," she says, "and as an archaeologist, the only mystery I see about the pyramids is that people still consider them a mystery. They are simply monumental tombs built for Egyptian pharaohs. That has been proven beyond any doubt. Whatever other mysteries there may have been, archaeology has solved."

Dr. Mertz is articulating what appears to be the

"scholarly consensus." In fact, a number of books have been written that state flatly that the various scholarly disciplines know exactly when, how, and by whom the pyramids were built. For good measure, they also believe they know the purpose of these gigantic structures. If that is true, Dr. Mertz is correct, there is no mystery.

But wait a minute. How was this scholarly opinion arrived at? Is it archaeology, history, or hearsay that has established the origin of the pyramids? Who or what is the authority for such a determination? Dr. Mertz says it is archaeology that has solved all the problems, but there are a number of experts who disagree. Perhaps we should hear from them before we accept the notion that the mystery of the pyramids has been solved.

Just about everyone has heard of or seen pictures of the Egyptian pyramids, but it is not certain that everyone knows just exactly what is so special about these great structures. Before we get too far into the arguments, let's make sure everyone knows why the world's foremost archaeologists, Egyptologists, architects, and structural engineers have spent much of their careers studying these "monuments." And why, if the mystery is solved, do they keep going back to the Great Pyramid year after year?

The pyramid of Khufu, or the Great Pyramid, was built, we are told, between 2600 and 2500 B.C. As it stands today, this pyramid is 451 feet high, but in its original form it topped out at 481 feet. Each of its four sides is precisely 756 feet long at the base, and the whole of it covers an area of thirteen acres. The pyramid is almost solid stone, six and a half million tons of it. There are 203 courses of limestone blocks, an estimated 2,300,000 of them, weighing up to fifteen tons each. Amazingly, despite its huge size, the deviation from dead level, measuring corner to corner, is approximately one fourth of an inch. Modern engineers can only shake their heads in amazement at the scope of this technological achievement.

(You might want to mark your place in the book at this point so you can refer back to it. All of these statistics become very important in tracing the mystery of how and when the Great Pyramid was built.)

The interior of the Great Pyramid (also called the Pyramid of Cheops, from the Greek name for Khufu) contains several small chambers that have been identified as the Queen's Chamber, an antechamber, and the King's Chamber. Interestingly, all of these are reached by way of an ascending passageway that was originally blocked by the builders with a huge granite plug. (Keep in mind, neither the king nor the queen nor the "*ante*" was ever found in this pyramid.)

For some distance ahead of the antechamber, the passageway opens up into what has been named the Grand Gallery. Further down, at the point of the blockage, another "descending" passageway leads to a subterranean chamber. This descending passageway then continues on a short distance to a dead end. Two air channels and a "well-shaft" connecting the ascending and descending passageways have also been identified. Above the King's chamber a pitched "roof" of granite supports the millions of tons of limestone over the chamber. Beneath this roof, five huge granite slabs, separated by granite blocks, serve as a ceiling to the chamber and provide several unique stress-relieving compartments.

All in all, inside and out, the Great Pyramid is a marvel of engineering and construction genius.

And all of this, according to Courtland Canby, author of *The Past Displayed*,[60] was achieved through painful trial and error. In his book Canby suggests that all other theorizing "deliberately discounts over a century of devoted work by the Egyptologists, whose findings clearly indicate that the Great Pyramid was built as a funerary monument for King Khufu (Cheops) of the Fourth Dynasty, and that it dates from around 2600 B.C."[61]

So now it is the Egyptologists who have solved the mystery.

Well, then, why not just accept the findings of the Egyptologists and archaeologists over the past century and let the pyramids, along with these early "trial and error" builders rest on their laurels? After all, they created a monument, not only to their king but to the indomitable spirit of ancient man as well.

That, unfortunately, is precisely the problem.

Egypt, in and around 2600 B.C., had precious little to work with. Their toolbox contained the hammer and adz (a shaping tool, possibly with diorite heads and cutting surfaces), chisels made of copper, possibly the square, the lever, and the incline plane. Other than the pyramids themselves, there is little to suggest the ancient Egyptians knew anything about geometry, let alone trigonometry and physics. And the science of geology was unknown. Yet all of these sciences virtually reach their zenith in the construction of the Great Pyramid.

The Great Pyramid is of a height that suggests dynamic geometry and a shape that directly implies static geometry. The floor of the King's Chamber is the

[60] *Cortland Canby*, The Past Displayed: A Journey through the Ancient World, *p. 195.*
[61] *Ibid.*

shape of a perfect "golden rectangle," which provides the necessary information to construct the Fibonacci series (an integer in the infinite sequence of which the first two terms are 1 and each succeeding term is the sum of the two immediately preceding, e.g., 1,1, 2, 3, 5, 8, 13 . . .) and the logarithmic spiral, the latter being a function of pi.[62] (The logarithmic spiral based on the Fibonacci series is derived when the radius of each quarter-turn of a spiral is determined by the length of the side of the square in which it is inscribed, and the value of this for each succeeding square is in turn determined by the Fibonacci series.) Could all of this be the happy result of trial and error and just plain dumb luck?

Basil Stewart, author of *The Mysteries of the Great Pyramids,* writes, "The plain fact is that we, today, with all our modern engineering appliances and resources, and putting aside the question of cost, would probably find the building of the Great Pyramid to the specification laid down in its geometrical plan, beyond us."[63]

But what of the other pyramids? Were they the precursors to the Great Pyramid? If Canby is correct, the trial and error structures would have come first, followed by the perfect construction of the Great Pyramid, made possible through the learning process.

There is another theory. This theory suggests that the Great Pyramid was already there in all its gleaming glory when the first Egyptians came on the scene and that the Egyptian kings tried unsuccessfully thereafter to imitate it. Near the pyramid of Cheops are two more pyramids, a smaller one usually attributed to Cheops's successor, Kephren, and another, even smaller, still

[62] *Max Toth and Greg Nielsen,* Pyramid Power, *p. 98.*
[63] *Basil Stewart,* History and Significance of the Great Pyramid, *p. 28.*

partly sheathed in red granite. These three, along with six much smaller and badly eroded structures supposed to have been built for Cheops's wives and daughters, comprise what is called the "Giza complex."[64] Roughly a hundred other pyramidal structures line the west bank of the Nile, some of them so badly eroded as to be barely recognizable as pyramids.

Todd Alexander, author of *Ancient Wonder, Modern Mystery,* rejects the traditional arguments advanced by Dr. Mertz and other Egyptologists. "What we are addressing here," says Alexander, "are the three great pyramids at Giza, not the hundreds of paltry attempts to imitate them. The bottom line is that not *one single thing* about the pyramids or the *builders* has been proven. There are two and only two indisputable facts: One, no dead king, or any other mummified corpse, has ever been found in any pyramid, and two, no absolute proof has ever been established for a construction date. Everything else about them remains a riddle. We don't know why, or who built the great pyramids at Giza, and most especially, we don't know *how.*"

So much for the scholarly consensus. And that brings up another interesting point. Most of what we do know about the early history of Egypt and the pyramids, aside from the hieroglyphic record left by the Egyptians themselves, comes from Herodotus, the legendary Greek historian who first saw the pyramid about 440 B.C. By that time the pyramids would have been as ancient to him as he is to us, but it is Herodotus who tells us that each of the pyramids' triangular faces was covered with a mantle of polished limestone, the joints so fine they could scarcely be seen.[65] What

---

[64] *Peter Tompkins,* Secrets of the Great Pyramid.
[65] *Ibid.* p. 2

the Great Pyramid looked like for the two thousand years before the visit of Herodotus is not recorded, however. No description has survived in any Egyptian text.

It is Herodotus, too, who gives the timetable for construction of the pyramid of Cheops. According to his account, 2.6 million blocks were quarried and brought to the site of the Great Pyramid over a twenty-year period. But brought how?

Here there is no scholarly consensus. Currently there are two schools of thought: One insists the blocks were "rolled" along a causeway on logs that were placed in front of the blocks, retrieved from the rear as the stone passed on, and placed in front again to give the huge stones a continuing path to roll on. Individuals who embrace this theory are known as "the rollers." The other theory is content to assume that hundreds, even thousands of Egyptians pulled the quarried stones up long ramps on skids of some sort. Scholars who agree with this idea are called "the rampers."

Each group is certain it has solved the problem of transporting the huge blocks of limestone (though they are less certain about the seventy-ton granite slabs above the King's Chamber in the Great Pyramid), and each uses specific hieroglyphic evidence to support its claims.

Basically, the "rampers" suggest that as the pyramid rose higher, the ramp was systematically extended and elevated as each level was completed. Thus, as the pyramid rose, the ramp rose along with it, gaining in height and length proportionate to the height of the pyramid. This theory seems to have originated with Herodotus, who was informed in Egypt that levies numbering a hundred thousand men were employed for periods of three months to transport stone from the quarries. According to Tompkins, "Herodotus says that to transport the rough blocks from the edge of the Nile to the top of the Giza plateau, a great causeway was built which required ten years to complete. The causeway was said to be three thousand feet long and sixty feet wide, of polished stone, over which sleds could pull the heavy stones."[66]

The theory is given further support by a hieroglyphic depiction found in the tomb of Djehutihotip, showing several score of Egyptians, harnessed in double rank to a colossal statue. In the relief, the statue is placed on a sled, the runners of which are being lubricated by liquid of some kind being poured in front of the sled to decrease the friction. This, say supporters of the "ramp" theory, is how the two-and-one-half- to fifteen-ton blocks were moved up the causeway and eventually up the pyramid.

The ramp theory, among other things, assumes an unlimited supply of manpower. But let's grant that for the moment and examine how the idea of ramps holds up mathematically. Dr. Joseph Davidovits, in his book, *The Pyramids: An Enigma Solved,* presents some interesting statistics with regard to this method of construction.[67] Dr. Davidovits is a chemist and carries out his research at the Geopolymer Institute in France, about a hundred miles north of Paris. According to Davidovits, "We know that sixty tons can easily be hauled over flat terrain. Fifty-five pounds of force are exerted to pull three hundred and thirty pounds, indicating that four hundred men were required to pull the [sixty-ton] colossus [represented in the above men-

---

[66] *Ibid.,* p. 222.
[67] *Joseph Davidovits and Margaret Morris,* The Pyramids: An Enigma Solved, p. 58.

tioned hieroglyph]. Using this system, an average six-ton block being dragged from the quarry to the Great Pyramid on flat ground would require only forty men. But the same operation on a ramp would be extremely complex."

Davidovits goes on to point out that inclined ramps of three-to-one and four-to-one were necessary. That would mean somewhere between one hundred and forty and two hundred men would be required to raise one block. At this point the rampers theory gets very interesting. According to the Herodotus account, 2.6 million blocks were transported over a twenty-year period. Take out your handy pocket calculator and follow along. In order to accomplish that feat the Egyptians would have to move 130,000 blocks per year, or an average of 1,400 blocks per day, and they would be going to an ever increasing height. Assuming teams of one hundred and fifty men per block, each team making four trips per day, that would require 52,500 men to be working together at one time. Squeezing this number of men together in an area only sixty feet wide (even strung out along the entire length of the cause-way), would make it impossible to get the job done. Furthermore, if the teams were capable of only two trips per day (which does not seem unlikely, given the nature of the task) 105,000 men would be required to be working in the same limited space.

But even using the lower number, 52,500 men all jammed together, shoulder to shoulder, pulling and sliding in mud, while maneuvering huge blocks of stone at great heights, presents a ridiculous scenario.[68]

The "rollers" are faced with similar problems, compounded by the fact that trees that might be used for

[68] *Ibid.*, p. 59.

such a purpose would be extremely difficult to come by. The date palms native to the Nile Delta were a food source and would not have been cut down simply to be used to transport stones. Assuming logs of some kind could be imported, the rollers are still faced with the difficulty of making the logs roll in soft sand. And even if that problem could be overcome by hardening the surface somehow, it is still likely that even the hardest wood is probably going to be crushed under the great weight of the stones. All of this before we even get to the ramps.

Davidovits himself proposes a rather unique solution to the problem. He believes the science that made the pyramids possible was chemistry or its predecessor, alchemy.

"The priest of Khnum," says Davidovits, "had long been adept at making extraordinary cements. Cement found in various courses of the Great Pyramid is forty-five hundred years old, yet it is still in good condition. The modern Portland cement used to repair ancient Egyptian monuments, by comparison, has cracked and degraded in only about fifty years.

"The pyramid blocks are not natural stone," Davidovits continues. "The blocks are actually exceptionally high-quality limestone concrete—synthetic stones—cast directly in place . . . no stone cutting or heavy hauling or hoisting was ever required for pyramid construction."

Dr. Davidovits goes on to point out that all of the chemicals and materials necessary to produce such a mixture are readily available and in abundance at or near the pyramid site.[69]

Dr. Davidovits stands alone in his theory of pyra-

[69] *Ibid.*, pp. 69–70.

mid construction, and so far he has been unable to explain certain anomalies, such as irregular shapes in some of the interior stones, as well as large gaps between some in-place stones. But even if the bulk of the stones were cast in place, we are left with the problem of transporting and elevating the several seventy-ton slabs of granite above the king's chamber in the Great Pyramid. Our research failed to turn up any corollary theories as to how these huge granite stones were put in place. Certainly ramping, rolling, or casting in place fails on several counts. Yet, like so many aspects of the pyramid mystery, the great, gray granite slabs are there, taunting us by their very existence.

This is a very old and very heated controversy. Even as Alexander the Great stood in awe before the Great Pyramid, his generals were already arguing over how they came to be. But whatever else they are, the pyramids are a reality—and realities can be measured and quantified.

Napoleon may have been one of the first to attempt to do that. Using only basic arithmetic, he concluded, as he watched several of his men climb to the top of the Great Pyramid, that it contained enough stone to build a wall three meters high and one meter thick around the whole of France. Mathematicians that traveled with him later confirmed this evaluation.

Still the controversy continues. Egyptologists and archaeologists cling steadfastly to the traditional theories of construction: thousands and thousands of men pushing and pulling massive stone blocks up long ramps and putting them in place with the precision of someone performing optical work. Some movie makers have tried to recreate this scene, and even in the world of make-believe the scenario is unbelievable.

Meanwhile many experts agree that mathematically, physically, and scientifically the Great Pyramid simply shouldn't be there at all, since it couldn't possibly be built.

But there it is, standing forty-two stories high and covering an area the size of ten football fields. It is an almost solid mass of intricately fitted stone blocks weighing from two and a half to fifteen tons. Think of it. That's enough stone to build thirty-five Empire State Buildings with a few *tons* left over. All of this was supposedly built by an ancient people with very little technology as we know it, and lacking even the saving grace of the wheel or iron tools. But as we begin to comprehend the size of the structure, the enormity of the task undertaken by these ancient builders takes on yet another dimension.

Greg Pyros, an architect with vast experience in the problems of large construction projects, points out that "before a structure of that size can be built, a geological study would have to be done to determine if the site could support the structure. It's doubtful that ancient Egyptians had any knowledge of modern geology, and without it, a structure that size would simply overwhelm the site it was built on. If it didn't crumble from lack of proper foundation, it would simply sink slowly into the ground."

Authors Max Toth and Greg Nielsen corroborate that idea. "The Egyptians must have been the world's best geologists," they say,[70] "far superior to those of today, since they were able to determine that the west bank of the Nile was the correct site for the pyramid complex. The amount of technical expertise required to determine that the huge area had a solid rock foundation is immense, and requires fantastically extensive

[70] *Max Toth and Greg Nielsen*, Pyramid Power, p. 73.

knowledge in the many fields associated with proper geological surveying."

Whoops! Must have been a trifling point the archaeologists and Egyptologists have overlooked.

While nothing has been built yet that rivals the size and weight of the pyramids, some comparisons can be made that give some sense of the importance of this aspect of the construction of the Great Pyramid.

"In modern construction," Pyros says, "engineers find a settling rate of six inches in one hundred years acceptable for office buildings. The U.S. Capitol, for example, has settled five inches during the past two hundred years. In *five thousand* years the Great Pyramid, weighing fourteen billion pounds, has settled less than one-half inch. Even with all of our modern technology, we are not able to achieve such amazing results."

It would appear that whoever the ancient genius was who chose the site at Giza, he knew more about site location and preparation than the best of the modern world's geologists. But there's much more to the site selection of the Great Pyramid than just the bedrock beneath it. Somebody might have just gotten lucky when he marked off the thirteen acres that situated the pyramid on such a firm foundation, but we also have to contend with the fact that it is located at the precise center of the earth's landmass and therefore less subject to earthquake and ground shift.

Amazing what a little trial and error can do. Now all that's left for the builders is to construct it to the exacting geometric standards mentioned earlier.

Let's see if we can make some comparisons here that will give a little clearer picture of the degree of accuracy the Great Pyramid represents. Dr. Ron Charles, archaeologist, historian, and engineer, has written extensively on the pyramids and other archaeological mysteries. He, too, believes the ancient builders have accomplished something modern construction techniques could not duplicate.

"In constructing the Great Pyramid," Dr. Charles says, "you must think of a square-based, forty-two story building covering seven square blocks in midtown Manhattan. Now each side of the square base of this building measures 756 feet. In modern construction if the builders can keep each side within two inches of plumb, that is, maintaining each side of the 756-foot base wall within two inches of being perfectly straight, it would be a tremendous achievement. But the Great Pyramid is only out of plumb by one quarter of an inch, which is totally impossible to duplicate in the construction field today."

Chuck Missler, an engineer and astronomer who holds graduate degrees in math, engineering, and business from UCLA, agrees. "The pyramid," he reminds us, "also has some descending passages. The one in the above-ground masonry block of the pyramid holds a straight line accurate to one fiftieth of an inch over its 150-foot length. Going through the bedrock below the pyramid, the straight-line accuracy is held to within one quarter of an inch for the entire 350-foot length. We don't know how they held to those parameters forty-six hundred years ago, but we probably couldn't do it today even with modern, laser-boring technology."

That is an amazing admission from a professional engineer, and helps us put into perspective the unbelievably precise work that was done on this huge edifice.

There's more. Originally the Great Pyramid was covered entirely with finely polished white limestone.

On his first expedition to Egypt under Julius Caesar, Mark Antony said the Great Pyramid could be seen from a distance of one hundred miles, shining in the sunlight like a precious jewel.

E. Randall Floyd, author of *The World's Greatest Mysteries,* tells us, "The 115,000 outer casing stones weighing up to ten tons each were removed in the fourteenth century to build the city of Cairo, leaving the pyramids at Giza as they are today. It is known, however, that these casing stones were fitted to tolerances of one two-thousandth of an inch. A razor blade could not be slipped between the joints. Such tolerances have never been duplicated since. In fact, the casing stones of the pyramid were fitted to a higher accuracy than the tolerances used for the heat shield of the space shuttle."

"The two- to ten-ton limestone blocks making up the two hundred and three layers composing the height of the pyramid were cut to an accuracy of one fiftieth of an inch," according to Missler. "What's more," he continues, "the mortar between the stones was usually so thin it can scarcely be detected with the naked eye. Yet it is so strong that even after forty-five hundred years of the ravages of sun, rain, and desert sandstorms, not to mention the ravages of man, the stones themselves will shatter before the mortar will yield."

Somehow the ancient architects and engineers that built the Great Pyramid had a grasp of things we simply do not understand even today. And, remember, up to this point we've been discussing only the method of construction of this magnificent building. Astronomers and mathematicians also find the structure itself absolutely mind-boggling. In this chapter we have only hinted at some of these characteristics of the structure.

Could the ancient Egyptians have known they were

solving the problem of squaring the circle? Did they know the significance of pi? Was the Fibonacci sequence familiar to them?

The answer to these and other questions provide even more surprising results. If there is no agreement on how the Great Pyramid was built, perhaps the precision with which it was constructed can tell us *why* it was built.

8

THE SCIENTIFIC PYRAMID

"When the gods created the cosmos they began by building Egypt and, having created it perfect, modeled the rest around it."

Livio Stecchini, *Notes on the Relation of Ancient Measures to the Great Pyramid.*

N APOLEON BONAPARTE SET OUT TO CONQUER Egypt with thousands of foot soldiers, two thousand cannon, and a hundred and seventy-five "savants," or scholars, as we would refer to them today. Whether or not he fully understood the significance of bringing these scholars to Egypt is open to debate; savants were not highly respected by Napoleon's contemporaries. But the very fact that astronomers, archaeologists, painters, and poets went along seems to suggest that Napoleon had more on his mind than trade routes and colonies.

Napoleon, like Alexander the Great and Herodotus before him, was fascinated by the wonders of ancient Egypt.[71] Judging from the number of savants in his party, and the various scientific disciplines represented, it is possible that Napoleon had some knowledge of the Akbar Ezzeman manuscript. This document is an ancient Arabic text that declares flatly that the Great Pyramid contains "the wisdom and acquirements in the different arts and sciences, the sciences of arithmetic and geometry, that they might remain as records for the benefit of those who could afterwards comprehend them. . . . the position of the stars and their cycles;

[71] *Gerald S. Hawkins*, Celestial Clues to Egyptian Riddles.

together with the history and chronicle of the time past (and) that which is to come."[72]

Apparently ancient Arabic cultures thought the pyramids were more than just oversized coffins. If the Akbar Ezzeman text has any validity at all, the Egyptians, or whoever built the Great Pyramid, certainly had more to go on than simple "trial and error." And while the scholarly consensus seems to be that the ancient Egyptians lacked a knowledge of advanced mathematics, the findings of some modern scientists would seem to suggest otherwise.

Livio Stecchini, a man who has spent his entire life researching the history of measures, wrote an abstract titled *Notes on the Relation of Ancient Measures to the Great Pyramid,* which appears in the appendix of Peter Tompkins's book, *Secrets of the Great Pyramid.* According to Stecchini, "Egypt is the country built according to a geometric plan. . . . Egyptians conceived of their country as having an exact geometric shape. They believed that when the gods created the cosmos they began by building Egypt and, having created it perfect, modeled the rest around it."[73]

This is an interesting concept in light of the fact that if you draw diagonal lines through the pyramid at right angles to each other and extend them to the Mediterranean, it very neatly encloses the entire delta within a triangle. Indeed, the description of the Nile Valley as a "delta" comes from the triangular shape of the fourth letter of the Greek alphabet.

"The geographical orientation of the Great Pyramid of Giza is perhaps its single most amazing characteristic," according to author and pyramid theorist, Anthony

[72] *August Tornquist,* Who Was the Architect, *p. 73.*
[73] *Peter Tompkins,* Secrets of the Great Pyramid, *appendix, p. 292.*

Hilder. "Its sides run almost exactly north to south and east to west, and the deviation is within three arc minutes from true north. Not magnetic north, but *true north itself.* By comparison, the famous Paris Observatory, built to the most exacting modern standards, has a deviation of *six* arc minutes, or twice the tiny error of the Great Pyramid. How could an ancient, quasi–Stone Age culture have been able to determine true north?"

So far no one has come up with a reasonable answer. But what makes it even more astonishing is that the three-arc-minute deviation could easily be due to earth shift. It is entirely possible that when the Great Pyramid was built it was aligned *perfectly* to true north.

What's more, that question is barely the tip of the pyramid, so to speak. E. Randall Floyd, journalist, and author of *100 of the World's Greatest Mysteries,* points out that the builders of the pyramids used a number of highly advanced mathematical concepts: "The Great Pyramid construction utilized mathematics not even discovered until thousands of years later. These include the Pythagorean theorem, the Fibonacci sequence, pi, differential calculus, trigonometry, the golden ratios, and more. How the Great Pyramid architect accessed these yet undiscovered mathematical concepts defies imagination."

Just as the construction techniques are still baffling, so is the relationship of the Great Pyramid to the Earth —and to the stars. Geographically it sits on the only intersecting line of longitude and latitude in the world that equally divides the Earth's landmasses and oceans. Could this location be just the result of chance, or could it, as many theorists insist, have been put there specifically as an astronomical observatory?

Bonnie Gaunt, author of *Stonehenge and the Great Pyramid,* tells us, "Whoever built the Great Pyramid knew the dimensions of this planet as they would not be known again until the seventeenth century of our era. They could measure the day, the year, and the procession of the equinoxes. They knew that the Earth was a sphere and how to compute latitude and longitude very accurately. Since, as far as we know, they did not have space vehicles, they must have had a phenomenal knowledge of the science of astronomy." It almost sounds as if evolution, at least on an intellectual scale, has been running backwards for the last five thousand years.

But if the Great Pyramid was to be used as an astronomical observatory, how was it aligned in the first place? That question has been the subject of intensive study by Egyptologist Zbynek Zaba. Rather than simply tombs, the pyramids, according to Zaba, are monuments incorporating the culture, science, and technology of the times in which they were built.[74]

Documents advanced by Zaba "prove beyond question" that the first thing done when erecting an important structure in Egypt was the ceremony of the "stretching of the cord," by which the north-south direction was determined and marked on the ground.[75] Is it possible that Egyptian priests or architects could, by some purely mechanical means, determine true north with more accuracy than modern astronomers? It would seem so.

In any case, Arab historians repeatedly suggest that the Great Pyramid was originally designed as an astronomical observatory and that it contained reproductions of the celestial spheres. In a book titled *The Great Pyramid, Observatory, Tomb and Temple,* written by

[74] *Tompkins,* Secrets of the Great Pyramid, *p. 150.*
[75] *Ibid.*

the British astronomer, Richard Anthony Proctor, a reference to the works of Roman philosopher Proculus is cited, suggesting that the Great Pyramid had been used for an observatory before its completion.[76]

That possibility was so simple that it was ignored by most academic Egyptologists, but in reality what the builders had done on the Giza plateau was first build a huge graduated slot (the Grand Gallery) perfectly aligned on the meridian through which they could observe the apparent movement of the stars. In Proctor's analysis the builders of the Great Pyramid had accomplished what he "considered the only sensible instrument short of a great modern telescope."[77]

Proctor's theory also provides an answer to a question that has plagued scientists for centuries. If the Great Pyramid was simply a tomb, what purpose was there in going to the enormous work of building the Grand Gallery? It is in no way essential to maintaining the structure, nor does its high, sloping walls appear to have anything to do with any of the other chambers.

In his book Proctor analyzes the problem from the standpoint of an astronomer rather than an architect and comes up with a startling conclusion. "Had an ancient astronomer wished for a large observation slot precisely bisected by a meridian through the north pole, so as to observe the transit of the heavenly bodies, what would he have requested of an architect? A very high slit with vertical walls, preferably narrower at the top; a gallery whose aperture, thanks to the reflected light of the polar star, could be designed so as to be exactly bisected by a true meridian.

"Looking up through such a slot, an observer could

[76] *Ibid.*, p. 147.
[77] *Ibid.*

watch the passage of the entire panoply of the zodiac, easily noting the transit of each star across a perfect meridian."[78]

The mathematical and astronomical precision of the pyramid construction appears to contradict the more commonly held theories. Think of it for a moment. We are being asked to accept the notion that, somehow, some Egyptian architect (Egyptologists like to give the credit to a man named Imhotep) by pure chance hit upon a spot of ground where several billion tons of stone could rest for centuries without shifting or sinking, and that he just coincidentally placed the center of it on the true north meridian, which bisects the landmasses of the earth. Then, by a system of trial and error, he hit upon the precise angle that would make the construction possible. And since he didn't have any knowledge of higher mathematics, the fact that both the ascending and descending passages are at the precise angle of the North Star (the ascending passage being a true reflection of the descending passage) and project downward at the thirtieth parallel, well, that must have been just a lucky guess as well.

The "trial and error" concept, it seems to me, fails on almost every point.

In the latter years of the nineteenth century, "Pyramidology" came into being. This is a study based on the theory that the Great Pyramid was a cosmic-force collector, operating on principles similar to the electrostatic condensers in modern electronics. This concept has drawn the interest of many qualified and scholarly people. Greg Nielsen, co-author of the number-one bestseller on pyramid energies, *Pyramid Power*, contends that "there is a helical vortex of en-

[78] *Ibid.,* p. 152.

ergy emanating from the apex of the pyramid, which actually expands in diameter as it rises higher and higher into the heavens.

"The first example of this apex energy," Nielsen says, "was demonstrated by British inventor, Sir W. Siemans, while standing on the apex of the Great Pyramid. He noticed that whenever he raised his hand and spread his fingers, he heard a ringing sound. If he raised just one finger, especially his index finger, he felt an irritating, prickly sensation in that finger. Siemans also noted that when he drank from the wine bottle he had brought along, he experienced a slight shock as the bottle touched his lips. The electrical activity intrigued Siemans so much that he took a wet newspaper and wrapped it around the bottle, converting it into a crude electrical accumulator which most high-school students would recognize as a Leyden jar. When Siemans held the converted wine bottle high above his head it accumulated tremendous amounts of static electricity, so much so that sparks began shooting from it.

"Siemans accidentally touched one of the Arab guides with the bottle, bringing about an instant labor-management problem. It gave the Arab such a jolt it knocked him senseless. Recovering quickly he took off down the pyramid as fast as his feet could carry him."

Nielsen concludes, "Although we don't know why or how, the Great Pyramid seems to be an accumulator of energies. What we are currently working on and may very well be able to prove shortly, is that the Great Pyramid acts like a resonating cavity which is somehow able to catch and focus unknown cosmic forces, like a giant lens."

Nielsen's theory that a spiraling mass of energy grows in diameter as it ascends into space is difficult to prove—or disprove, since we have no mechanism for measuring whatever form of energy it might be. But with so many intriguing possibilities, does it still seem reasonable that the Giza complex is nothing more than a massive graveyard for royalty? Could it be the Great Pyramid was in fact there before the pharaohs came along?

Dr. Barbara Mertz insists that "in spite of the bizarre and science-fictional theories about these pyramids at Giza, they were and are nothing more than funerary monuments. The largest was built by Khufu, or Cheops, as the Greeks called him; the other two large ones were built by his son and his grandson. The minor pyramids were built for wives and others of the royal families. The sphinx was erected by Khafre, the builder of the second pyramid, and the face bears a distinct resemblance to his own. Giza is a funerary complex. Nothing more, nothing less."

That of course, could all be quite true. But it's interesting to note that the same Egyptologists who seem to be more than willing to accept the unsupported assertion by Herodotus that the pyramids were built in just twenty years tend to ignore another of his historic assertions. In addition to his writings about the Great Pyramid, Herodotus also recorded that the actual burial vault that Cheops constructed for himself was an "underground apartment" on an "island formed by drawing water from the Nile by a channel." If Herodotus is reliable in one instance, why not the next?

According to E. Raymond Capt, "The underground vault described is believed to be a subterranean vault about three hundred yards from the pyramid's Mortuary Temple, known as 'Campbell's Tomb.' Running around this vault is a deep trench, seventy-three feet

deep and five feet, four inches wide, which is filled
with water when the Nile floods."[79]

J. David Davis, author and ancient historian, also
believes the "funerary complex" thesis lacks merit.
"There is a funerary complex at Giza," Davis agrees,
"but this hardly proves that Giza is *only* a funerary
complex. It would be much the same as considering
the cathedral of Notre Dame a funerary complex because there is a graveyard beside it. Also, attributing
the sphinx to the pharaoh Khafre has become untena-
ble. Recent archaeological and geological discoveries
demonstrate that the sphinx is at least ten thousand
years old and maybe even *twenty thousand* years old."

If the pyramids existed before the Egyptians, then
this might explain the funerary buildings and the minor
pyramids at Giza. If the early Egyptians considered the
pyramids a sacred gift from the gods, they might naturally want to be buried near them and in the same sort
of structure. But this theory opens up many more
questions.

"First," states Dr. Ron Charles, "we must clearly
understand that no bodies have ever been found in any
of the Giza pyramids or in any other Egyptian pyramid
for that matter. Furthermore, there is no hard evidence anywhere that the pyramids were ever intended
as the burial tombs of the pharaoh kings, although the
standard archaeological argument is that these tomb
chambers were robbed of their contents. In light of
what we know today, this does not seem likely. In fact,
just the dating and attributing of the three Giza pyramids to the Fourth Dynasty of pharaohs appears to be
based on an archaeological fraud."

Actually what Charles is referring to is graffiti sup-

[79] E. *Raymond Capt*, Study in Pyramidology, *p.* 27.

posedly left behind on one of the interior walls by one of the Egyptian workers or supervisors. For over a hundred and fifty years this splotch of graffiti has been the determining factor in the "scholarly consensus." Happily, a man by the name of Walter M. Allen knows something of this alleged fraud.

"Concerning the hieroglyphic graffiti written inside the Great Pyramid in red paint, which Egyptologists use to this day to identify the pyramid with Khufu," says Allen, "I can assure you that it's a forgery and not authentic. My great-grandfather was an eyewitness to the forgery when on May 28, 1837, he witnessed a Mr. Hill, with brush and red paint, simulate the royal name. When my great-grandfather objected, he was fired and banned from the site. An amusing sideline to the story is that Hill ended up writing 'Rh-u-fu' instead of 'Kh-u-fu,' which would have been like taking the name of God in vain. It would have never happened authentically."

But even today modern Egyptologists hazard their reputations on the misspelled forgery as being the evidence that the Great Pyramid is King Khufu's tomb. But if it wasn't designed and built as a tomb for the king, what was its purpose?

According to Bonnie Gaunt, "The Great Pyramid is designed very differently from the others. All the other pyramids have underground chambers, whereas the Great Pyramid has three above-ground chambers, meaning the use for this pyramid was different."

One of those uses, we have seen, might well have been as an astronomical observatory. Could the basic construction also have been designed as a repository of mathematics for later generations as suggested in the ancient Arabic manuscript mentioned earlier?

Chuck Missler notes, "All kinds of measurements

have been taken that seem to portray a model of the solar system. The concave sides appear to be a representation of the three separate lengths of Earth years, (1) the solar year, which is 365.242 days, (2) the sidereal year, which is about 20 minutes longer due to motions of the Sun and, (3) the anomalistic year, which is the year of the equinoxes and turns out to be five minutes longer than our actual year. When measured in 'sacred cubits' (twenty-five inches) the base and the sides turn out to have ratios that exactly match the length of those years. For example, the direct measure of the base (of the Great Pyramid) is exactly 365.242 sacred cubits. People have been baffled by that. They have discovered that the pyramid anticipates the value of pi, many many times and in different ways. It is also the solution to the classical dilemma of squaring the circle; that is by taking the radius of a circle that's the height of the pyramid, the pyramid would subtend a square whose perimeter is equal to the circumference. All of this comes about because of the magic angle, 51 degrees, 51 minutes, and 14.3 seconds, which just happens to be the angle on which the Great Pyramid is built. In short, the sophistication of the Great Pyramid is amazing."

Amazing may be too tame a word. But we might have to settle for that, since no single word seems to do the Great Pyramid justice anyway. And what is even more tantalizing is the realization that there could still be other secrets yet to be uncovered in the Great Pyramid. They are there, according to the ancient Arabic text, for those "who can comprehend."

There are also, however, a number of misconceptions about the pyramids, and one that stands out prominently is the mythical "curse of the pharaohs." This idea grows out of the activities associated with opening the tombs, such as Tutankhamen's, in the Valley of the Kings, some three hundred and fifty miles distant from the Great Pyramid of Giza.

"The 'curse of the pharaohs' story," according to J. David Davis, a theology graduate of Tennessee Temple University who did archaeological work in Israel from 1986 to 1992, "begins in the 1920s when two Englishmen, Howard Carter and Lord Carnarvon, discovered the tomb of Pharaoh Tutankhamen. Among the spectacular riches, Carter and Carnarvon uncovered a tablet on which a dire curse had been written: 'Death will slay with his wings whoever disturbs the peace of Pharaoh.'

"The warning did not make them nervous, but they were afraid their native assistants might panic and quit. They crossed out any mention of the tablets discovery from their records and tossed it into the rubble. The stone with the frightening message has never been seen again. The whole incident might have been forgotten forever had not some three dozen scholars and others connected with the excavation died sudden and mysterious deaths. Twenty-two of them, within the first seven years of opening the tomb. Several within hours.

"Carnarvon and Carter were about to uncover the mummy itself, when Lord Carnarvon became deathly ill. Although suspecting an infection, doctors were uncertain of a diagnosis. He died before his son could reach his bedside and precisely at the moment of his death, an unexplainable power blackout occurred all over Cairo.

"Another victim was American architect Arthur Mace, who had been the person to rip out the last piece of a wall blocking the entry to the tomb. He died in the same hotel and with the same symptoms as Carnarvon, feverish and in a sudden coma.

"The morning after Carter had shown his friend George Gould the tomb, Gould awoke with a high fever. By nightfall he was dead. Radiologist Archibald Douglas Reed was the first to cut the mummy's wrappings and X-ray it. Reed died aboard ship on his way home to England. Carter's secretary Richard Bethell died of sudden circulatory collapse."

What could have caused these untimely and coincidental deaths among the invaders of King Tut's sacred tomb? Could they have been caused naturally, by the men inhaling an ancient bacterium or virus perhaps?

Dr. Ezzeddin Taha, an eminent physician and biologist in Cairo, held a press conference in 1962 wherein he claimed discovery of an ancient, microscopic fungus that had probably survived in a dormant state for thousands of years. This fungus, he surmised, was the killer —not some ancient curse. Furthermore, the fungus could be controlled by modern antibiotics. Ironically, Dr. Taha died during the period in which he was running his fungus experiments. His car went out of control on an isolated desert road. The autopsy report listed that same circulatory collapse that had killed the others as the cause of his death.

Could it be that there *is* something to the "curse of the pharaohs"?

Whether there is or not, it must be pointed out that since no pharaoh has ever been found in any pyramid, and since there have been literally thousands, perhaps millions of hours of exploration in and around the pyramids, the pyramids are apparently exempt from whatever curse there might be.

But we are still faced with a major dilemma. If the ancient Egyptians did not build the pyramids, who did? Egyptologists and archaeologists insist it was the ancient Egyptians, while at the same time insisting that they lacked the mathematical and astronomical expertise to do the job. Luck, trial and error, and a lot of manpower, they tell us, is all it really took. Some argue for ramps, some for rollers, but few of them it seems, are seriously looking for other explanations.

Max Toth and Greg Nielsen, in their book *Pyramid Power,* speak to this problem very forthrightly:

"We believe that present-day theorists have allowed themselves to become so preoccupied with their own theories, and are so busy defending any challenges to them, that they are unable to deal with other hypotheses which might very well be as sound as their own.

"It seems to us that so long as Egyptologists continue to squabble over the methods of construction used to build the Great Pyramid, with the members of each school of thought tenaciously and blindly clinging to their own theories, like small children stubbornly hanging on to old, soiled teddy bears, the mystery, if there is one at all, will never be solved."

We can only applaud and move forward.

In the next chapter the search for the builders of the pyramids takes a dramatic leap. Could it be that the pyramid-builders of Earth, in fact, have a very unearthly origin? Who could have counted the planets from Pluto inward toward the Sun, and told the Sumerians ten thousand years ago, that the Earth was planet number seven? Is there modern, scientific evidence of life on other planets in our solar system?

9

VISITORS FROM OUTER SPACE

"When all rational explanations have been exhausted, whatever remains, no matter how improbable, must be the truth."

—Sir Arthur Conan Doyle

RECENTLY THE WORLD OF EGYPTOLOGY RECEIVED a jolt to some long-held conclusions. Fascinating new findings have turned up that may finally begin to unlock the mysteries of the pyramids.

Dr. Herbert Haas, director of the Radiocarbon Laboratory at Southern Methodist University, is one of the experts who has devoted a great deal of effort to establishing accurate dates for the construction of the pyramids as well as other ancient constructions. According to Dr. Haas, "Scholars have always insisted that the so-called 'Bent Pyramid' attributed to the pharaoh Zoser was the first pyramid erected in Egypt; that the Great Pyramid was not built until several hundred years after. Now it turns out that, according to their own carbon-dating methods (used on mortar samples), it has been established conclusively that the Great Pyramid is *at least* four hundred fifty years older than Zoser's 'Bent Pyramid.' That means that instead of being the seventh or eighth pyramid built in Egypt, the Great Pyramid was the first. Which, in turn, means that those scholars who have suggested all along that the smaller pyramids were failed attempts to re-create the Great Pyramid in all its perfection were probably right."

The radiocarbon test data was just the beginning. Having opened up the whole argument of *when* the pyramids were built and once again finding the "scholarly consensus" to be wanting, other scientists began to take an interest in the whole pyramid complex.

"In 1991," according to J. David Davis, "a detailed survey by a team of eminent geologists and geophysicists made another astounding discovery. They determined that the Great Sphinx was built around *10,000* B.C., and actually suffered water damage from fierce flooding in the area following *the last ice age,* more than five thousand years before the first Egyptian kingdom came into being."

Was the sphinx, which is believed to have been carved out of a single extrusion of living rock, actually the first structure of the complex? If so, could there be some significance in relation to other modern discoveries? Intriguing questions indeed. Later on we'll see if this ancient guardian of the desert could somehow be connected to discoveries in space.

The more we learn about the Giza complex, the more unsure we are of the conventional theories explaining the mysteries of the structures and its Great Pyramid. But if the conventional theories do not explain the purpose of the pyramids, what do more contemporary theories have to offer?

Perhaps if there were some definitive agreement on the purpose of the Great Pyramid the task would become more manageable. Given the number of theories pertaining to the purpose of this magnificent edifice, however, such agreement might be a long time coming.

August Tournquist, for example, points out that, quite apart from their being used as tombs (if indeed they ever were), there are a number of very practical problems the Great Pyramid resolved for those who might have lived in its shadow.

"The Great Pyramid, whatever else it might be,"

Tournquist says, "is a sundial, a calendar, and an astronomical observatory. At its original height of 481 feet,
the pyramid cast a shadow 268 feet long in mid-winter,
diminishing almost to zero in the spring, and could be
used to mark the hours of the day, the seasons, and the
exact length of the year."

Zecharia Sitchin, author of *The Twelfth Planet* and
Stairway to Heaven, proposes an entirely different possibility in his writings. Hearkening back to ancient Sumerian texts, Sitchin suggests they had astronomical
information we do not possess even today.[80] Modern
astronomy asserts that our solar system consists of the
Sun and ten planets (counting the Moon as one), "but
that is not what the Sumerians said," Sitchin writes.
"They claimed that our system was made up of the Sun
and *eleven* planets (counting the Moon), and held
steadfastly to the opinion that, in addition to the planets known to us today, there has been a *twelfth* member of the solar system—the home planet of the
Nephilim."

It should be remembered that the first and oldest
civilized culture on earth was the Sumerian, which not
only left written records but had a highly advanced
astronomical system. Archaeology doesn't have much
to say as to how this might have come about, but the
question is intriguing. How could a "pre-everything"
culture just suddenly appear, complete with a complex
written language, an economic system, and a well-or-
dered society? Sitchin believes they may have given us
the answer themselves.

"Based on the evidence provided by the Sumerian
texts," Sitchin says, "it appears that the Giza pyramids
were built as beacons by extraterrestrials as a part of a

[80] *Zecharia Sitchin,* The Twelfth Planet, *p. 178.*

mission-control landing corridor, ending at a landing spaceport in the Sinai Desert."

Could the ancient Sumerians have been the descendants of interstellar travelers who used the "seventh" planet as a sort of interplanetary "bus stop"?

There are still other theories. Earlier we discussed the findings of British astronomer Richard Proctor, who demonstrated, using ancient Egyptian records, that the Great Pyramid had indeed been used as an astronomical observatory. At some point in its construction it seems the Great Pyramid was used for mapping the heavens through use of both the descending passage and the Grand Gallery. That some astronomical purpose was at least a part of the design of the Great Pyramid seems undeniable.

Consider the theory that the Great Pyramid was an interplanetary communicator. Roger Oakland, author and science lecturer, suggests it might have been designed as a giant radio transmitter-receiver.

"The Great Pyramid," says Oakland, "is essentially a ziggurat, a stepped pyramid such as the Tower of Babel. There are many of these found all over the ancient world. Their sole purpose was to allow pagan priests and kings to communicate with the gods of the universe. They are essentially crystalline structures and therefore highly receptive to radio-like energy waves or even cosmic microwaves. The Great Pyramid at Giza, with its five granite slabs above the king's chamber, could very easily be a massive transmitter-receiver, tuned to some distant part of the universe of which we are still ignorant."

There is, it seems, no lack of theories concerning the purpose of the Great Pyramid at Giza, ranging from the preposterous to the ingenious. All of them, however, are connected one way or another to the mystery surrounding the building of the structures themselves. Does it seem possible that the task could have been accomplished by the ancient Egyptians?

The Greek historian Herodotus, remember, wrote that the Egyptians of the fifth century B.C. told him that a crew of a hundred thousand men (and probably women) took twenty years to build the Great Pyramid. What's more, Herodotus seems certain that these crews were replaced every three months. The assertion is without any corroborating evidence or support, but modern Egyptologists and archaeologists seem content to accept it without argument.

Dr. Rita Evelyn Freed, curator of the Department of Egyptian and Ancient Near Eastern Art at the Museum of Fine Arts in Boston, believes we should examine the Herodotus documents a little more closely.

"We know," Dr. Freed tells us, "that the Egyptians of the Fourth Dynasty had nowhere near the population to supply such a vast number of laborers. The great English archaeologist, Flinders Petrie, unearthed barracks for about four thousand workmen, and that would be a much more likely number."

Once again, the reality of the times and the capabilities of the people seem to strongly suggest that there was something or someone else at work on the Great Pyramid than just the Egyptians themselves.

Given that observation, let's review once again the traditional and currently accepted (among Egyptologists) theory of pyramid construction. According to this notion there is no mystery at all about the methods employed to build the pyramids. The limestone packing blocks used for the construction core came from nearby quarries. These quarries are from three to thirty miles distant from the site. They were moved on huge sleds or pulled across a bed of rolling logs. The stones that came from distant quarries were barged down river to the site. A great causeway led from the river landing, and the stones were moved up its mile-length by pure muscle-power.

Once the stones were on site, they were levered up from tier to tier and then set in place. The process, from the leveling of the site to the setting of the capstone was incredibly labor-intensive.

Traditionalists grant that such an accomplishment would probably be the greatest single effort of men working together ever recorded—a fantastic effort even—but they insist it is still a very human one.

Needless to say, there are a number of very competent people who have considerable difficulty with these notions. Margaret Morris, for example, is assistant director at the Institute for Applied Archaeological Sciences in Detroit, Michigan and, co-author of *The Pyramids: An Enigma Solved,* referred to in an earlier chapter. Ms. Morris stops just short of suggesting these assertions are pure hogwash.

"I can't comprehend that any respected scientist could believe such a premise." According to Morris, "The only metal tools these ancient people had were made out of soft copper. There is no way in this world, regardless of the size of the work force, that anyone is going to cut and dress quarried stone weighing from two and a half to ten tons to tolerances of one two thousandths of an inch with copper chisels. Some granite blocks in the King's Chamber weight up to forty tons and would be even more difficult to shape with copper tools.

"These people had no knowledge of the wheel, use of draft animals, no pulleys, surveying equipment, winches, derricks, or block and tackle. The only mechanical devices they had were the lever, the roller, and the inclined plane.

"Let's say they could keep a work force of ten thousand laborers at work day in and day out (and that's probably twice as many as they could possibly have had), then allowing an average of one working hour of the entire labor force to quarry, dress, move, and set one block, a ten-hour day would give us ten blocks a day, or 3,500 blocks a year. At that rate it would have taken some 715 years just to build the core structure.

"A more likely crew would have been five thousand men, setting five blocks a day. At that rate Khufu would have had to wait nearly seventeen hundred years to see the capstone set on his pyramid. To build the Great Pyramid in twenty years, as some archaeologists claim, would have meant setting one of those huge stones every three and one-half minutes, twenty-four hours a day. That would require a technology we certainly don't have today."

The statistical arguments are difficult to ignore and even more difficult to refute. Remember, the number of stones in the Great Pyramid is not in doubt. The traditionalists, nevertheless, seem willing to accept the Herodotus history without question. That being the case, their theories are cast into a huge and irrefutable mathematical hole. And keep in mind, Morris was only talking about the time required to *set* the stones. Now we're back to the matter of getting the stones into a position where they could be set.

Chuck Missler reminds us that "the generally accepted academic viewpoints are equally divided between the 'rollers' and the 'rampers.' These two theories are being taught in schools right now as fact when they are not even substantial theories. And then there is a widespread general belief, which Hollywood has helped to promote, that hundreds of thousands of slaves were used to build the pyramids. Nothing could be further from the truth."

David Teuling, author of *A Sign and a Witness,* agrees. "The Egyptians of the Fourth Dynasty were neither a formidable military nation nor a very aggressive one, but even if they were, there were not enough potential slaves within a five-thousand-mile radius to have supplied the work force needed. The number of workers required to build the greatest construction on earth in twenty years would have bankrupted Egypt."

Greg Pyros, whom we met earlier, finds the "ramp" idea difficult to accept also. "With the ramper school of Egyptology," Pyros writes, "we are asked to believe that a mile-long ramp was built, rising in slope with the progress upward of the pyramid. If it takes a hundred men to drag a 2.5 ton rock along a smooth, level road bed, then the effort will increase geometrically with each degree of elevation. One degree will require two hundred men, two degrees will require four hundred men, and so on. By the time we reach the pitch of ten degrees needed to reach the top, it will require 51,200 men to pull a single rock up a ramp.

"Actually it would have required more effort to build the ramp than to build the pyramid, and even as much effort to dismantle it. Obviously, there would have been some six billion pounds of construction garbage to get rid of afterwards. Where is it? Does anyone know?"

Even the most adamant ramp theorists have been unable to answer those questions. But what about the "rollers"? Couldn't their theory that the stones have been brought to the site on rollers be true?

David Teuling doesn't think so. "With enough manpower and under optimum conditions, moving a given stone in this manner can be demonstrated, but some rather obvious considerations should have dispelled this notion long ago. The only trees available in ancient Egypt were date palms. As a food source, it is unlikely they would have been cut down, but even if they had been, they would have made very poor logs.

"Importing logs is a solution, of course, but that would have required more shipping than Egypt has ever possessed in its entire history. Twenty-five million trees would have been needed. Besides all of that, it is virtually impossible to roll a log in sand or on crude mud-and-stone-chip roads. But even if they could be rolled, the great weight of the stones would have crushed the logs to pulp within the first few miles."

The problem seems to compound with each set of experts that examines it.

Let's look at what we've discovered so far. First of all, the Egyptians did not have the tools capable of shaping the stone. Second, there were not nearly enough Egyptians (including the possibility of slaves) to do the job in any reasonable length of time. And finally, the methods suggested for moving and setting the stones are both mathematically and functionally impossible.

We are reminded of something Sir Arthur Conan Doyle put in the mouth of his famous detective, Sherlock Holmes: "When all rational explanations have been exhausted, whatever remains, no matter how improbable, must be the truth."

Since the pyramids exist, there must have been another, totally different method of lifting and moving these tremendously heavy stones—a device that would make the moving of these massive weights feasible. If the ancient Egyptians did not have such a device, there seems to be only one likely conclusion: The Egyptians did not build the Great Pyramid.

August Tournquist sees evidence for that conclusion in what is *not* in the records.

"The Great Pyramid," he writes, "was the greatest single undertaking in the whole history of mankind, and yet there is not one picture or drawing, not one artifact, not one inventory or tally sheet to tell of its construction. The Egyptians left us some three hundred years of written and pictorial history, covering virtually everything that happened in their culture, from babies being born to plowing and harvesting, building, weaving, sacrificing, praying, and embalming, but nothing about the Great Pyramid."

The key question is inescapable: If the ancient Egyptians did not build the Great Pyramid, who did? Could it be that we have found the answer in a recent discovery on another planet?

Richard Hoagland is an investigator, science writer, lecturer, and author of *The Monuments of Mars—A City on the Edge of Forever*. His investigations have led to some astonishing conclusions—conclusions that Zecharia Sitchin's ancient Sumerians might have found quite comforting.

Hoagland is the prime moving force in leading a collective band of scientists, international scholars, and world governments to an active interest in what he describes as the "monuments of Mars," which include a giant face on the planet's surface that is seemingly associated with a complex of geometric structures referred to by the experts as "Cydonia." Hoagland, by the way, did not discover the "face on Mars." That honor belongs to various experts studying the Viking photos of the Red Planet.

According to Hoagland, "A NASA Viking scientist,

Dr. Tobias Owen, actually discovered the first of these 'monuments' in 1976: a gigantic, mile-long, human-looking head, lying in a northern Martian desert. In 1979 two NASA-contracted imaging analysts, Vincent DiPietro and Gregory Molennaar, discovered that there were *two* photos of the 'face' taken at *two different angles* by the Viking spacecraft. They also noted a massive, pyramidal structure close at hand which is now known as the D&M Pyramid. Their findings were quickly dismissed by NASA as an optical illusion."

NASA, the organization that had taken the photographs and had full charge of them simply chose to ignore, if not impugn what they seemed to be showing the world—evidence of something other than random or natural configurations on the surface of Mars.

Dr. Mark Carlotto, a computer-imaging expert with Analytic Sciences Corporation, tried to take issue with this posture but had very little success.

"After years of fruitless debate," Dr. Carlotto told us, "I decided to use a state-of-the-art, 3-D computer modeling technique that now strongly indicates the 'face' could be, in fact, a real, *three-dimensional,* human-looking 'sculpture' lying on the Martian surface—a 'sculpture' fifteen hundred feet high and over a mile long."

While a number of scientists continue to pooh-pooh the idea that something "man-made" could exist on Mars, Hoagland's interest was unabated, and he continued to analyze all of the Viking photos that he could get his hands on that pertained to Cydonia.

"In the seventeen years since Viking first photographed this object," Hoagland insists, "I and my colleagues have found, using similar analytical techniques, a number of additional 'anomalous' structures at Cydonia. And we have shown, using the most modern computer-image processing available and rigorous mathematical analysis, that these Cydonia structures show clear evidence of being highly geometric.

"Furthermore, we now know they are intimately connected to each other by an *identical geometry*. Geometry is the key, the one true signature of intelligent life that planetary scientists now look for on all planets. In simple terms: intelligent life creates 'things,' things like buildings, cities, pyramids—that are inescapably composed of repeating *geometric* structure.

"The face on Mars, its nearby pyramids, the entire Cydonia complex, we've determined, is simply brimming with this elegant, repeating geometric structure."

If that's true, it is one of the most exciting and far-reaching discoveries in the history of the world. Think of it. Certainly no one on Earth went to Mars and built structures. If they are, in fact, buildings, statures, structures of any kind built by intelligent beings, it is proof positive that we are not alone in the cosmos.

But how do geometric structures on Mars relate to the construction of the Great Pyramid on Earth? Part of the answer is found in Zecharia Sitchin's book, *The Twelfth Planet*. Sitchin makes the point that the ancient Sumerians, "without actual instruments, nevertheless had the sophisticated astronomical and mathematical know-how required of a spherical astronomy and geometry."[81]

In 1925 the world's astronomical community agreed to divide the heavens as seen from Earth into three regions, northern, central, and southern, and to group the stars therein into eighty-eight constellations. According to Sitchin, "There was nothing new in this arrangement, for the Sumerians were the first to divide

[81] *Ibid.*, p. 187.

the heavens into three bands . . . the northern, the central, and the southern. The present-day central band, the band of the twelve constellations of the zodiac, corresponds exactly to the 'Way of Anu,' in which the Sumerians grouped the stars into twelve houses."[82]

But Sitchin's investigations get even more astounding. "A Sumerian tablet in the Berlin Museum (VAT.7847) begins the list of zodiacal constellations with that of Leo, taking us back to circa 11,000 B.C., when man had just begun to till the land.

"This is indeed fantastic astronomical sophistication at an impossible time. Just as it is evident that the Sumerian astronomers possessed knowledge that they could not possibly have acquired on their own. Also, there is evidence to show that a good deal of their knowledge was of no practical use to them. Who in ancient Sumer really needed to establish a celestial equator for example?"[83]

The Sumerians apparently had other astronomical information that was of no use to them. A forty-five-hundred-year-old Sumerian depiction of the solar system clearly shows Uranus, Neptune, and Pluto in their relative positions and (except for Pluto) size. Had this depiction been studied two hundred years ago, astronomers would have thought the Sumerians totally uninformed and very imaginative. Now we know those planets are there. The depiction also shows "that there was—or has been—another major planet between Mars and Jupiter."[84]

Again, according to Sitchin, "Toward the end of the eighteenth century, even before Neptune had been

[82] *Ibid., p. 188.*
[83] *Ibid., p. 197.*
[84] *Ibid., p. 206.*

discovered, several astronomers demonstrated that 'the planets were placed at certain distances from the Sun according to some definite law.' This suggestion, which came to be know as Bode's Law, convinced astronomers that a planet ought to revolve in a place where hitherto no planet had been known to exist, that is, between the orbits of Mars and Jupiter.

"Nearly three thousand asteroids have been counted orbiting the Sun in what is now called the asteroid belt. Beyond any doubt, this is the debris of a planet that had shattered to pieces. While astronomers are certain that such a planet existed, they are unable to explain its disappearance.

"The answers to these puzzles," Sitchin insists, "have been handed down to us from antiquity."[85]

Hoagland himself refers to Sitchin's works and finds them intriguing, referring to Sitchin as "my other guide." "The blurbs on his book *The Stairway to Heaven*," say Hoagland, "termed him [Sitchin] a man with a profound knowledge of modern and ancient Hebrew . . . the Old Testament . . . history and archaeology of the Near East [who] attended the London School of Economics.

"I soon discovered," Hoagland recounts, "that it was Sitchin's thesis that the two high cultures of the Near East—Egypt and Sumer—owed their existence to 'advanced visitors from another planet.' "[86]

Hoagland also pays tribute to what he calls "the solid scholarship" employed by Sitchin and finds in his writings support for the concept of an interstellar connection between the Cydonia complex on Mars and the Giza complex on Earth.

[85] *Ibid.*, p. 209.
[86] Richard C. Hoagland, The Monuments of Mars, *pp. 289–291.*

"The most solid and most stunning connection between the monuments of Mars, and the monuments of Earth," Hoagland exults, "we've now found to lie in Egypt. The fundamental mathematical relationships communicated by the structures at Cydonia, are now eerily *replicated* in the Giza complex here on Earth, including the very placement of the sphinx. Even the key latitude of Giza north of the equator is now directly linked to the D&M Pyramid latitude at Cydonia on Mars. That, in itself, is now the single most striking statement of 'intelligence' on Mars we've found . . . if not evidence of some truly important connection to the Earth."

Hoagland and his team have gone even further: They've done detailed imaging analyses of the "face" on Mars and compared it literally to the sphinx. In doing so, they have discovered that the two, striking "man/lion" images, located literally millions of miles apart, contain amazing visual and symbolic similarities.

"It is difficult to believe," Hoagland writes, "that all of this is merely due to 'chance.' There's just too much documented linkage between the 'monuments of Mars,' and the Giza complex here on Earth to accept that it's all just coincidence. That's why all of us are bringing so much pressure to bear on NASA, to specifically and exhaustively photograph the Cydonia area on the next Mars mission in two years."

(The 1993 probe was launched and was promptly "lost" by NASA. The communications equipment failed, and as of this writing the probe has not been found.)

Could it be that the Great Pyramid at Giza is a replication of the D&M Pyramid at Cydonia on Mars? The idea at first appears preposterous. Intelligent beings coming to Earth to build . . . what? We don't even know what the word "pyramid" means. The world has simply allowed the structure to define the term. Could it be a navigational beacon? A transceiver (transmitter-receiver) of some sort? And if so, are the descendants of the builders of this magnificent structure still using it for its originally intended purpose?

Once you let yourself accept the notion that there could be intelligent life on planets other than Earth, a host of questions invade the mind. If there should prove to be a connection between the Giza and Cydonia and their associated pyramids, then who were the space-traveling builders, and—perhaps more importantly—where are they now? Is the city of Cairo related to Giza in the same way that the face-pyramid's complex is to Cydonia? We know that the basic atmosphere of the Earth has changed in the distant past. Could Mars have once been a more hospitable planet? Is it essential that intelligent beings be capable of living only in an atmosphere like that found on Earth?

Some mysteries, upon exhaustive examination, lose their pull on our sense of curiosity. Rightly or wrongly, we tend to either get bored with the whole idea or simply come to the conclusion, as most archaeologists and Egyptologists seem to have done, that the mystery is solved.

The Great Pyramid of Giza, in my mind, does not fall into that category. This gigantic and marvelous structure has been measured, probed, and analyzed beyond anything else on the face of the Earth, yet we still face it with the same questioning awe as Herodotus, Alexander the Great, and Napoleon. Far from solving the mystery, modern technology, specifically space technology, has only added one more intriguing chore to the already impossible task. Who built it? Why? How? The questions echo and re-echo down through the ages. The answers, if there are any, were swallowed up long ago by the drifting desert sands.

The Great Pyramid of Giza is undoubtedly one of the world's most fascinating puzzles and will remain so until the ingenuity of today's "experts" catches up with that of the ancient builders. Given the current pace of our understanding, that could easily be another thousand years.

Incidentally, there is another element to this mystery that makes it impossible for us to just turn and walk away. It reaches out from antiquity like a shadow falling across the centuries, daring us to hold it up to the light. The name "Cairo," it seems, is an old Seleucid Arab word that means . . . *Mars!!*

10

ALIENS—REAL OR IMAGINED?

"They flew like saucers would if you skipped them across the water."

Kenneth Arnold, 1947

1. The pyramid of Khufu, or the Great Pyramid, is thought to have been built between 2600 B.C. and 2500 B.C.

Other than the pyramids, there is little to suggest the ancient Egyptians knew anything about geometry, trigonometry, physics, or geology. However, all of these sciences were used in the construction of the Great Pyramid. COURTESY OF TODD ALEXANDER

2a & 2b. The Great Pyramid is the only pyramid that has above-ground chambers instead of underground chambers. The chambers in the Great Pyramid have been thought to have many different purposes depending on which expert's opinion you accept. Many experts believe that the Great Pyramid was built as a burial monument even though a mummy has never been found within its walls. Other experts believe these rooms were originally designed as astronomical observatories or repositories of mathematics for later generations. COURTESY OF TODD ALEXANDER

2a. The King's Chamber with the coffer. The walls are made up of exactly 100 red granite blocks. All of them are polished and fitted perfectly. No two blocks are the same size, and in the south and north walls are carved two air tunnels that bring in fresh air from the outside.

2b. At the top of the Grand Gallery one can look directly through the antechamber into part of the King's Chamber.

3. There is enough stone in the Great Pyramid to build 35 Empire State Buildings with a few tons left over, an astonishing accomplishment considering it was built by an ancient people who did not possess iron tools or simple technology.

The Great Pyramid was originally 481 feet tall, each of its four sides precisely 756 feet long at the base, and it covers 13 acres. There are 203 courses of limestone blocks, an estimated 2,300,000 stones, weighing up to 15 tons each. COURTESY OF HENRY S. WIEBER

4. The Bermuda Triangle, purportedly located between Miami, Bermuda, and Puerto Rico, has been said to have caused the disappearance of hundreds of ships and planes and taken thousands of lives. COURTESY OF SUN INTERNATIONAL PICTURES, INC.

5. Stonehenge is one of the world's greatest mysteries. To this day we do not know how these multi-ton slabs of diorite came to be in the middle of a desolate English plain.

Myth says the wizard Merlin brought the stones, which were thought to have mystical powers, from Ireland by means of his "engines." COURTESY OF ROBERT ALEXANDER AND BONNIE GAUNT

6. To this day no one knows how these gigantic Easter Island statues were moved or made to stand upright. These statues stand up to 32 feet tall and weigh up to 90 tons. COURTESY OF THE BETTMANN ARCHIVE/UPI

7. One hundred forty years after Easter Island was discovered, wooden tablets were found, covered with the characters of an unknown language.

This board, known as a "talking board," could be evidence that Polynesians created a written language over 2,000 years ago. COURTESY OF THE BETTMANN ARCHIVE/UPI

8. Bigfoot has been spotted in just about every state in the Union. The creature is said to stand between 8 and 12 feet tall and appears to be very shy. According to reports, he is able to travel at great speed, has an awful smell, and, of course, leaves footprints that range from 16 to 22 inches heel to toe and up to 8 inches wide. COURTESY OF THE BETTMANN ARCHIVE/UPI

9a   **9b**

9a & 9b. The Loch Ness monster is thought by some experts to be the extinct plesiosaur. The reported long neck, tiny head, thick body, and four flippers seem to resemble this departed dinosaur. COURTESY OF THE BETTMANN ARCHIVE/UPI

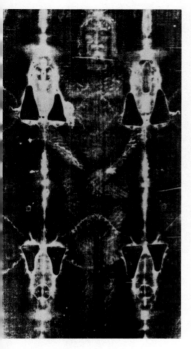

10. In 1898 the Shroud of Turin was finally photographed. Until that time the image on the cloth could hardly be seen. If someone viewed the shroud from too close or too far away, the image disappeared. When the shroud appeared on the photographer's negative, however, it became a positive image. The likeness on the cloth could be seen in full detail for the first time in history. COURTESY OF BARRIE SCHWORTZ

11a & 11b. In 1532 the shroud was nearly destroyed by fire. Molten silver dripped onto the cloth. The resulting series of burn marks down both sides of the shroud's entire length are similar to the paper cutouts we made as children, suggesting the cloth was neatly folded at the time of the fire. COURTESY OF BARRIE SCHWORTZ

11a

11b

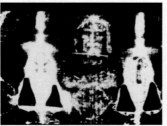
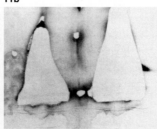

12. Michel de Nostredame (1503–1566), French physician and astrologer, famous for his book of rhymed prophesies titled *Centuries* (1555). COURTESY OF THE BETTMANN ARCHIVE/UPI

13. Today the tomb of Nostradamus stands in quiet remembrance of this healer and prophet. But 225 years following the death of Nostradamus a band of partisan rebels for some unknown reason dug up his grave. When they opened the coffin, they were stunned to see a brass plaque held in place by bony fingers. It read MAY 1791, the exact month and year his grave was desecrated. COURTESY OF DOLORES CANNON AND MARGARETHA LETTERHAG

$\mathbf{H}$AVING RAISED THE POSSIBILITY OF SOME ALIEN visitation in the pre-dawn of recorded history, and having hinted that such an event may have had something to do with the astonishing capabilities apparent in the remnants of those ancient cultures, it only seems fair that we should take some time to examine the mystery of visitors from outer space.

Far from being a modern phenomenon, this is, rather, a mystery that seems to transcend time. Virtually every written record, from antiquity to the present, including the Holy Bible, contains some reference that can be construed as a description of beings from another world.

Sitchin, in interpreting what are perhaps the oldest of all earthly written records, the Sumerian tablets from Ninevah, describes a cosmology that suggests the gods of Heaven and Earth not only originated in the heavens but could also return to the heavenly abode. The concept might easily be written off as imaginative superstitions except for the fact that the documents describe in some detail who came to Earth with the gods and what their responsibilities were. They are duly noted as "one Prime Minister, three Commanders in charge of the *Mu's* (rocket ships), two Commanders of the Weapons, two Great Masters of Written Knowledge, one Minister of the Purse, two Chief Justices, two 'who with sound impress,' and two Chief Scribes, with five Assistant scribes."[87]

Such remarkable detail would seem to go far beyond the simple necessities of superstition. One of the great mysteries of the Sumerian existence has always been the fact that their culture just seems to suddenly be there. And when it appeared, it came complete with a written language, a high degree of mathematical skill, and a superb understanding of astronomy, all of which is easily explained in the quotation cited at the beginning of this chapter. We seem unwilling however, to take the text of the tablets at face value.

On Christmas Eve, 1968, Commander James Lovell, resting comfortably in the cockpit of *Apollo 8* on his way to the Moon, was patched into the whole world as he read aloud the familiar lines of Genesis, Chapter 1: "In the beginning God created the heavens and the earth . . ." These astronauts were the first men ever to see Earth as God must have seen it as He completed His work. Men, for the first time, so far as we know, looked down upon a sparkling blue marble laced with wisps of white and hung against the deep black void of space.

The pictures of our globe that have since come back from that and subsequent space missions are familiar to every grade-school child today, but for a Sumerian, five thousand years ago, perhaps even as much as eleven thousand years ago, to have a settled knowledge of Earth as a sphere nestled among twelve other planets orbiting the Sun, boggles the mind.

Consider the fear expressed by the men involved in the epic voyage of Columbus. Barely five hundred

[87] *Sitchin*, The Twelfth Planet, *p. 174.*

years ago they looked at the horizon each day and won-dered when they would fall off the edge of the Earth. The realization comes swiftly that there was knowledge possessed by the ancients that was truly remarkable.

As the human race takes its first halting baby steps into the void of the cosmos, it seems to me to be the height of arrogance to suggest that we earthlings are the only beings in all the universe capable of such an undertaking. Generation after generation seems to in-sist that certainly no one or no "thing" could have ever preceded us. Certainly there is no evidence that any-one ever preceded us into space. Or is there?

Some of our foremost scientists appear quite con-tent with the formula that "nothing, plus nobody, times flying chance, equals everything" (used with thanks to whoever it was that invented that theorem). Blithely ignoring a number of written records to the contrary, we push forward, grudgingly accepting Galileo and Co-pernicus, but otherwise holding ourselves to be the only beings in the universe with intelligence.

Intelligence, would, it seems to me, preclude any such conclusion.

Why then, do we blanche at the mere suggestion that there is a civilization, or perhaps hundreds or thousands of civilizations, out there in the cosmos that not only can do what we are just beginning to attempt, but indeed have been doing it for thousands of our Earth years? What if our planet just happens to be a place where people from these civilizations stopped to rest? Are we any less if some ancient astronaut decided to stay? What if some advanced society, knowing what our evolutionary struggle would be, just dropped off a few clues to help us when we got smart enough to figure them out? Would that take away from our ac-

188 MYSTERIES OF THE ANCIENT WORLD

complishments? And what if they come back from time to time, just to see how we're doing?

Let's go back to the Great Pyramid of Giza for just a moment.

Many of today's scientists find a direct correlation between the mathematics and astronomy of the Great Pyramid and the enigmatic construction in the south of England known as Stonehenge. But how could that be? The two structures are thousands of miles apart, they look nothing at all alike, and they were apparently constructed at different periods of time. The only thing they seem to have in common is that somehow people who shouldn't have known how, nor had the means to build them, managed to place gigantic stones on top of one another.

And, according to Bonnie Gaunt, author of two books on the connection between Stonehenge and the Great Pyramid, the people involved in each had a common language, the language of mathematics. "In ancient times," Gaunt tells us, "Pythagoras, the fifth century B.C. mathematician said, 'Numbers are the language of the universe.' And he taught his students their importance as language. Indeed, numbers are the very building blocks of creation, but they are more than this. They are a language that communicates through time and space—an external language—a language of beginning. Sir James Jeans, the British physicist, declared, 'The Great Architect of the universe now begins to appear as a pure mathematician.' "[88]

The dialogue of those examining the mystery of Stonehenge sounds amazingly similar to that of those discussing the Great Pyramid:

"The means of construction alone is awesome. It is

[88] *Bonnie Gaunt,* Stonehenge and the Great Pyramid, p. 2.

not enough that we should grapple with the 'what' and the 'why,' but Stonehenge also compels us to ask 'how.' How did these stones get there."[89]

There are a number of legends and myths cited: "The great Merlin, wizard of King Arthur's Court, transported them from Ireland by means of his 'engines.' And the stones themselves were thought to have magical, curative powers. [But today] we live in a world of reality, and the stones are very real. They were placed there by real people, like you and me."[90]

For the reader who might be unfamiliar with this ancient mystery, a brief description is in order. Stonehenge is an open structure consisting of several concentric circles with two inner circles opened and spread to form U-shaped arrangements. The innermost arrangement of stones is called the "bluestone horseshoe." Outside the arrangement of bluestones and dwarfing them in size, stand the huge stones of the trilithon horseshoe. These are free-standing sets of two upright stones topped by a crosspiece called a lintel. There are five of these trilithons. They form a U-shaped set of frames through which the sunrise, sunset, moonrise, and moonset can be viewed at the equinoxes and solstices. Surrounding the horseshoes is the bluestone circle, and immediately outside the bluestone circle is the sarsen circle. The sarsen circle was originally composed of thirty upright stones and thirty lintels. The inner faces of these uprights, for some unknown reason, were dressed and highly polished.

The mean circumference of this remarkable circle is 316.8 feet. Then, far out beyond the sarsen circle, lies the Aubrey circle, a circle of fifty-six small holes.

[89] *Bonnie Gaunt*, Stonehenge: A Closer Look, *p. 6.*
[90] *Ibid.*

Standing approximately on line with the Aubrey circle were, at one time, four unhewn monoliths that formed the corners of a rectangle perpendicular to the summer sunrise. Only two of these stones remain today, and one of them is lying on its face. To the northeast of the Aubrey circle, standing alone and separate, is the heel stone, a vital part of the monument, since it serves as a marker for sunrise at the summer solstice.[91]

The trilithon stones are the tallest stones in the monument and, the lone remaining stone of the great central trilithon towers above them all. It weighs fifty tons. How stones of such great size came to be on the desolate plain where they now stand is the stuff legends are made of, and of legends there are plenty, but easily the most enduring is the Merlin legend.

After dispatching some fifteen thousand men to Ireland at Merlin's urging, so the story goes, the king of Briton waited for their return with some apprehension. After all, Merlin had told him the great stones had been brought to Ireland from Africa by giants who lived in Ireland for a time. Each of them, Merlin assured the king, carried a full measure of magic.

But fifteen thousand men were insufficient for the task, not being able to move the stones so much as a foot. Whereupon Merlin, with his amazing "engines," laid the stones down as lightly as a feather and transported them to their present site.[92]

Given our earlier discussion, the legend does have the elements that suggest some extraterrestrial help. One thing is certain, however: The stones are there. Many of the huge lintels are still in place, and how these multi-ton hunks of diorite wound up in the mid-

---

[91] *Gaunt,* Stonehenge and the Great Pyramid, *p. 17.*
[92] *Gerald S. Hawkins,* Stonehenge Decoded.

dle of a desolate English plain is an absolute mystery. No one has even the slightest clue.

Those facts being inescapable, what does all this have to do with the pyramids in Egypt? The question is best asked by author Gaunt: "Is there any correlation between these two ancient monuments? Was the one known to the builder of the other? Did they, by any stretch of the imagination, share a common architect?"

To begin with, Stonehenge is at latitude north, 51 degrees, 17 minutes, and at this precise latitude, the solstice movements of the Sun and Moon form a rectangle precisely in line with the four corner or "station" stones of the monument. A few miles north or a few miles south and this would not be the case. How did the builder know the only latitude in the Northern Hemisphere that would make this unique geometry possible? Furthermore, by bisecting this rectangle from the northwest corner through the southeast corner, you draw a line that, if followed without deviation, would take you directly to the Great Pyramid of Giza.[93]

As noted earlier, the angle of the Great Pyramid from base to apex is 51 degrees, 51 minutes, 14.3 seconds. Some have called it the pi angle because it gives to the height the same ratio to its square base as the radius of a circle bears to its circumference. As it happens, this is also the angle of the summer-solstice sunrise to the north at Stonehenge. Gaunt asks, "How did the builder of Stonehenge know of the pyramid angle? Or did he? The alignment of summer-solstice sunrise, as Professor Hawkins has so succinctly stated, 'is not man-maneuverable,' and, we might add, neither is the direction of north. Bear in mind that this angle between sunrise and north exists at Stonehenge and not

[93] *Gaunt,* Stonehenge: A Closer Look, *pp. 32–33.*

at Al-Gizeh [Giza] in Egypt, yet the builder of the Great Pyramid used this angle long before Stonehenge was built."[94]

But the trail of "coincidence" doesn't end there. The latest carbon-dating techniques place the beginning of the construction of Stonehenge immediately following the completion of the Great Pyramid. Again, according to Gaunt, "This brings us face to face with the astounding fact that the builder of the Great Pyramid knew the angle of summer-solstice sunrise relative to north in the remote southern plain of the British Isles before Stonehenge came into existence.

"It is interesting to note also," Gaunt continues, "that the complete circle of Stonehenge, including the ditch which surrounds it, fits precisely into the triangle of the pyramid, just scribbling the three sides."[95]

These and many other remarkable geometric similarities seem to suggest that the builders of the Great Pyramid and the builder of Stonehenge, at the very least, shared a common mathematical and perhaps astronomical language. Could they be one and the same? Could the "gods" of the ancient Sumerian texts and the "gods" that piloted the "chariots" of Erich von Daniken (in his book *Chariots of the Gods*) share a common genesis?

In that much maligned but highly successful book, von Daniken broadly suggests that modern man owes a far greater debt to "visitors from outer space" than we are willing to acknowledge. He gives examples of this thesis that are as sobering as they are startling.

For example, von Daniken tells us, "At the beginning of the eighteenth century ancient maps which had

[94] *Ibid.*
[95] *Ibid.* p. 36.

belonged to an officer in the Turkish navy, Admiral Piri, known as Piri Re'is, were found in the Topkapi Palace. Two atlases preserved in the Berlin State Library which contain exact reproductions of the Mediterranean and region around the Dead Sea also came from Piri Re'is.

"All these maps," von Daniken reminds us, "were handed over to American cartographer Arlington H. Mallery for examination. Mallery confirmed the remarkable fact that all the geographical data were present but not drawn in the right places. He sought the help of a Mr. Walters, cartographer in the U.S. Navy Hydrographic Bureau. Mallery and Walters constructed a grid and transferred the maps to a modern globe. They made a sensational discovery. The maps were absolutely accurate—and not only with regard to the Mediterranean and the Dead Sea. The coasts of North and South America and even the contours of the Antarctic were also precisely delineated on the Piri Re'is maps. The maps not only reproduced the outlines of the continents but also showed the topography of the interiors. Mountain ranges, mountain peaks, islands, rivers, and plateaus were drawn in with extreme accuracy.

"In 1957, the Geophysical Year, the maps were handed over to Jesuit Father Lineham, who is both director of the Weston Observatory and a cartographer in the U.S. Navy. After scrupulous tests, Father Lineham, too, could only confirm that the maps were fantastically accurate. What is more, the mountain ranges in the Antarctic, which already figure on the Piri Re'is maps, were not discovered until 1952. These mountains have been covered in ice for untold years, and the present-day maps were drawn with the aid of echo-sounding equipment.

"Comparison with modern photographs of our globe taken from satellites showed that the originals of the Piri Re'is' maps must have been aerial photographs taken from a very great height. How can that be explained?" von Daniken asks.[96]

How indeed? Here we have physical evidence—"hard copy" proof, if you will, that somehow, someone was able to see the Earth from a different perspective, and that person (or persons) was intelligent enough to record what he or she saw, not just as a map, but as a *global* map.

Certainly no one alive today knows of anyone who was taking high-altitude aerial photography prior to the eighteenth century. And no one seems to know just how the copy of the maps came into the possession of the Turkish admiral. But how they came into his possession is irrelevant. Since he had them prior to the year 1700, their accuracy is still astonishing, as is the very fact of their existence.

If interplanetary travelers were interested in this planet, wouldn't they first examine or create some cartography? The inescapable, logical answer is, almost certainly.

In today's world the sighting of "otherworldly" craft has taken on new and almost "cultic" significance. "Flying saucers," or "unidentified flying objects" (UFOs), are a daily, even hourly occurrence. For over twenty years the U.S. Air Force maintained a department (Project Bluebook) dedicated solely to tracking down and identifying reports coming in from all over the country relating to mysterious flying craft with unusual, unworldly, and often frightening properties.

"Ninety percent of those reports," a former mem-

[96] *Erich von Daniken,* Chariots of the Gods, *pp. 14–15.*

ber of the Project Bluebook team told me, "were easily and quickly identified with some natural or man-made event. But the other ten percent, we just don't know." My friend, who still does consulting work for the military, didn't want to be identified, but he did concede that "ten percent . . . even *one* percent, would be a significant number." In other words, there are a lot of things flying around out there that no one can identify. We don't know what they are or where they come from, or what they're doing here. It is a sobering realization.

At present there are two computer networks that provide reports of sightings from all over the globe. A recent request for a printout of the current library resulted in a report of no less than 226 pages. Reports came from Victor Harbour, Australia, to Petaluma, California, and virtually all points in between.

The United States by no means has an exclusive when it comes to these strange events. On the morning of June 30, 1908, something huge and terrifying exploded over the region of Tunguska in remote Siberia. A witness saw an elongated flaming object trailing dust. The blast shattered windowpanes and sent a searing wind roaring across the landscape, felling trees like matchsticks. Scientists would later estimate the power of the blast to be equivalent to a twenty-megaton nuclear bomb. The Tunguska explosion has remained a mystery.[97]

October 13, 1917, turned out to be a rainy, drizzly day in Fatima, Portugal. By afternoon, a crowd of fifty thousand people had gathered because of three young peasant children who said they had spoken to the Virgin Mary. She had told them, the children said, that

[97] *Time-Life Books*, The UFO Phenomenon, *pp. 23–24.*

she would "reveal" herself on that day "so everyone would believe."

Just before five o'clock P.M. the huge crowd watched in amazement as the clouds parted. There in the sky above them a huge silver disk was spinning like a windmill. The object glittered and danced about in the sky, throwing off an intense heat. The bewildered onlookers shielded their eyes; some fell to their knees, afraid to look upon the miracle. Others gasped in amazement as their rain-soaked clothing dried in just a matter of minutes.

The remarkable display continued for several minutes, then suddenly the whirling disk plunged toward the earth, turned upward in a huge arc, climbed back into the sky and disappeared into the sun.[98]

Did "everyone" believe? It is likely that everyone who was there did. And Fatima remains, to this day, one of Christendom's most venerated shrines, attracting even the pope on various occasions.

But the era of the "flying saucer" didn't begin officially until June 24, 1947. Kenneth Arnold, a 32-year-old pilot from Boise, Idaho, was flying his single-engine plane at ninety-two hundred feet over the Cascade Mountains of Washington. It was, according to all reports, a fine sunny afternoon. Suddenly a blue-white flash engulfed him. Arnold braced for the shock of what he was certain was a huge explosion, but nothing came. He looked about at the undisturbed Earth and sky and began to relax and breathe a little easier. Then another brilliant flash lit up his cockpit.

This time, ahead of him and to the north, he saw a formation of dazzling objects skimming the mountain tops at incredible speed. Every once in a while one of

[98] *Ibid.*

the objects would bank and reflect a blaze of sunlight from its mirrorlike surface. It was this reflection that had riveted his attention. At first he thought they were some of the new "jet" fighters he'd been hearing about, but they moved with such speed and precision that he decided to check it out. He looked at his clock: it was exactly one minute till three o'clock P.M. The first object shot past Mount Rainier, and he marked the second hand on the clock in front of him. When the last object flashed past Mount Adams, he marked the time elapsed at a minute and forty-two seconds. Checking the map, he found the two mountains were forty-seven miles apart. A quick calculation told him the speed of the objects was 1,656 miles per hour, much faster than any jet he had ever heard of.

Once on the ground in Yakima, Arnold raced to tell his friends what he had seen, and by the time he reached Pendleton, Oregon, later that afternoon, reporters were already waiting for him when he landed. When asked to describe the mysterious objects, he said, "They flew like a saucer would if you skipped it across the water."[99]

The era of the "flying saucer" was born.

Less than a month later an event took place that redefined the study of UFOs forever. Over the Fourth of July weekend in 1947, near Roswell, New Mexico, many UFO investigators believe a "flying saucer" crashed.

Over the years I have worked personally with historians, researchers, and witnesses to this event on two motion-picture projects and a book (*Hangar 18*). Only recently, after years of denial and official silence from Washington, have UFO researchers finally put together

[99] *Ibid.*, p. 36.

the pieces of this most mysterious puzzle. For nearly
four decades the world has been left to wonder if the
United States government has in its possession the
crashed UFO *and* the bodies of its alien crew. There is
still no official word. Nor will the government say
whether or not evidence of these events is secreted
away in fabled Hangar 18 at Wright-Patterson Air
Force Base near Dayton, Ohio. But in a climate less
repressive than in years past, recent research has gotten closer to the answers than ever before. The conclusion seems to be that, indeed, something that either
the government cannot or will not explain happened on
that fateful Fourth of July. And whatever it was definitely has otherworldly implications. Until the government opens the doors of Hangar 18 or invites investigators into the cold-storage lockers in Dayton, the
questions will continue to be asked.

Did a flying saucer crash near Roswell, New Mexico, in 1947? Were the bodies of aliens retrieved? Is
the craft itself still in the possession of our government? Have they learned to make it fly? Many UFO
investigators and a few of the surviving participants in
the original investigation believe the answer to all of
those questions is yes!

There is another puzzle that has come to light just
in the past two decades that may or may not be associated with the subject of aliens among us. Those who
have investigated this particular phenomenon find it as
intriguing as any of the stories of UFO sightings, perhaps even more so.

For this discussion we must return to Richard C.
Hoagland and his book, *The Monuments of Mars*. Ac-
cording to Hoagland, on August 3, 1990, in Central
England, a striking "crop glyph" just . . . appeared.
Suddenly the previously simple (if baffling) phenome-

non of "crop circles" took on an "explosive geometric evolution."[100]

Crop circles began appearing in 1975 and have baffled scientists ever since. The name derives from the fact that these "circles" are always etched in a standing agricultural field, usually several acres in size. The geometric designs are gently swirled into some strange geometric pattern. Very large, and appearing literally overnight with no sign of entrance or exit on the field, the circles are made by crop stalks pressed down, but not broken, and sometimes, to everyone's amazement, they will be bent in opposing directions in the same glyph.

Most of the early designs were simply what the name implies, circles, but the "Cheesefoot Head" crop circle changed all that. Now a new name, "glyphs," was required. In this instance four arcs were connected by straight lines that bisected two small circles, with a much larger circle containing an intricate geometric design in between them. The size and symmetry of the design astounded those who saw it. Below the smaller arcs the straight line continued to yet another circle, and beyond that the glyph ended in a small "Y" shape.

Hoagland measured the central angle of the four arcs, bracketing the smaller circles and straddling the largest circle on the axis. He discovered, to his amazement, that the angles present in the glyph were identical to two of the key angles measured at Cydonia. Even more amazing, the result of dividing these angles into one another and examining the radian measure of one angle revealed a "message" that was indisputably redundant, "tetrahedral," "biological," and—identical to that present at Cydonia.

[100] *Richard C. Hoagland,* The Monuments of Mars, *plate 41.*

"Subsequent measurement of scores of additional 'circles' appearing both in 1990 and 1991 demonstrate beyond doubt," Hoagland says, "that 'crop glyphs' are clearly (if inexplicably) attempting to communicate on Earth."[101]

(Recently, [October 1993], a group claimed responsibility for creating the crop circles in an attempt to debunk this strange phenomenon. But when asked to demonstrate how they did it, they could not duplicate the feat. Followers of the crop-circle phenomenon are quick to point out also that the number of circles the group claimed to have made was only a fraction of the total. The debunkers, it seems, were themselves quickly debunked.)

Could it be that as we get closer to the answers, our "visitors" give us more clues to work with? Or will we discover at last that there is, in fact, some rational and logical explanation for these seeming mysteries that is not "otherworldly"?

One man who seems to take the latter view is Jacques Vallee. In his book, *Messengers of Deception,* Vallee takes a position that is hardly satisfying to either side of the argument, but is interesting nonetheless:

1. Unidentified flying objects operate according to an understanding of our universe that transcends ordinary space-time physics. If we are living in an "Associative Universe," as I am suggesting, then we must expect such paranormal effects, possibly triggered by and accessible to human consciousness. This would explain both the "impossible" movements of UFOs and the psychological phenomena of contact.

[101] *Ibid.*

2. The main effect of UFOs on their witnesses is a conditioning process. Through exposure to its powerful imagery, man appears to be acquiring new forms of behavior and new models of his relationship to the world of nature. Although the source of this condition seems to be a technology, the actual mechanism still eludes us. Whether or not it is controlled by human beings is an open question.

3. The social process caused by the belief in the phenomenon takes the form of new sects, movements and "contact" cults. Close observation of these cults shows that they are monitored and in some cases deliberately manipulated by occult groups, government organizations, and extremist political movements.[102]

It is that last proposition that has caused the most concern. "The public," Vallee says, "has two usual positions on UFOs—either 'it's all nonsense,' or 'we are visited by creatures from another planet.' Until today, the first position has been the stronger one. A majority of the public and practically every scientist has long thought that UFOs were nonsense. Now things are changing. So many people have seen strange phenomena that a new belief has been born. Scientific opinion cannot stop this shifting of power . . . In the naive words of a *New York Times* science editor, 'We are not alone!'

"There is another system," Vallee insists. "It is sending us messengers of deception. They are not necessarily coming from nearby stars. *In terms of the effect on us, it doesn't matter where they come from*

---

[102] *Jaques Vallee*, Messengers of Deception, *preface.*

[his italics]. I even suspect that 'where' and 'when' have no meaning here. How could we be alone? The black box of science has stopped ticking. People look up toward the stars in eager expectation. . . . Yet we shouldn't rejoice too soon. Perhaps we will get the visitors we deserve."[103]

David Swift, a sociologist, writing an epilogue to Vallee's book explains that "although Jacques Vallee concludes that UFOs are real, he does not think they are spaceships; instead he suggests that they are physical devices for manipulating human beliefs, and that the manipulators may be people here on earth."[104]

It is an interesting thesis, and certainly deserves attention. The difficulty however, is in trying to discover how these earthly "manipulators" manage to do such unearthly things. In my view, the question is still open. It is a mystery that dates back to antiquity but has all the currency of a new novel by Ludlum. And once you begin leafing through its pages, it becomes extremely difficult to put it down.

Are there aliens among us? If there are, are they our progenitors or our protagonists? At least one space scientist was able to design a workable spaceship based solely on Ezekiel's biblical description of the "wheel within a wheel." Could it be that these so-called aliens are not "alien" at all?

[103] *Ibid., pp. 245–246.*
[104] *Ibid., p. 247.*

11

ATLANTIS—A WORLD WITHIN A WORLD

"[I]n a single day and night of destruction all the warlike men in a body sank into the earth, and the island of Atlantis, in like manner, disappeared in the depths of the sea."

Plato

MORNING DID NOT REALLY "BREAK" OVER THE IS-
land kingdom of Atlantis; rather, it rolled quietly down
from the top of Cleito's Mountain and gently nudged
the citizens awake. Poseidon, god of the sea, and his
ten sons would have it no other way.

Poseidon, who governed earthquakes as well as the
seas, had been given Atlantis to rule, where he fell
under the spell of a beautiful mortal maiden named
Cleito. He built her a magnificent home on the hill
overlooking the plains of Atlantis, and to prevent anyone from reaching her home, he encircled the hill with
alternating rings of land and water, "two of land and
three of water, which he turned as with a lathe."

Poseidon and Cleito had ten children, five sets of
male twins, and Poseidon divided Atlantis and its adjacent islands among his ten sons to rule as a confeder-
acy. Atlas, the firstborn of the eldest twins, gave his
name to Atlantis and ruled as chief king.[105]

In the beginning, Atlantis, the nearest thing to paradise on the face of the Earth, was governed by wisdom and virtue, and the land as well as the people
responded to these honorable traits. Fruits and vegeta-
bles grew abundantly, flowers and herbs bloomed ev-

[105] *Roy Stemmans,* Atlantis and the Lost Lands, *p. 13.*

erywhere on wooded slopes or verdant plains. Animals, both wild and tame, roamed the hills and meadows that were liberally sprinkled with sparkling rivers and deep, cool lakes.

Atlantis was rich in precious metals, and all the people were wealthier than any people before or since. They raised great temples to the gods and decorated them with silver, gold, and burnished brass. The royal palace was breathtaking in its lavish furnishings and wondrous beauty. In addition, great feats of engineering were commonplace in Atlantis, and a complex system of waterways and bridges linked the very heart of the city with the open sea.

This was a kingdom known far and wide because of the steady stream of ships from other lands that were constantly coming to its inviting ports.

In short, the people of Atlantis had everything anyone could ever want.[106]

And thus begins one of the world's most durable legends, told by one of the world's most respected philosophers and thinkers.

Plato, generally regarded as one of the fathers of Western thought, is the sole direct source for the legend of Atlantis.[107] The story appears in two of the dialogues that Plato began originally, according to most scholars, as a trilogy. The subject of Atlantis is introduced in *Timaeus*, and ends abruptly, in mid-sentence, in *Critias*. The work, whatever it was intended to be, was never finished.

The dialogues credit the origination of the story to Solon, the famous lawgiver of Greece, who was renowned for his honesty. Solon, according to the record,

[106] *Ibid.*
[107] *Reader's Digest*, The World's Last Mysteries.

received the story from an Egyptian priest whom he visited in the city of Sais, an Egyptian city of the Nile Delta having close ties with Athens.

Solon was a real person, known to have visited Egypt sometime around 590 B.C., some hundred and fifty years prior to Plato's recounting of the story. Scholarship is divided over Plato's relationship to the great lawgiver. Some suggest he was a great-grandson or at a least distant relative of Solon,[108] while others suggest Plato was a distant relative of Critias the Elder, a poet and historian whose "great-grandson," in the dialogues, is given the responsibility for the retelling of the story.[109]

In *Timaeus* there is a brief account of what the priests had told Solon. According to ancient Egyptian records there had been a great empire in about 9600 B.C., based on an island west of the Pillars of Hercules, (the Strait of Gibraltar) that was larger than Libya (North Africa) and Asia Minor combined. This empire, called Atlantis, ruled over lands that had been conquered from North Africa as far as Egypt and southward through Europe to the Greek borders. Only here did Athens, standing alone, defeat the Atlantean army.[110]

Then the Egyptian priest told Solon (who told Critias, whose great-grandson Critias, is now telling the story through Plato's dialogue), "[T]here occurred afterward violent earthquakes and floods; and in a single day and night of destruction all the warlike men in a body sank into the earth, and the island of Atlantis in like manner disappeared in the depths of the sea. For

---

[108] *Eberhard Zangger, The Flood from Heaven, p. 11.*
[109] *Stemmans, Atlantis and the Lost Lands, p. 13.*
[110] *Ibid.*

which reason the sea in those parts is impassable and impenetrable, because there is so much shallow mud in the way, caused by the subsidence of the island."[111]

From this marvelously told tale has sprung the seemingly indestructible legend of Atlantis. But why should anyone, let alone generations of serious-minded scientists and philosophers, believe that the story is anything more than a fanciful tale devised by Plato as a backdrop for illustrating his own beliefs regarding governance and politics? Plato was, after all, a powerful storyteller who used the device of "dialogues" between well-known characters to further his own philosophical ideas. (Socrates is one of the participants in the *Timaeus* dialogue.) Why wasn't the tale of Atlantis simply assigned to the realms of fiction by scholars who followed Plato?

The mere fact that it wasn't—that now, twenty-three hundred years later—it is still regarded as a factual account of real people and real events, attests to the power of the story. It should be remembered, too, that Plato receives the "facts" of Atlantis more or less directly from Solon, one of the greatest and most highly regarded of all of the ancient Greek lawgivers. Solon, among other things, was noted for his absolute integrity. Furthermore, Plato has no less a luminary than Socrates himself saying that the story has "the very great advantage of being a fact and not a fiction." Added to all of this is Plato's own reputation for honesty and truth, which was not inconsiderable.

There is another aspect of Plato's account of Atlantis that makes it difficult to dismiss out of hand. The second dialogue, *Critias,* is filled with rich detail. The structure of the city, and even individual buildings are

[111] *Ibid.*

described in minute detail. The social, political, and religious organizations of the people are painted in such vivid terms as to bear the stamp of authenticity. We are told of the red, white, and black stones used in the buildings, of statues of gold so high their heads touched the roof of the temple, of the ornamentation of simple buildings as well as of palaces and temples. Such detail one would expect only in a factual account.

Still, it is difficult to imagine that great scholars and explorers would stake their reputations on just that story alone. (Keep in mind that every book or article about Atlantis that has ever been written or published is based on Plato's account.) It is at this point that the mystery deepens. The scholars have, over the centuries, made discoveries of their own, and these discoveries have generated a host of questions that *might* be answered if the story of Atlantis is true.

To quote from Roy Stemman's interesting work:

"Why, ask the scholars, are there so many remarkable similarities between the ancient cultures of the Old and New Worlds? Why do we find the same plants and animals on continents thousands of miles apart when there is no known way for them to have been transported there? How did the primitive peoples of many lands construct technological marvels, such as Stonehenge in Britain, the huge statues of Easter Island in the Pacific, and the strange sacred cities of the Andes? Were they helped by a technically sophisticated race that has since disappeared? Above all, why do the legends of people the world over tell the same story of an overwhelming natural disaster and the arrival of godlike beings who brought with them a new culture from afar? Could the catastrophe that sank Atlantis have sent tidal waves throughout the globe, causing terrible havoc and destruction? And were the 'gods' the remnants of the Atlantean race—the few survivors who were not on or near the island continent when it was engulfed?

"Even without Plato's account," Stemman suggests, "the quest for answers to these mysteries might have led to the belief of some 'missing link' between the continents. Nevertheless, it is the Greek philosopher's story that lies at the heart of all arguments for or against the existence of such a lost continent."[112]

But what could have brought about such a disaster? Several theories have been proposed that link the destruction to known natural calamities that would seem to conform to the information given to Solon by the Egyptian priest. These theories, over the centuries, have placed the lost continent of Atlantis just about every place on the globe. We must remember, however, that Atlantis was protected by one of the chief gods. Poseidon was answerable only to Zeus. Surely they would not have permitted the destruction of such a favored race. Plato, in the last paragraphs of the *Critias* dialogue, suggests they brought it on themselves.

"[T]hey lost their comeliness through being unable to bear the burden of their possessions, and they became ugly to look upon, in the eyes of him who has the gift of sight; for they had lost the fairest of their goods from the most precious of their parts; but in the eyes of those who have no gift of perceiving what is the truly happy life, it was then above all that they appeared to be superlatively fair and blessed, filled as they were with lawless ambition and power. And Zeus, the God of gods, who reigns by Law, inasmuch as he has the gift of perceiving such things, marked how this righteous race was in evil plight, and desired to inflict punishment

[112] *Ibid.*, p. 10.

upon them, to the end that when chastised they might strike a truer note. Wherefore he assembled together all the gods into that abode which they honor most, standing as it does at the center of all the universe, and beholding all things that partake of generation; and when he had assembled them, he spake thus—"[113]

And thus the story ends. Plato never returned to finish it. Instead he went on to write his last dialogue, *The Laws*.

But if Plato could walk away from the story, why can't the rest of the world? Perhaps the answer to that question lies in all the other unanswered questions. Whatever the reason, there seems to be no end of scholars, explorers, adventurers, even clairvoyants, who are unwilling to let Atlantis rest.

Literally thousands of books have been written and nearly as many theories advanced as to what could have happened, as well as where and why it happened. (Only the most dour critics continue to question whether or not it in fact did happen.) And the fascination seems to be worldwide.

Scientists in Siberia, for example, have come up with a theory regarding the disappearance of Atlantis that also suggests an explanation for several other ancient mysteries. It also touches, albeit lightly, on Sitchin's postulation of a twelfth planet.

The theory notes that ancient Greek writings refer to a time during which no Moon graced the heavens. Certain legends of African Bushmen corroborate these writings. Also . . .

There are Native American legends that speak of a time, prior to some major catastrophe, when the Earth

[113] *Zangger*, The Flood from Heaven, p. 36.

was much nearer to the Sun, the greater warmth making clothing unnecessary. And . . .

A crater near Antarctica appears to have been caused by a meteorite of some sort, but no foreign matter was discovered in or around the site, suggesting that something hit the Earth, but at such an angle and velocity as to permit it to carom off like a billiard ball.

Taking these legends into account, the Siberian scientists suggest that the comet that is known to have torn through the solar system around 1500 B.C. slammed into a planet they call "Phaeton," then in orbit between Mars and Jupiter (shades of Sitchin!). Phaeton was pushed out of orbit and fell into the Earth's gravitational field. It fell to Earth and slammed into the ground in what is now Antarctica, creating the mysterious crater and drastically altering the orientation of the Earth's axis. But the angle and velocity of Phaeton was such that it bounced off the surface and found an orbit, becoming Earth's moon. The force of this collision and the resultant shift in the Earth's rotation could well have caused such massive geological changes that the continent on which Atlantis was located was indeed swallowed up beneath the ocean.

Interestingly enough, an old Greek legend states that Phaeton, the son of the sun god, requested that he be allowed to drive his father's chariot one day. The boy was unable to control it and came too close to the Earth and flames shot up from the ground. The people were terrified and appealed to the gods for intervention. The goddess of the Earth spoke to Zeus, who in response to her pleading, took up his lightning bolts and shot Phaeton down from the skies. Could the ancient Greek storytellers have been describing the events suggested by the Siberians' theory?

But is there any evidence to suggest the Earth's axis

has changed markedly? Well, ancient waterclocks discovered in Egypt and totally unworkable there would have been completely accurate if they had been used at the Earth's equator.

One of the earliest and most successful Atlantologists (the story has named a new science as well as an ocean) was an American politician and member of Congress named Ignatius Donnelly. Donnelly published his thesis in 1882 and immediately gathered to himself a large and loyal following—and a storm of controversy.

In *Atlantis: The Antediluvian World,* Donnelly brought together all the contemporary sciences: archaeology, mythology, linguistics, ethnology, geology, zoology, and botany, to prove that the pre-Columbian civilizations of America and ancient Egyptian cultures had a common origin, and that that origin could only be Atlantis. Everything from the mysterious breeding habits of eels, to the tall, white-skinned aborigines of the Canary Islands was held out as proof of Donnelly's "scientific" analysis.[114]

Today the fundamental base upon which all of Donnelly's theories are constructed—that Atlantis was in the mid-Atlantic—has been substantially refuted. Oceanographic studies of the entire thirty-six million square miles of the Atlantic show that nowhere is there evidence of any such continent or any cataclysmic event that might have destroyed one.[115]

The idea that Atlantis lay somewhere in the Atlantic Ocean was resurrected in 1968, however, with the discovery of huge underwater stone walls, obviously man-made, submerged off the island of North Bimini in the

[114] *Reader's Digest,* The World's Last Mysteries.
[115] *Ibid.*

Bahamas. Followers of Edgar Cayce, the American clairvoyant, were quick to recall that in the early 1940s Cayce had predicted that some part of Atlantis would rise again in 1968.

Edgar Cayce provides one of the more interesting interludes in the Atlantis mystery. A professional photographer by trade, Cayce had a widespread reputation as healer. He would go into a deep hypnotic trance and while in that trance come up with remarkably effective diagnoses and treatments for various problems and ailments about which he had no knowledge. Most of his "patients" were personally unknown to him as well. Frequently all he had was a name, address, and a brief description of the problem. His effectiveness was well documented, and even today Cayce's son continues his father's work through an organization called ARE (Association of Research and Enlightenment), located in Virginia.

While in his hypnotic trances, Cayce revealed many fascinating aspects of Atlantis and its occupants, from which, he said, many of his clients were descendants. Some were even "reincarnated" Atlanteans.

That Cayce strongly believed in the prior existence of the continent of Atlantis is indisputable. And his many "readings" on the subject provide some interesting insights or overlays on the original story. Cayce believed their world had been destroyed in 50,000 B.C., again in 28,000 B.C. and most recently in 10,000 B.C. This latest date correlates to within a thousand years or so of Plato's record of the destruction. Coincidentally perhaps, it also places Atlanteans in a time period that would have permitted them to have at least helped with the carving of the sphinx (if the new dating of that monument is accurate), and, using Plato's dating, it also puts them in a chronological position to be of help to ancient Sumer (around 11,500 B.C.) when, scholars say, the Sumerian language just seems to have materialized.

Cayce's contention was that most Atlanteans escaped the disaster because their technology permitted their knowing in advance what was coming. Accordingly, they spread throughout the region, to Greece, Egypt (and Sumer, of course), as well as westward into Mexico, Peru, and the Americas. According to Cayce, Atlanteans and their descendants all have one thing in common, an extraordinary grasp of technical matters. Echoing the theme of the last paragraphs of Plato's story, Cayce suggests that it was the scientists and technologists of Atlantis who brought about their own destruction through misuse of the great knowledge they had acquired.

The editors of *The World's Last Mysteries* ask what is perhaps the most relevant question in this regard: "Is it possible that Cayce's vision was in fact a premonition: that he was looking not at the remote past but at the immediate future of industrialized America? His message does appear to be a clear warning to modern society."[116] The question deserves consideration.

There is, however, one modern scientist who believes he has solved the mystery. Dr. Eberhard Zangger, a noted geoarchaeologist with many years of field work in the Mediterranean, has, according to his book, *The Flood from Heaven,* discovered the true nature of Plato's story, and the real location of Atlantis.

The whole thing, says Dr. Zangger, was just a linguistic misunderstanding. Two ancient individuals— one Greek, the other Egyptian—simply didn't understand each other that clearly, and Solon brought back a story that he should have been familiar with, the story

[116] *Ibid.*

of the Trojan War, and passed it on as something new. By the time it reached Plato, some hundred and fifty years later, he didn't recognize it either, at least not right away.

Dr. Zangger describes his findings in his own words:

"Plato described the Atlantis legend as having originated in the sixth century B.C. during a conversation between the Greek statesman Solon and a priest in Sais, at that time the capital of Egypt. After his visit to Egypt, Solon had planned to turn the narrative into an epic poem, but he never succeeded. His unfinished manuscript was handed down over a few generations until Plato, a descendant of Solon, circulated it a few years before his death in 347 B.C. Although Plato realized the secondary nature of the account, he appears to have been fully convinced of its accuracy. If Plato's suggested transmission is correct, the 2,500-year-old confusion around Atlantis may have resulted from a simple misunderstanding between two very old men, Solon and a Saitian priest, who were chatting about history and were not quite able to comprehend the meaning of their sources. Solon was fascinated by the story only because he was misguided. If he had realized that the priest was speaking about the Trojan War, he would perhaps not have taken notes of the conversation in his diary."

There you have it. According to Dr. Zangger, "Plato's account of Atlantis was in fact a retelling of the story of the Trojan War."[117]

Zangger goes on to suggest that at some point Plato realized he was telling a story with which he was all too

---

[117] *Zangger*, The Flood from Heaven, *p. 11.*

familiar and simply dropped it in mid-sentence to go on to other things.

It might be well to point out here that Troy and the entire saga of the Trojan War was also once thought to be pure fiction, the invention of a composite author called Homer. Then in 1871 a German archaeologist, Heinrich Schliemann, with a copy of Homer's *Iliad* in one hand and a spade in the other, excavated in Hissarlik, in northwestern Turkey, uncovering the city of Troy exactly where Homer said it was.

Dr. Zangger's book was first published in Europe in 1992. The full impact of his research and findings has perhaps not yet had time to penetrate the core of Atlantean theorists and investigators. Whether it will have much impact is open to question. After all, the story has been around for nearly two and a half millennia and seems to gain interest with each new discovery, real or imagined.

Was there a lost continent of Atlantis? Did survivors of this unique and powerful society gain knowledge and power that in the end destroyed them? Did their survivors dot the globe with architectural and scientific masterpieces that modern man has yet to duplicate?

Whether or not it was the Atlanteans, whoever built the Great Pyramid and Stonehenge and the Mayan and Olmec temples had a marvelous grasp of mathematics and geometry, as well as other sciences previously thought to have been discovered by more modern scholars. Perhaps these builders are all the same people, or members of the same race, a race that has left its footprints all over the planet Earth.

Were they Atlanteans? Were they visitors from another planet? Were the first Atlanteans visitors from another planet? The truth is, we don't know. And in this instance at least, the evidence appears to be on the side of the skeptics. Still, one can't help wondering what Plato might have done if he could have foreseen the enormous impact his story would have on the world. Would he have finished it, and in so doing removed the mystery? Or did he purposely walk away from the story, leaving Atlantis at the mercy of Zeus in order to create the mystery?

Maybe he just couldn't think of anything that Zeus might have said and, weary of the tale, went on to something else. It is interesting to note, however, that the story ends on the point of Zeus setting up a meeting of the gods. It is unlikely that even the great Solon would have been privy to that conversation.

12

THE BERMUDA TRIANGLE

*"Could it be that something or someone . . .
is collecting people like specimens?"*

Charles Berlitz

SOME YEARS AGO I HAD THE PLEASURE OF WORKING with Charles Berlitz on the motion picture version of his bestselling novel, *The Bermuda Triangle*. Over a period of several months I gained some familiarity with that part of the Atlantic Ocean, which has swallowed up hundreds of ships and planes and taken literally thousands of lives. It is this record of loss and devastation that has made the "Bermuda Triangle" synonymous with ancient and sinister mystery. The very name conjures up visions of ghostly ships plying the seas with no one on board, or airplanes disappearing in the blink of an eye, never to be seen again. And even though the written record begins over five hundred years ago, the stories are as modern as day-before-yesterday, and quite possibly, day-after-tomorrow.

Is there some malevolent force unique to this spot on the globe? Could there be something that preys on travelers in these waters—something that can snatch a whole squadron of planes from the sky or swallow up a giant ship with equal ease? Those who have experienced some of the strange events that occur in the Triangle will tell you they don't really know, but they are not quick to volunteer to go back and find out either.

We know for a fact that strange occurrences were

already being reported as far back as 1492 in this other-wise very pleasant part of the world. The records of Columbus indicate that he and his men were alarmed by strange lights in the night sky and the sudden erratic behavior of their compass. Perhaps they thought that they had entered into that terrible "Devil's Sea" they had been warned about before leaving Spain.

We can only guess at what dark fears may have clutched at the hearts of these intrepid men whose courage had already been severely tested by frightful months of wandering in a trackless sea. But from Co-lumbus's logs and reports we know that his expedition encountered many of the same mysterious phenomena in the Bermuda Triangle that continue to haunt mod-ern mariners even as we approach the twenty-first cen-tury.

The notations in those logs might have been written off as the fearful imaginings of officers and men too long in the grip of their forced isolation. But Columbus also recorded that the island natives, like the Caribs and Arawaks of Puerto Rico were, and had long been, familiar with strange occurrences in this part of the world. Their legends and folklore contained many sto-ries of "sky gods" and "green-fire boats" that could fly in the sky . . . or under the water.

We may be stretching the definition of "ancient" here just a bit, but it is fair to say that this not some-thing that flew onto the front pages of our collective consciousness on the wings of modern aircraft. Quite the opposite. But these primitive people must have gotten the notion of flying ships and green-fire boats from somewhere.

Of course strange and mysterious events and just plain old-fashioned "vanishings" are still being reported today, but the fears engendered by such events stretch back to the very beginnings of the record. Men, ships, and planes have vanished in this part of the Atlantic Ocean for hundreds of years, with no explanations for many of the disappearances. Since 1945 alone, there have been over a thousand "vanishings" of everything from huge naval vessels to private boats, from commercial airliners to small planes, not to mention the staggering number of people aboard these craft. That they were lost in the ocean is bad enough, but the fact that they simply disappeared without leaving a single trace adds something ominous to these disastrous events.

But are these disappearances the result of some sinister and unknowable force? Or are they just tragic, but quite understandable catastrophes? Lawrence D. Kusche, librarian at Arizona State University and author of *The Bermuda Triangle: Mystery Solved*, is one expert who takes the latter view.

"To begin with," Kusche writes, "there is no such place as the 'Bermuda Triangle.' The term was coined by Vincent Gaddis in 1964. It appeared first in *Argosy* magazine in an article that contained a series of highly imaginative, quasi-facts and modern myths that later became a chapter in a book that was also written by Gaddis. That was like letting the genie out of the bottle. A spate of books followed, with every writer adding bits and pieces of more rumors, hearsay, and garbled stories to hype quite ordinary disappearances and tragedies into a manufactured mystery, which was really no mystery at all. Unless, of course, bad weather can be considered a mystery."

Dr. Dean D. Churchill, assistant professor of Meteorology and Physical Oceanography at the University of

Miami, shares that view. According to Dr. Churchill, "The area of the Atlantic Ocean known as the Bermuda Triangle is often referred to as a 'Foul Weather Factory.' Sudden and very powerful squalls are completely unpredictable, and even though they don't last very long they can be devastating."

There can be no doubt that weather plays an important part in both sea and air losses in the Bermuda Triangle, but can it be blamed for the staggering number of disappearances? And what of the many other odd occurrences on record that have nothing to do with weather at all?

"There are forces operating in this part of the Atlantic Ocean," Charles Berlitz tells us, "that are neither understood nor explainable by modern science. What's more, they may have been occurring for thousands of years before the voyage of Columbus."

Many of the strange and unexplained occurrences are reflected in the folk legend of the natives of the area, but the actual record of "vanishings" goes back to at least 1609. In that year, the good ship *Sea Venture*, on a voyage from England to America, carrying a full manifest of passengers bound for Virginia, was shipwrecked just off the island of Bermuda. Members of the crew were able to salvage the longboat, and on September first of that year, with members of the crew, experienced mariners all, manning it, the small vessel set out to reach the mainland five hundred miles away to bring back help. There was, according to reports, a fair wind, and the boat quickly slipped beyond the horizon . . . never to be seen or heard from again.

Ships of the U.S. Navy were vanishing as early as 1800, and in his book, Berlitz lists at least twelve cases of major vessels that have disappeared and seven cases of ships found drifting, intact and apparently abandoned, with not a living soul on board.[118]

Berlitz describes one of these events.

"The log of His Majesty's ship, Harwhal, May 16, 1767. 'For a fortnight we have been becalmed in the midst of this damnable Sargasso Sea and the patience of men and officers alike is sorely tried. We seem to be clasped,' the Captain wrote, 'within the grasp of some strange force that will not let us go. Though we have not had the whisper of a breeze for days, oddly there is the sound of wind about us. Strange lights, appearing as huge, glowing green puffs, were sighted on the modish last night.'

"The Captain interrupted his notations when the watch topside shouted that they had spotted a ship coming toward them, fully rigged and apparently with bellied sails. The approaching ship was recognized as the *Westbury Star,* out of Liverpool. There was no appearance of life on board. The frigate captain tried signaling and calling, but there was no answer. The log continues with this contradictory comment: 'Though there was not a living soul on deck the sails were neatly trimmed and the *Westbury Star* was tacking to a brisk wind as she passed within a few hundred yards.' The Captain's log entry ends with these plain words: '. . . but upon my honor there was not the slightest breeze to ripple our own rigging.'"

Does it seem possible that the wind could permit the ghost ship to tack by with bellied sails, while a hundred yards away there was not the slightest breeze? It is, of course, happenings like these that have given the Bermuda Triangle its eerie reputation and spawned an entire genre of "sea stories" by authors such as Jack

[118] *Charles Berlitz,* Enigmas and Mysteries.

London. Ghostly galleons with tattered sails glide silently into puffs of fog and disappear. Skeletons command schooners, and even islands can be made to appear and disappear in a writer's fertile imagination. But the story of the American schooner *Ellen Austin* didn't spring from a writer's imagination. It came directly from the heart of the Bermuda Triangle.

Richard Winer, another long-time researcher in this area, and author of *The Devil's Triangle* (the other name by which this mysterious piece of the Atlantic is known), tells the tale.

"The American schooner *Ellen Austin* was bound for Spanish and Portuguese ports in the early fall of 1881, when the ship's crew was surprised by the sudden appearance of another ship off the starboard beam. They called their captain, and when he joined them they hailed the vessel and scanned the topside deck. Getting no answer they put over a boarding party.

"The rigging was intact and the ship was seaworthy and trim. Everything seemed normal . . . except there was not a living thing aboard. Sailors always have a superstitious foreboding about derelicts, but this ship represented a salvage claim worth a small fortune to the captain and crew of the *Ellen Austin*. A salvage, or 'prize' crew, as it was sometimes called, was left aboard while the others made their way back to the *Ellen Austin*.

"But before they could get under way, a ferocious squall suddenly hit without warning. It was all the crew could do to save the *Ellen Austin*. The fury of the storm blew itself out in less than half an hour, passing as quickly as it had come. Then came the stunning discovery. The prize derelict, along with the salvage crew . . . were gone. It had completely disappeared. Both the officers and men of the *Ellen Austin* would later testify that it was as if it had vanished into thin air. Not so much as a broken plank could be seen on the surface of the water."

It is hard to imagine a ship, even one engulfed by a raging storm, going down without leaving so much as a piece of rigging to mark the spot. Yet this is apparently what happened. And the crew of the *Ellen Austin* is not the only crew to tell of such an occurrence. Most ships and planes lost in the Triangle, it seems, disappear without a trace.

The list of lost ships and derelicts—just those missing in modern times—is staggering. Why do crews and passengers just simply vanish without a trace? Charles Berlitz, after studying the phenomena for many years, asked, "Could it be that something or some*one* . . . is collecting people like specimens?"

Some of the events that have taken place in the Triangle seem to not only defy logic but the laws of physics as well. Captain Don Henry, a tugboat captain and salvage expert based in Florida, tells one of the most interesting of all the Triangle's many weird and harrowing stories.

"We were coming back to Miami from Puerto Rico on the tug *Good News* . . . towing an empty barge of twenty-five hundred tons on a thousand-foot hawser (tow rope) out behind. You couldn't want for a nicer day at sea. I was in my cabin with the mate at the helm when all of a sudden the electrical system went crazy. So I went down below to check the generator. Everything was running fine . . . nothing wrong with the breakers . . . then I heard all this shouting topside so I headed up immediately. The mate was pretty shook up. The compass and all the instruments had just gone berserk. Nothing was working worth a hoot."

Captain Henry and his mate were both somewhere

just this side of panic by this time, and then the once placid ocean and clear sky took on a different hue.

"Suddenly everything looked odd," Henry recalls. "I mean the water, the sky, the horizon, everything, all just blended together like a foggy picture.

"My biggest concern was losing the tow. But I had two thousand horses under me in the big twin diesels and I ran them up to the redline. All I wanted to do was to get the hell-and-gone out of there. But it was like something was holding us, sort of like a tug of war. We were churning up green water but we were going no place fast."

The captain didn't know what was going on, but all around him was a thick, greenish fog. The seas were churning as if they had suddenly been caught up in a storm, but the most disturbing thing was the fact that they seemed frozen in place. The tug was working at maximum power, but as far as Henry could tell he was just churning up a wake.

"We were just about at our wit's end," Henry told us, "when we came out of that weird fog and the storm just quits. I headed aft to check on the tow, and what I saw made the hair stand up on the back of my neck. That towing hawser was standing out stiff, as if there were something still pulling on it, but there was nothing there. It just went straight back to . . . nothing. We hauled it in hand over hand and it finally fell onto the deck, sheared clean. A minute later the barge broke out into the open and behind it . . . in that strange clump of fog . . . the water was still all stirred up. I figured I could see about eleven miles in every direction, and I swear, there was no fog anywhere else."

By this time Captain Henry was totally perplexed. He'd spent most of his life at sea, but this was something entirely different than anything he had ever experienced, and he wasn't through yet. There was one more jolt still to come.

"The storm had taken all the warmth out of the air and a real chill had set in," he continued, "but when I touched one of the metal rails, it liked to of fried my hand. I'll tell ya, the Triangle only happened to me once, but I don't need another time to make me a believer."

That seems to be the attitude of most survivors of an encounter with the Bermuda Triangle. A "once is enough" feeling that in some cases keeps men from ever returning there again.

Oh, by the way, there was yet another interesting result of Captain Don Henry's encounter with the Bermuda Triangle. When he got back to port he had to throw away every battery on the tug. They were all completely drained. Nobody, including the captain and his mate, has the slightest clue as to why they should all have suddenly and simultaneously gone dead.

There are many such seagoing encounters experienced in these waters. However, some of the most remarkable mysteries have to do with aircraft: large and small, military, commercial and private. But since most of the tales that come out of the Triangle deal with disasters, let's start with one that has a happy ending.

In November of 1964, Chuck Wakely, currently a charter flight operator, and at the time, senior pilot for a charter flight airline, may have escaped one of the Bermuda Triangle's most puzzling snares. Like Don Henry, Wakely is convinced that there is something going on in that part of the world, and that it isn't all happening at sea level.

"There is definitely something I can't explain that occurs in this area," Wakely told us, "and it is definitely electromagnetic in nature. A few years back I was pilot-ing for Sunline Aviation in Miami. I had dropped off some people on a charter to Nassau and was heading back. It was a beautiful night. Clear as a bell—stars everywhere. Then just over Andros Island I notice this kind of glowing on my wings. I thought at first it was some kind of effect from the instrument lights, then in a couple of minutes the whole aircraft started glowing."

Wakely was an experienced pilot and a veteran of many many trips across this particular expanse of ocean. It was not in his nature to panic, but what hap-pened next did make him . . . well . . . a little anx-ious.

"My instruments didn't just malfunction," Wakely said, "they went completely crazy. By then the aircraft was glowing so intensely I could no longer see stars or even the horizon. I just took my hands off the controls and let the plane fly itself. After a while the glow just sort of faded and everything returned to normal."

Looking back on it, what does Chuck Wakely think now about his experience in the Bermuda Triangle?

"These things have happened to a lot of us, though professional pilots don't like to talk about them for all sorts of reasons. But there are darned few of us who don't think there's *something* out there."

Whatever it is that's out there doesn't seem to be particularly affected by the size or type of aircraft, nor is it particular about the kind of tricks it plays.

On approach to Miami International Airport one clear, starry night, a National Airlines flight suddenly disappeared from the radar screens. It reappeared just as suddenly, but that was just the beginning of one of the Triangle's most inexplicable mysteries; a mystery that demonstrated very clearly that strange occurrences are by no means limited to the private pilots and small aircraft that routinely fly through the Bermuda Triangle.

Miami International is one of the busiest airports in the world, and it has its share of strange stories to tell. And, remember, as we pass this story on to you, that we're talking about highly experienced pilots and the world's most advanced technical equipment.

Dee Riggs, an investigative reporter and writer, remembers what happened on this particular night.

"The Triangle has a long history of what we like to call 'time-warp' incidents," Riggs says, "such as unexplainable incidents in which time just doesn't behave itself. Like the happening we're talking about here. It was a lovely spring night and somehow there was a 'time lapse' that no can explain."

As prudence and regulations require, the pilot and copilot of this particular flight, approaching Miami from the north and out over the Triangle, began their check procedures.

"National Airlines, Flight 727, a passenger jet," Riggs remembers, "was on approach to landing from the northeast. They asked the Miami air traffic controller for a time check, and set the instrument panel clock. They were twenty minutes out and right on schedule. The copilot reported later that he noticed a strange-looking mist had enveloped the plane, but aside from its unique appearance, nothing seemed out of the ordinary.

"Meanwhile, back at the Miami Air Traffic Control Center, Flight 727 just suddenly disappeared from the radar screen. The operator immediately set emergency procedures in motion. Within minutes the Coast Guard was alerted, Search and Rescue leaped into action, and all of the emergency procedures a modern airport can provide were poised and prepared for the worst.

"Back in the cockpit of National Airlines 727, things were proceeding without incident. Well, almost without incident. A stewardess, checking the scheduled arrival with the captain, was told she had just performed her last cabin check, including several passenger chores, in less than three minutes. And the copilot was more than a little puzzled to discover the mist that had surrounded the plane was now gone. Not just gone from around the plane—gone from the sky."

Completely oblivious to the situations of each other, the people at Miami International were preparing for a major disaster, while on the plane, the passengers and crew were casually preparing for a routine landing.

Riggs continues: "It had been precisely ten minutes since Flight 727 dropped off the radar scope at the Air Traffic Control Center. A major air-sea rescue operation was about to get under way when, as suddenly as it had disappeared, Flight 727 reappeared on the scope."

Someone suggested that perhaps there had been an equipment malfunction, but thousands of lives depend on these scopes, and they are tested and checked thoroughly and routinely. There was no equipment malfunction detected. But that wouldn't have explained what happened next anyway.

"The plane landed without incident," Riggs remembers, "and the crew was understandably concerned about all the emergency equipment. No one on board the aircraft had any sense of anything being wrong . . . until one of the supervisors told them they were ten minutes late."

Both the pilot and the copilot were incredulous. They clearly remembered setting the cockpit clock in accordance with the airport time check. Suspecting that maybe one of the controllers had been on shift too long or that one of the supervisors was just giving them a hard time, they took an investigator and went back into the cockpit.

Riggs concludes: "In spite of the fact that just twenty minutes earlier they had set their clock on a Miami control tower check, the instrument panel clock —and all of the crew's watches—were exactly ten minutes slow."

No one on board the plane or on the ground had a clue as to what could have caused the time lapse. Some experts, noting that our planet operates on electromagnetism, have wondered if the Bermuda Triangle and certain other areas, might not create vortices where material objects can drop into—or out of—another time-space continuum. That sounds impossible, but the facts are, the plane disappeared from radar for at least ten minutes and all of the clocks and watches on board the plane lost ten minutes in a twenty-minute time span. No one has even tried to explain the strange green mist reported by the copilot.

And before we are too quick to reject the "time-space continuum" theory, there is another "Triangle incident" that no one has been able to explain.

Carolyn Cascio, a licensed pilot, flying a light plane with one passenger, was clearly seen by two employees of the airport at Grand Turk Island. But try as she might, the airport manager could not get the pilot to answer her radio signal.

On the ground, both the airport manager and an employee watched as the plane circled overhead easily within their visual range.

Time after time the airport manager keyed the microphone: "This is Grand Turk, calling the aircraft overhead . . . do you read me?"

There was no response.

"Cessna, this is Grand Turk, identify yourself please . . . Over."

The pilot ignored the repeated request, but both the startled airport manager and an employee heard the mike on the plane key open and comments made by Carolyn Cascio to her passenger came through loud and clear.

"I don't understand it," she said, "this should be Grand Turk, but there's nothing there. It's the right place on the map and the shape is right, but this island looks uninhabited—no buildings . . . roads . . . nothing."

The airport manager tried again to make radio contact, but it was as if he were talking into a dead mike. He could only watch and listen as time and again the obviously concerned and increasingly desperate pilot expressed disbelief that what was below her was not Grand Turk Island. Yet it was obvious that she could see nothing on it. No buildings, no landing strip, nothing.

"It has to be Grand Turk," she said, as the disbelieving airport manager listened in, "but it's not there. It looks like Grand Turk, but it just can't be."

Growing more desperate himself, the airport manager repeated over and over that it was Grand Turk Airport and they were copying her transmissions. But apparently, Carolyn Cascio was seeing the island, not as it is now, but rather as it was in some distant past.

The airport manager and employee could only watch helplessly as the totally confused pilot simply banked the aircraft away and flew out of sight . . . never to be heard from again.

In fact there were a number of observers on Grand Turk at the time who said the plane circled for more than half an hour before disappearing. Which leaves us with a disturbing question: If observers could clearly see the plane, how is it the pilot could not see the buildings, roads, and runway on Grand Turk?

That brings us to perhaps the most famous of the unsolved mysteries of the Bermuda Triangle. Once again we turn to Charles Berlitz, whose exhaustive research into this event probably makes him the definitive expert on the disappearance of Flight 19.

"The naval air station at Fort Lauderdale, Florida," Berlitz tells us, "was the scene of one of the most spectacular mysteries of the Bermuda Triangle. It all began rather routinely on December 5, 1945. An advanced training flight was scheduled for takeoff at fourteen hundred hours. Five pilots and ten crew members were scheduled to go up. Ironically, their course was to be a simple triangle with an expected flight time of two hours. The flight leader was Lieutenant Charles Taylor, an experienced combat pilot with over twenty-five hundred hours of flying time."

But the mystery of Flight 19 actually begins before the planes ever left the ground. For reasons not even he understood, marine corporal Alan Kosnar requested relief from the flight. After some discussion with superior officers, permission was granted. That left the enlisted crew for the flight at nine, yet records would show later that the full complement of ten men left with Flight 19.

Berlitz continues: "Flight 19 completed the first leg of the flight plan and turned north. Suddenly all of the aircraft began experiencing problems with their instruments. Some forty miles away, Lieutenant Robert Cox, a training instructor, picked up their transmission, but for some reason they couldn't hear him. Cox called the base station in Fort Lauderdale, which now had lost contact with Flight 19. Immediately emergency procedures went into effect. Base operations continued to receive Lieutenant Cox's transmissions, which told them Flight 19 was lost and disoriented, but they could not get through to Taylor or any of his pilots."

Ham radio operators up and down the coast were also tuned in to the lost flight and monitored their frequency. Then, as night fell, one of them caught the last words ever to be heard from Flight 19. The message, according to Berlitz, was cryptic and ominous: "Don't come after us . . . they look like . . ." The transmission faded in a burst of static.

"Even as the last words were being transmitted," Berlitz continues, "a huge search and rescue mission was launched. A big Martin mariner with a crew of thirteen, one of the first planes to lift off in search of the lost squadron, suddenly disappeared from radar, and like Flight 19, was never heard from again.

"The greatest search effort in the history of the navy was now underway. Thousands of square miles of ocean were scoured, but it all came to nothing. In the end, Flight 19 and the Martin mariner, twenty-two (or twenty-three according to the official record) men in all disappeared without a trace, as if they had passed through some window into another dimension."

Incredible as it seems, five skilled combat pilots on a routine two-hour training mission somehow got lost and were never heard from again. For over forty years the story has ended there, locked deep in the mystery of the Bermuda Triangle.

Others who have investigated this incident have come up with their own theories of what happened. Some claim there was a storm that day and that Taylor, the most experienced of the pilots, was nonetheless new to the Fort Lauderdale complex and didn't know the area. The theory rests on the assumption that Taylor, the flight leader, would rely on his own sense of the terrain below him rather than on his instruments. This argument is bolstered by the fact that Taylor reported all his instruments were malfunctioning, which would mean he would have to rely on what he could see and try to navigate accordingly.

One report suggests one of the younger pilots more familiar with the area was heard to tell Taylor that "if we go east, we'll get home." But based on where they think Flight 19's last position was, that would have taken them further into the Atlantic.

There is a good deal of discussion about these frantic transmissions, and not all investigators agree on what was said and by whom. It must be remembered that much of what came over the radio was reported second-hand by Lieutenant Cox. There are those who suggest, too, that Taylor, who was unfamiliar with the topography, was actually in charge of four "rookie" pilots, not a group of hardened combat pilots. The truth is, just about the only thing everyone agrees on is that Flight 19 and the Martin mariner did, in fact, disappear on that day somewhere in the Bermuda Triangle and no trace of them has been found . . . until now!

Maybe!

On May 8, 1991, the *Deep See,* a research and exploration vessel ten miles off the coast of Fort Lauderdale, picked up a computer-generated outline of an airplane lying on the seabed 750 feet below. The distinctive rear gun turret marked the plane as a navy Avenger. Two hundred yards away the sonar began picking up a second plane—and a third—all Avengers. Over the next twenty-four hours the crew spotted five in all, lying within a one-mile radius.

National news magazines trumpeted the find as the solution to one of the greatest mysteries in the history of aviation—found at last, Flight 19, not ten miles from their home base off the coast of Fort Lauderdale.

In fact, the *Deep See*'s underwater camera identified the letters FT on the fuselage of one of the sunken planes, the designation for the Fort Lauderdale base. On another, the number 28, the number of Taylor's plane, was clearly discernible. And even though 139 Avengers were lost off the coast of Florida during the war years, the news reports strongly suggested the mystery of Flight 19 had been solved. But to some, the mystery had only deepened.

Time magazine, in its June 17, 1991 issue, under the heading "Bermuda Triangle," headlined a follow-up story, "It's Still the Lost Squadron." According to this report, while the preliminary evidence seemed to support the experts' conclusion that they had at last discovered Flight 19, the high-tech salvagers who found the planes announced they were not the Lost Squadron after all. Rather, they appeared to be five separate aircraft that had crashed within one-and-a-half miles of each other on individual training missions.

It does seem inconceivable that five experienced pilots would all be so disoriented they couldn't see the lights of Fort Lauderdale only ten miles away, storm or no storm. Certainly at least one of those aircraft could have glided the ten miles to Fort Lauderdale. Could this belated discovery have been *staged* at this late date for our benefit? If so, why? Roger Shockley, author, lecturer, and UFOlogist, has some intriguing ideas.

"One of the favorite theories," Shockley says, "among the scholars and intellectuals of the seventeenth and eighteenth century was the concept of dual civilizations. The theory, which Darwin picked up on, is that one life-form came out of the sea to become man, and another remained in the sea to become a separate race. The mythology and legends of every single society of the human race, including the Stone Age cultures, believed a race of people lived under the sea. Is it possible," Shockley asks, "that the world is shared by both air-breathing and water-breathing animals? We humans are only one of many air-breathing species, and the biological scientists and engineers already have the techniques to modify our race into water-breathers. The answer to the ancient mystery of the Bermuda Triangle might be right under our noses, literally. Those waters may simply be a gateway between our world above and theirs below."

Another theory suggests the planes were somehow scooped up by alien craft, perhaps for study of their armament and flight capability. Then they were returned and placed on the ocean floor near their home base. The pilots of the five navy Avengers are, according to this theory, still captives of the aliens.

An interesting theory, perhaps, but not one to turn the head of Graham Hawkes, who according to the *Time* article, headed the search for the five aircraft found in 1991. "I don't know where Flight 19 is," *Time* quotes Hawkes as saying, "but it's certainly in the ocean and not up with the aliens anywhere."

That may be, but it is a fact, nonetheless, that no mention of bodies was ever included in any of the reports of the five aircraft that were discovered by the *Deep See*. The questions will have to go unanswered yet a while longer.

One of the very real risks in trying to deal with something as mind-boggling as the Bermuda Triangle is that so many unexplainable incidents have taken place that we tend to shrug them all off as a group. Investigators over the years, in trying to prove everything, leave themselves open to the criticism of having proven nothing. But taking that posture might prove to be a mistake also. There are things going on in the Bermuda Triangle right now that could have the makings of tomorrow's headlines.

At this very moment there are over one hundred special research projects being conducted by international teams of scientists in this section of the Atlantic. Indeed, the 1990s may be the time we finally determine some answers to the mystery of the Bermuda Triangle that satisfy everyone.

In the meantime, having been there, and having spent many hours poring over the research, I am personally persuaded that scientists have pretty well solved the mystery already. The stories are engaging, even exciting to contemplate, but in the final analysis we are left with the question so frequently asked by Lawrence Kusche: Has anything really happened here that can't be satisfactorily explained by weather phenomena or a naturally occurring electromagnetic vortex? We do know, for example that the line longitude, 80 degrees west, at the western boundary of the Bermuda Triangle, is one of the few places on earth where a compass needle does indicate both magnetic north and true north.

Stripped of all the emotionalism, the various accounts produce two clear factors. The area is, unarguably, subject to frequent and violent storms; and it is characterized by known electromagnetic anomalies. These factors, coupled with man's natural inclination to enlarge upon what he doesn't understand, leads me to believe that the Bermuda Triangle is less *mystery* than it is *misunderstanding*.

There are, in fact, much more engaging puzzles to solve, as we will readily demonstrate in the next chapter.

13

EASTER ISLAND

"They walked."

Easter Islanders' answer to the question: How did the statues get there?

IT IS HARDLY MORE THAN A VOLCANIC SPECK, LOST in the vastness of the Pacific Ocean, yet it is called "the Navel of the World." Completely isolated on what must be one of the loneliest spots on Earth, the ancient inhabitants of this triangular shaped piece of lava rock managed to establish the only written Polynesian language known (if indeed it is a language), to create a complex society, and to populate their island with huge, monolithic stone statues.

But before we get to the mystery of the statues, there are other questions that leap to mind, not the least of which is, why would anyone want to live here in the first place?

Easter Island sits in almost frightening isolation. Their nearest neighbor is Pitcairn Island (made famous as the refuge of the *Bounty* mutineers), and that lies twelve hundred miles to the west, with nothing in between but the Pacific Ocean. To the east lies the northern coast of Chile, twenty-three hundred miles across the open sea. It would be hard to imagine a spot more distant from anyone, anything, or anyplace. But even if it were within shouting distance of friendly shores, there is precious little to recommend it for human habitation. The island mainly consists of three volcanoes, which the natives call Rano Raraku, Rano Kao, and Rano Aroi. It is barely thirteen miles long and no more than seven miles across at its widest point. There are no fresh-water rivers or streams, and the salt winds that roar across the island prevent the growth of any tall trees or plants. The soil is porous, and boulders are everywhere, as if they had been scattered about by a giant pepper mill. So far as anyone can determine, there weren't even any wild animals for the first settlers to hunt for subsistence. There was only the ocean, everywhere. Yet a people not only survived here, they multiplied, creating a society with a complex social structure and an art form that is unique in all the world.

As might be expected, the people of Easter Island were completely unknown to the rest of the world for many years. Then, in 1722, on the evening of Easter Sunday, a Dutch navigator by the name of Jacob Roggeveen spotted the tiny dot of land in the deepening twilight. Curious but cautious, Roggeveen and his men spent their first night at the island anchored off-shore, safe on board their ship.

The following morning, the watch on Roggeveen's ship spotted several fires dotting the shore. As the sun slowly chased away the shadows, the admiral and his men were stunned by what they saw. Islanders of differing colors prostrated themselves before giant stone statues, each carved with the face of a man. Many of the statues appeared to be wearing a gigantic stone "hat." The statues faced inland and dwarfed the people, whom Roggeveen assumed were worshipping the images.

It was Roggeveen who named the island *Paasch Eyland,* or Easter Island, for the day he had first sighted it.

Roggeveen and his men stayed at the island only a

few hours, but they did take time to examine the statues, which were all very similar in appearance. He reported that they were basically huge, elongated figures of various heights. Some of them were buried so deeply that only the head, with freakishly long ears, could be seen. Others stood on raised platforms, as many as fifteen in a row, with the great stone "topknots" precariously perched on top of their heads. Roggeveen couldn't have known it, but the largest of these huge monoliths was thirty-three feet tall and weighed eighty tons. The topknot, carved out of stone from a different quarry, measured six feet in height, three feet in width and weighed twelve tons. More surprised by the strange statues than intrigued, Roggeveen and his men just shook their heads, got back aboard their ships, and sailed away. An investigation of this amazing phenomenon would have to wait for another day and another, more imaginative explorer.

While the origin of the statues is readily apparent, due to a number of them still lying unfinished in the living rock of Rano Raraku, the fact is that to this day no one knows how these gigantic statues were moved or made to stand upright, let alone how the topknots were put in place. Some very interesting theories have been put forward, however—but I'm getting ahead of the story.

Over the more than two and a half centuries since Admiral Roggeveen discovered Easter Island, several intriguing theories as to the origins of the people and their enigmatic culture have emerged. The scholarly consensus (I love that phrase—it has such a reverent ring one almost hates to see it debunked . . . almost) is that the Easter Islanders are descendants of Polynesians who settled the island somewhere around the twelfth century. And, indeed, the islanders' legends tell of their ancestors arriving in canoes from the Marquesas Islands, two thousand miles to the northwest.[119]

But given the island's isolation and the unique and enigmatic statues that populate the entire island (some six hundred of them), it is perhaps not too surprising that a somewhat more imaginative concept of their origins has developed over the years.

In fact, one of the more amazing aspects of the islanders noted at the time of Jacob Roggeveen's discovery is that they all seemed as mystified by the statues as the Dutch sailors were. Certainly none of them bore any resemblance to the faces on the statues, nor had the current islanders made any attempt to complete any of the two hundred unfinished statues, (one of them an enormous sixty-six feet in length) still lying in the caldera of Rano Raraku.[120]

Their legends, however, told of a time when two distinct peoples inhabited the island. One group, the "Long Ears," were so called because they elongated their ears by placing heavy weights in them. Additional weight was added as the ear lobes grew longer. These were the first people to come to the island. Later another group arrived. They were the "Short Ears," a people who didn't share their neighbors' penchant for disfiguration.

According to the legend, the Long Ears, who had begun the carving of the great statues (called *Moai*), made slaves of the Short Ears and forced them to do the arduous work of carving the statues out of the living rock in the side of the mountain. But that job was child's play compared to the task of moving them to the appropriate site. This part of the legend is supported

[119] *American Heritage*, Mysteries of the Past, p. 137.
[120] *Roy Stemman*, Atlantis and the Lost Lands, p. 68.

by the fact that all the statues have the elongated ears characteristic of the Long Ear people. It does seem likely that, given a choice, at least some of the statues would represent the Short Ears, since they were the ones doing the carving.

But like all tyrants, the Long Ears came to a bad end. The Short Ears rebelled when they were ordered to clear the Poike peninsula of rocks to make it suitable for farming. Easter Island, as noted earlier, is virtually covered with rocks and small boulders. Poike peninsula, in fact, is the only place on the island today that is virtually rock-free. But according to the legend, it was farmland dearly bought.

The Short Ears, so the story goes, went to work at the task, but they grumbled and plotted a rebellion. When the Long Ears heard about it, they dug a ditch across the neck of the peninsula and filled it with dry wood. Their plan was to set fire to the wood and create a barrier between them and any attackers. But the plan went awry. With the help of a woman spy, the Short Ears learned of the ploy and many of them sneaked across the ditch and got behind the Long Ears' encampment while others created a diversion. When the Long Ears decided they were under attack, they set fire to the wood, only to discover, much to their chagrin, that they were already surrounded. All of the Long Ears, men, women and children, were driven into the fiery ditch and destroyed. Only one man of the Long Ears was permitted to survive. He married a Short Ears woman, and their descendants live on the island to this day.[121]

From a historical and cultural standpoint, that's not a particularly uplifting story, but it gets worse. Accord-

[121] *National Geographic Society,* Mysteries of the Ancient World, *p. 212.*

ing to the editors of National Geographic's *Mysteries of the Ancient World,* the battle of Poike Ditch started a chain reaction that nearly destroyed Easter Island. Men of the extended-family groupings that lived along the coast adopted one or more of the Moai as their own, presumably as a god of some sort, and began raiding one another's settlements, toppling the other group's Moai. Then actual warfare began, with bands of "warriors" roaming the island, raiding and killing. Not even women and children were spared.

It wasn't long until it was unsafe to work the taro fields and food became scarce. The islanders solved the problem by turning to cannibalism. Having made their tiny island a bloody battleground, they turned to the only food source available to them, their fellow islanders. Easter Island is, in fact, one of the few places in the world where cannibalism seems to have had little or no religious or magical significance. It was simply a matter of acquiring food.[122]

The ancestors of the inhabitants of Easter Island figure prominently in a number of legends about the Earth's early civilization and its origins. One of the more prominent places Easter Island at the southeasterly tip of a great Pacific continent called *Mu* (or *Lemuria*) that disappeared into the sea thousands of years ago. (The Pacific Ocean's version of Atlantis?)

In *Atlantis and the Lost Lands,* published by Danbury Press, a division of Groiler Enterprises, Inc., a comprehensive account of the Mu theory has recently been published. In theory at least, the legend of Mu has its beginnings in scholarly research.

In 1864 a French scholar, the Abbé Charles-Etienne Brasseur of Bourbourg, came across an

[122] *Ibid.*

abridged copy of a treatise on the Mayan civilizations. This treatise contained a copy of a "Mayan alphabet." The discovery of this alphabet excited Brasseur, who reportedly had a keen interest in the civilizations of the new world.

"Armed with the alphabet and a lively imagination," the record says, Brasseur began a translation of the *Tro-Cortesianus Codex* preserved in Madrid. According to his translation, the book was a tale of a volcanic catastrophe and of a land that sank beneath the waves. There were two symbols in the Mayan manuscript that Brasseur was unable to account for. They did however, bear a faint resemblance to the "M" and the "U" in the previously discovered alphabet. In a most unpoetic way, Brasseur put them together and called the lost continent the land of "Mu."

The original alphabet discovered by Brasseur has been shown to be based on erroneous principles, and Brasseur's translation has likewise been discredited, but somehow, like Plato's description of Atlantis, the story lives on. Interestingly, Brasseur believed Mu to be the name once used for Atlantis. Others, however, have adopted the story—or perhaps we should say adapted the story—to a South Pacific continent. But it gets even better.

Brasseur's contemporary, Augustus Le Plongeon, a physician and archaeologist, attempted his own translation of the *Codex*, drawing on the work of Brasseur and a liberal interpretation of pictures found on the walls of ruins in the Mayan city of Chichén Itzá.

According to the editors of the article, "Le Plongeon's 'translation' retraced the story of the sunken continent of Mu with an extravagance that made Brasseur's account pale in comparison. At the heart of his account is the rivalry of two Muvian princes, Coh and Aac, for the hand of their sister, Moo, the queen of Mu. Prince Coh won, but was killed by his jealous brother, who immediately took over the country from Queen Moo.

"At the height of this drama, the continent began to sink. Moo fled to Egypt, where she built the sphinx as a memorial to Prince Coh, and, under the name of Isis, founded the Egyptian civilization."[123]

Wow! Mu, the Mayans, and the Egyptians all bound up in a single codex. That is some translation. Fortunately, it is not the only explanation for either the Egyptian culture or Easter Island.

In 1906 a university professor in New Zealand, J. MacMillan Brown, a geologist, archaeologist, and anthropologist, came up with another theory to explain the mystery of Easter Island. It is a good deal more prosaic, but in some respects equally fantastic. Professor Brown argues that there once was either a continent or a densely populated archipelago in the South Pacific inhabited by white men, and that Easter Island was used as a collective burial ground. We're not quite sure what happened to the continent or the archipelago; presumably there was more sinking into the sea that took place. And Professor Brown doesn't explain why anyone would choose such a rock-filled chunk of land for a burial ground. But perhaps the biggest difficulty with this idea is that no burial ground has ever been found. At least not one big enough to handle the collective needs of a "densely populated" archipelago.

But easily the most influential of all the Mu theorists was a man by the name of James Churchward, who in 1926 published a book entitled *The Lost Continent of Mu,* in which he claimed the land of Mu as the

---

[123] *Stemman,* Atlantis and the Lost Lands, *pp. 68–69.*

true cradle of civilization for the world. If there is a "Plato" of the legend of Mu, it is Churchward.

Among other things, Churchward claimed Mu had a population of 64,000,000, that it was the real location of the Garden of Eden, that it was flourishing fifty thousand years ago, and that it was, in fact, the Motherland of man.[124]

The map included in Churchward's book, which, incidentally, is still in print, shows Easter Island as the furthest southeastern tip of the continent of Mu. His book is still considered to be the final authority on things Muvian.

So much for the theories and speculation. It's time now to find out what, if anything, the scientific community has done to create a better understanding of Easter Island and its inhabitants. Unfortunately, the answer is, not much.

Thor Heyerdahl has probably done more than anyone else, though. A very careful scientist, he undertook a thorough archaeological study on his expedition to Easter Island in 1955. He concluded that the key to the many questions still surrounding Easter Island lay in the fact that of all the inhabited Polynesian islands, it is the nearest to South America and the farthest from Asia.

Basically, Heyerdahl theorizes that South American Indians landed on Easter Island in two waves, bringing with them their culture, gods, skills, and the custom of extending their ears. He points to two curious facts: (1) Totora reeds are growing in the craters on Easter Island, the only place in the Pacific where they are found. They do, however, grow on the shores of Lake Titicaca in the Andes, and (2) Heyerdahl's workmen

[124] *Ibid.*

uncovered a curious statue in Rano Raraku that is unique on the entire island. The statue is of a man kneeling and bearded. It is much smaller than any of the other statues and according to Heyerdahl is similar to sculptures, again, near Lake Titicaca.[125]

Heyerdahl, of course, has his detractors, but his approach to solving the mystery of Easter Island not only makes use of the legends of the island, but it carefully considers the scientific realities as well. It does not, however, require the sinking of a massive continent, or an appeal to Isis, to support his conclusions.

There is rather general agreement on one thing, and that is that at some point in time the Easter Islanders gave up the worship of the Moai and turned to a form of worship involving birds, specifically the island terns.

One can only imagine how it all started. Perhaps it was something to fill the void between the destruction of the Moai and the subsequent social disorder brought about by the shifting away from their traditional gods. But for whatever reason, the island's most important religious ritual was practiced right up until the late 1860s.

The ritual was held each year at a place called Orongo, on the seaward side of the volcano Rano Kao. It was held solely to determine who the "Bird Man" would be for the coming year, though it's difficult to understand why anyone would want the "honor."

Candidates for the exalted position were volunteers from the island's most important families. A great celebration would take place, after which the volunteers or their representatives (the important families almost always had a representative) would swim approximately a half-mile to the farthest of three islets just off the tip of the main island. There they would wait, hiding in caves for as many days as necessary until the return of the sooty terns that nested on the islet. The idea was to raid a tern's nest, steal an egg, then swim back to the island through shark-infested waters—without breaking the egg. The first man to do so won the coveted honor. He, or the man he represented, became the Bird Man.

And what did this remarkable feat get him? Well, when he "won," his hair, eyebrows, and eyelashes were shaved, his face was painted red and black, and he was placed in a thatched hut where he lived absolutely alone for one full year. When he emerged, he was supposedly filled with wisdom and power, and he became an honored and respected elder.[126] (Presumably he was filled with enough wisdom not to go back and do it again, since none of the reports mentions anyone ever being selected Bird Man twice.)

Today Easter Islanders, perhaps influenced by the large numbers of tourists that make their way there each year, have begun to take pride in their ancient heritage. Then, too, the ongoing research that has taken place almost without interruption since Thor Heyerdahl's expedition in 1955 seems to have added a measure of cultural pride. Young men who attend school as far away as Santiago, Chile, have come back to participate in the island's artistic reawakening.

That artistic heritage, in spite of everything else we know, or think we know, about Easter Island, has left the world a mystery that has yet to be solved with any degree of satisfaction. Even though the origin of the great statues presents few difficulties, how they man-

[126] *Ibid., p. 211.*

aged to get down from the rim of the caldera and across the rocky terrain to the seashore is a question that puzzles everyone, including the islanders themselves. When Heyerdahl asked them how it was done, the almost universal answer was, "They walked."

They walked? Fifty tons of perpendicular rock walked?

Perhaps they did. Certainly the statues that are by the seashore betray no telltale scars to suggest they were pulled or pushed over the rock-filled terrain. Modern attempts to move the statues haven't been able to duplicate the feat. And what about the top-knots? They are carved from completely different rock and come from a different caldera. Some of them weigh ten tons or more. How were they put in place? Then there's the matter of the *ahus,* the large, intricately constructed pedestals some of the statues were placed upon. Who built them? And why raise some of the statues and bury others up to their chest?

The answers to those and other questions that make the mystery of Easter Island so intriguing, are still to be found . . . perhaps in the next chapter.

14

THE GREAT STONE STATUES

"I should still like to see a group of Easter Island men lift one of those red, five- to eleven-ton topknots the height of a four-story building and seat it on top a statue's head."

Erich von Daniken

I‍MPRESSIVE IN THEIR SIZE AND NUMBER, THE GREAT stone statues of Easter Island, by their very presence, have mystified all who have seen them for centuries. In 1914 the English explorer, Kathryn Ruoutledge wrote,

> In Easter Island the past is the present. It is impossible to escape from it; the inhabitants of today are less real than the men who have gone. The shadows of the departed builders still possess the land. Voluntarily or involuntarily, the sojourner must hold commune with these old workers. The whole air vibrates with a vast purpose and energy that is no more. What was it? Why was it?

And we might add, how? How did all of this come to be? The lost continent of Mu notwithstanding, and in spite of all the work done by Thor Heyerdahl and others, the fact is that the origin of the Polynesian race is lost in antiquity. We do know, however, that long before Columbus set sail they were already populating the islands of Polynesia, from New Zealand through Samoa, Tonga, Tahiti, and on to Hawaii. Somehow, in the latter part of the seventh century, one of these groups, perhaps the group from the Marquesas, struck out across the open ocean and landed on Easter Island. In point of fact, the Polynesians are only one of several races in and around the Pacific Rim whose origins have not been found. Erich von Daniken, however, believes the answer is before our very eyes. "No one ever talks about the culture that was there for five hundred years before the Polynesians appeared on the scene," he says. "I believe the great cultural achievements of the Easter Islanders came about through contact with visitors from outside our realm of understanding. In religious literature they are referred to as the 'Nephilim' or the 'Watchers.' In reality they are visitors from another planet."

"Reality" is an elusive thing when dealing with the twin barriers of time and distance. Probably the most truthful thing we can say at the moment is that we don't know.

But we do know that this harsh volcanic island is home to over six hundred stone statues, twelve to thirty-two feet tall, weighing from twenty to ninety tons. Many of these Moai were carefully fitted with red granite "topknots" or head coverings that are separately carved from an entirely different kind of rock and appear to have been put in place after the statue was erected—an unbelievable achievement when you consider these topknots weigh from five to eleven tons by themselves. The fact is that what the ancient Easter Islanders did would be difficult to accomplish even with modern power equipment.

Why would a primitive people expend their meager resources in such an effort?

Dr. Evan Llewelyn, a historical sociologist, points out, "Every culture since time immemorial has raised statues to their gods and great personages. The Easter Islanders were no different." According to Llewelyn, "The organized social structure of their society was religious, with a well-defined upper class that called themselves *Hanau Eepe,* or 'Long Ears,' because they extended their ear lobes with heavy ornamentation. The lower classes were called *Hanau Momoko,* or 'Short Ears.' It is revealing that all of the stone heads are of the 'Long Ears.' "

Elizabeth R. Wheaton, a science librarian and researcher, concedes the latter point, but suggests there might be something to von Daniken's theory. "It is quite true," Wheaton writes, "that the giant statues depict the 'Long Ears' only, but recent archaeological discoveries have revealed skeletons of a much larger-boned culture, which would seem to support the legend of an earlier race of people on Easter Island."

An earlier race perhaps, but how much earlier? And where did they come from? Could they be the "Nephilim," (also referred to as "giants" in the biblical literature) suggested by von Daniken? Could they be Churchward's super-race from the land of Mu? Or perhaps even colonizers from outer space?

All we really have is a tiny dot of an island, located, literally, a "thousand miles from nowhere," with a society of unknown origin, carving hundreds of giant statues for some unknown reason. All of the statues are virtually the same design, but some of them are buried up to their necks while others stand proudly on raised platforms (*ahus*), or altars. As near as anyone can tell, the buried statues are as long and heavy as those still standing upright, but how and why they were stuck in the ground simply adds to the puzzle. No one, it seems, has the solution.

And then there are those crowning red stone topknots. What could account for the almost eerie uniformity of design but the widely varying method of display? And perhaps more important, how were the statues transported from the crater of Rano Raraku to their current position on the seashore, staring brood-ingly back at the island's interior?

The one mystery that seems to have been solved is how the statues were carved. Over the past hundred years science has pretty well determined how this was accomplished. Dr. Elroy Randall, an anthropologist at the University of Wyoming explains, "The early sculp-tors, using obsidian and other hard-stone tools, chipped away at the volcanic rock inside and outside the crater of Rano Raraku, which is the mountain where all the statues were carved. We know this because many stat-utes (over two hundred of them) still lie here where they were started, simply left on the mountainside or in the crater and never finished.

"Even the stone tools that were used to do the work appear to have just been dropped and left where they lay. But there is no question that all of the statues on Easter Island were carved out of the living rock left by this extinct volcano. The bigger question is, how did they get them from the mountain to the coastal plat-forms where many of them were still standing when Jacob Roggeveen first saw them in 1722?"

How indeed? Some of these great stone monoliths are ten miles from the hillside where they originated. Some of them even came from the downslope *inside* the crater, making the task of moving them even more difficult. The native explanation that "they walked" from the mountain to the shore, understandably per-haps, gets a cold reception from the experts who have tried to solve the mystery. Still, turning our collective noses up at native legends, I have learned, frequently results in collective embarrassment.

Some experts have suggested that in spite of the sorry state of the island's current ecology, at one time it was heavily timbered and covered with lush growth. The forests, so this theory goes, could have easily provided logs to facilitate rolling the statues and large levers for raising them up once they arrived at their destination.

That view of the island's pre-history is very much in doubt, but others have suggested that lush vegetation of a bygone era could have acted as a natural lubricant for sliding the fifteen- to twenty-ton monsters along the ground without the aid of logs. But then there is that pesky reality we have to deal with: There are no marks on the chest or back of any of the statues that would suggest they were pushed or pulled over the harsh ground. Even with tons of sweet potatoes or grasses or whatever to act as a lubricant, the rocks underneath would have left deep gouges in the carved statues.

Maybe we shouldn't discard so readily the answer the islanders gave. Maybe they did "walk." A man with the unlikely name of Pavel Pavel took the islanders at their word and performed an experiment in which seventeen men moved one of the statues from side to side, in an upright position, using a system of ropes and pulleys. Pavel demonstrated that the statues could be tilted as much as seventy degrees to either side without falling. He also suggested the topknots could have been put in place a similar fashion.

This theory has two things to recommend it. First, it would have taken less manpower, and that could be important since it is believed the island never supported more than ten thousand people, even at its peak population. Second, the only structural wear and tear on the statues appears to be on the flat bottom they all have in common. The natives, seeing the statues moved in this fashion, might very well describe the process as "walking."

And yet, more recent experiments suggest something different.

William Mulloy, an American anthropologist, was a member of Thor Heyerdahl's 1955 expedition to Easter Island and has developed his own theory.

"I believe the statues were transported, prone, and head first," Mulloy said, "after being placed on a Y-shaped sled, probably made from a tree fork. Once lashed to its sled, the statue would then be pulled by a series of ropes along a prepared road covered with reeds or grass for lubrication."

A reasonable hypothesis, perhaps, but it still leaves the problem of getting the statue on the sled, and then getting it upright—and then getting the topknot in place. With regard to this latter problem, it has been suggested that the stone topknots were lashed in place and raised along with the statue as one unit.[127]

But let's think about that for a moment. A sculpture proportional to and only twice as tall as its neighbor weighs eight times as much.[128] Given that small fact of physics, the task of raising the statues to an upright position with an additional five to ten tons at the very top seems to stretch the bounds of credibility. Also, the neck portion of the statues is the narrowest and therefore weakest point. Wouldn't that maximize the weight-to-stress ratio and put the greatest additional burden on the only possible break point? The theorists who suggest this particular method of getting the topknots in place are silent on these questions.

[127] Charles Lebaron, "The Giants of Easter Island" in Reader's Digest, The World's Last Mysteries.
[128] National Geographic Society, Mysteries of the Ancient World, p. 204.

Von Daniken tends to shun all the current theories. "I have not seen or read anything," he says, "that presents a convincing case of what or who the statues are . . . and how they were moved and put in place. I should still like to see a group of Easter Island men lift one of those red, five- to eleven-ton topknots the height of a four-story building and seat it on top a statue's head. Until then I choose to believe that perhaps it might have been the 'Nephilim,' who may well have been the fathers to a race of large, white, red-haired people that are at the heart of the mystery of Easter Island."

Von Daniken's theory brings up another interesting point. The Heyerdahl expedition reported that the village leader was a white man with red hair who claimed to be a descendent of the "Long Ears." Could the topknot have had some special ceremonial significance? We know that the statue carvers went twenty miles to the other side of the island to cut the topknots from the red lava rock found only in the crater there. What we don't know is what the head covering represents—beyond, that is, an enormous additional engineering job for the statue makers.

Von Daniken asks another question regarding the positioning of the Easter Island statues that leaves most of the theorists shaking their heads, and we'll get to that in just a moment, but for now let's continue with the puzzle of how the statues were moved.

An experiment suggested by Mulloy in 1956 did, in fact, result in one of the statues being raised. A dozen islanders were challenged to replace a twenty-five-ton statue on its altar. They accomplished the feat in eighteen days by building a masonry platform under the belly of the statue and levering it up with sixteen-foot-long tree trunks.[129] The statue did not, however, have the topknot lashed in place, and the effort resulted in a great deal of scarring to the front of the statue, something that is not in evidence on the other statues on the island.

Laura Patton, an archaeologist and Easter Island investigator, doesn't think the topknots were raised up with the statues. According to Patton, "Scientists usually label something that can't be explained with a given premise, an 'anomaly,' a definition that fits the so-called 'topknots' on the statues of Easter Island. These cylindrical stones are called *pukaos*. The *pukao* was placed on top of the statue after it was raised to an upright position. Most investigators have assumed it was some sort of ceremonial hat. The natives have always insisted however (though they were not believed), that the 'Long Ears,' the ruling class, were white-skinned and red-headed. It seems obvious that the pukao was not a ceremonial hat at all, but rather represented a topknot of red hair."

Does that then give credence to von Daniken's theory of the "Nephilim" or Churchward's theory about the descendants of "Mu"? All of that additional work and effort just to represent red hair would seem to suggest the "Long Ears," or ruling class, or their ancestors, or whoever the statues represent, were considered worthy of enormous veneration. Certainly it was an engineering feat of immense proportions, even by today's standards.

Dr. Mulloy has calculated that to carve, transport, and raise one of the average-size statues, given the tools and methods the islanders had to work with,

---

[129] *Charles Lebaron, "The Giants of Easter Island" in Reader's Digest, The World's Last Mysteries.*

would take twenty-three thousand man-days.[130] And there are hundreds of these great statues. Given the fact the island population was somewhere in the neighborhood of seven to ten thousand at its height (probably two thirds of those being women and children), the work must have gone on for centuries.

But why did the islanders quit carving the statues? Could it have been that the "Short Ears," slaves for so long, upon doing away with their oppressors, just walked away from the work? Floyd Thompson, a young Peace Corps volunteer working on the island, said, "The conviction is unshakable that one day the work simply stopped." Other investigators agree. The handpicks and adzes made of andesitic basalt that the carvers used to shape the great statues lie scattered about the hillside by the dozens,[131] as if the workers just dropped their tools and walked away, never to return.

But now we have another compelling mystery. It is an apparent fact that whoever carved the statues kept at it generation after generation, probably for hundreds of years. Yet the evidence suggests that not only did the work stop, the entire social and religious structure was abandoned.

According to Peggy Mann, author and researcher, "Within a period of just four short years, from 1770, when a Spanish ship visited the island, and 1774, when Captain Cook arrived, hundreds of the statues had been toppled. Centuries of culture were overturned in the historical blink of an eye. It is an event unprecedented in human history. People simply do not give up the beliefs and traditions of generations, but apparently these people did."

[130] *Ibid.*
[131] *National Geographic Society*, Mysteries of the Ancient World, p. 204.

To a cultural anthropologist that is an astonishing turn of events. It's as if all of Christendom suddenly buried their crucifixes and toppled the statues of Christ. It's a cultural phenomenon that is unimaginable, yet it appears to have happened on Easter Island.

If, as many investigators believe, the statue carving didn't cease until around A.D., 1690, and they were still worshipping at the base of the Moai in 1722 when Jacob Roggeveen arrived, what could have happened in such a short period of time to turn them against such time-honored veneration? After all, it was not just the religious cosmology that was being overturned, but years of work by ancestors that many of those still living must have known and remembered.

In the case of Easter Island, mystery is piled upon mystery. Here's another one. The Easter Islanders were apparently tireless workers with great building skills, as evidenced in the intricate stonework found in many of the *ahu,* or altars. But for some unknown reason they lived like rats, burrowed into caves or in cramped, boat-shaped huts. Hiding in caves to escape the cannibalistic tendencies of neighboring groups may make some sense, but why continue such discomfort out in the open terrain of the island?

"Why these small, boat-shaped houses struck the fancy of the islanders is indeed a mystery," writes Peggy Mann. "They could not have been comfortable. They had no windows, and the roof was so low it was impossible to stand up. Entrance was made by crawling through a small opening on all fours. The foundation consists of stones about a foot long, laid level with the surface in two lines converging at each end. In every stone of the foundation is one or two holes into which a stake was inserted. The stakes or branches were then bent to meet in an arched roof. Reeds woven through the framework formed walls and ceilings. The finished house not only had the shape of a canoe, it was about the size of a canoe.

"Why, when they could produce miracles of stone construction in altars fourteen feet high and five hundred feet long; why, when without knowledge of the wheel or any engineering devices, they could drag the giant statues unscathed across stony fields to set them up on these altars; why, when they could perform such building feats as raising a ten-ton topknot to rest on the head of a statue three stories high; why did they choose to live in these low, crowded, hot, stinking, boat-shaped houses?"

"The answer," von Daniken responds, "is obvious. The Polynesians simply didn't possess those skills." According to von Daniken, "Some of the altar-pedestals the statues rest on have been dated to the first century of the Common Era [A.D.]."

At this point Von Daniken asks the question that has so far been ignored by all of the experts. "If only the Polynesians, who didn't arrive until the end of the seventh century, carved these statues, then who built the pedestals six hundred years before?"

Who indeed? The venerable Captain Cook reported the stonework on the pedestals "was not inferior to the best plain piece of masonry we have in England."

And so, the mystery deepens. Now we have huge stone statues, forty feet tall and weighing up to sixty tons, as many as fifteen of them standing upright and all in a row. They are perched on large intricately constructed stone and masonry pedestals built hundreds of years before, and to top it off, literally, giant stone headpieces of up to eleven tons rest solidly on the heads of each of the statues.

To be sure, that's not the condition of many of the statues today, but the evidence is clear that at one time many of the statues were placed upon the *ahu* in just this fashion. What caused the islanders to topple most of them and bury others deep in the ground is just another part of the mystery. To this point in time there are a lot of theories and guesses, but real answers are few and far between.

Intriguing as these stone statues are, they are not the only treasure to be uncovered on this incredible island. The "talking boards," discovered in the nineteenth century, generated another mystery that remains with us to this day.

These "talking boards," as the islanders call them, are inscribed wooden tablets covered with minute ideographs that turn back and upside down at the end of each line and appear to form one continuous sweep of "writing."

It was a hundred and forty years after Easter Island was discovered that this remarkable mystery came to light. The simple wooden tablets were covered with the characters of what appear to be an unknown language. In the 1860s a French missionary by the name of Eyraud spotted the tablets and discovered the islanders were using them for firewood. He recognized immediately that these tablets could be the irreplaceable keys to the history of the island. The problem was that there was no one left alive who knew how to read them.

Scholars were keenly interested in the find, but as the years passed without any progress being made toward translation, some dismissed the markings as simple decoration. Finally a German scholar, Thomas Barthel, took up the challenge by following a clue from the previous century. He learned that a French bishop had found an Easter Islander on Tahiti who could chant songs from four of the boards. The bishop had translated each song into Polynesian. Barthel determined to find the bishop's notes.

Finally, after tracking the bishop's notebook from Tahiti to France, to Belgium to Italy, he found it in a monastery near Rome. He would later write, "Those lines of Polynesian syllables in the bishop's shaky hand became my Rosetta stone. I'll never forget the moment when the first textual fragments began to make sense."

By 1960 Barthel began publishing his translations, which, he said, were mostly prayers to gods, instructions to priests, and accounts of island mythology.[132]

It appeared that some of the mysteries of Easter Island might at last be uncovered, but it was not to be. Too few boards remain (only twenty-one of them) to confirm Barthel's translations, and many other scholars, as might be expected, have rejected them outright.

In spite of the scholarly squabbles that are still going on, the "talking boards" are significant by their very existence. The fact is, there has never been anything discovered on any Polynesian island or among any other Polynesian group to suggest any sort of written language. The "talking boards" are explicit evidence that of all the Polynesians, if indeed they are Polynesians, it was the Easter Islanders alone who created a written language some two thousand years ago.

Even after centuries of study and investigation, the questions keep coming. What compelled the islanders to produce such a wealth of religious art and architecture on such a colossal scale? What were the seeds of this magnificent culture's destruction? Above all, in a world in which it is taken for granted that great civilizations usually develop through intensive cultural ex-

[132] *Reader's Digest,* The World's Last Mysteries, p. 103.

change, how did such an astonishing culture evolve on the most remote inhabited island on the globe?

In spite of all the speculation, in spite of all the theories, postulations, studies and scholarly papers, we are left with the realization that the achievements of this ancient culture may remain cloaked in mystery forever. A complete understanding of the history and people of Easter Island seems to be beyond our reach. Perhaps it is precisely that realization that keeps us looking for answers and makes the many mysteries of Easter Island worth investigating.

Next time someone proposes vacationing in some little out-of-the-way place, you might suggest Easter Island. Anyone interested in our world, what makes it work, and what has made it an exciting place to live since time immemorial will find Easter Island fascinating.

15

MYSTERIOUS MONSTERS

"It is a temptation to suppose they must be the fabulous Loch Ness monsters, now observed for the first time in their underwater activities."

Dr. H. Braithwaite, Birmingham University

A NUMBER OF YEARS AGO, I DECIDED TO PRODUCE a feature film dealing with the subject of this chapter; in fact, I titled the film *Mysterious Monsters*. We were fortunate enough to engage the services of Mr. Peter Graves, star of the hit television series "Mission Impossible," to be our investigator and narrator. Mr. Graves was appropriately skeptical but agreed to go to some of the places where these monsters had been seen and, wherever possible, talk to the people who had seen them. We also asked him to interview experts in various fields who had devoted their time and expertise to solving the mystery of these not so mythical beasts.

A star of Peter Graves's magnitude is not ordinarily anxious to search out the likes of "Bigfoot" ("Sasquatch," as he is called in Canada), nor the Loch Ness monster, the Abominable Snowman, nor Ogopogo. Ogopogo??? (Yes, there is such a monster, or so many people believe, in a huge lake in Canada.) Those kinds of associations do not ordinarily add luster to a star's portfolio. But in addition to his skepticism, Peter shared the same sense of curiosity that brought us to the project in the first place. It was this combination of curiosity and skepticism that made Peter Graves the perfect investigator and narrator for our film.

The results of our investigation surprised all of us in

one way or another, and I think it's safe to say there might still be a few surprises left for both the skeptic and the believer. So let's update our look at these mysterious monsters from all over the world that many people claim to have seen, smelled, and photographed and see what progress, if any, has been made in determining their reality.

Since "Bigfoot" is likely to be the one most readers are familiar with, we'll begin with this much discussed phenomenon of the American Northwest. Actually, confining Bigfoot to the Northwest is inaccurate. According to published reports, a Bigfoot of one description or another has been spotted in just about every state in the union. He, she, or it cannot be said to be "native" to any one place. Even though the name changes, the basic description does not.

That description is of a humanlike figure completely covered with hair and standing anywhere from eight to twelve feet tall. The creature is apparently shy, since it never attacks but always runs away from those who spot it, and according to those who have seen it moving, it does so with surprising speed, walking upright, like a man, taking huge and deliberate strides. Bigfoot derives his name from footprints that have been discovered, measured, and put in plaster casts. They range from sixteen to twenty-two inches, heel to toe, and can be as wide as eight inches. Oh yes, there is one more characteristic that is more or less uniform in all the reports. Bigfoot smells terrible.

The name "Sasquatch," by which these hairy monsters are known in Canada, comes from an Indian word that roughly translates to "hairy giant."

Apparently, the folklore of Native Americans has been populated with stories of a Bigfoot monster for centuries. Native legends of South and Central America likewise abound with similar creatures. Dr. John Napier, a long-time curator of the primate collection in the Smithsonian Institution wrote a book titled *Bigfoot,* published in 1973, stating, "Although . . . there has been a tremendous revival of public interest since these creatures have come to the attention of the 'white settlers,' it is a reasonable assumption, from what we know of early written records that, like Peyton Place, the story of Sasquatch has been continuing for a great many years."[133]

It is difficult to pinpoint all the origins of the legends of the various natives, but the introduction of the Bigfoot story into our own culture can be dated precisely. Explorer David Thompson is the first "white man" to report seeing a Bigfoot track. Thompson was making his way across the Canadian Rockies in 1811 in an attempt to reach the Columbia River. Suddenly, and quite unexpectedly, he came upon a set of footprints that stopped him dead in his tracks. He was a man familiar with the wilderness and the creatures that inhabit it, but there were a number of things about these tracks that made his blood run cold. First of all, they measured nearly fourteen inches long and eight inches wide. At first he thought he'd come across the biggest grizzly bear in the history of the world, but on closer inspection these tracks exhibited only a four-toe impression, not the standard five-toe imprint left by grizzlies, and they seemed to be spaced too far apart to accommodate a grizzly bear's relatively short hind legs. Furthermore, there was no evidence that the tracks had been made by something walking on all fours.

Thompson was near what is now Jasper, in the province of Alberta, and being a trader as well as an

[133] *Angus Hall, "Wild Men of the Woods," in* Monsters & Mythic Beasts.

explorer, he lost no time in spreading the word. Given his description, everyone agreed it couldn't have been a bear. For a while the story of Thompson's tracks were tossed around the campfires and cookstoves, but eventually even the hardiest storytellers lost interest and the tale faded into obscurity.

Little more is heard about the great northern Sasquatches for over seventy years. Then, in July of 1884 an account of the capture of a Sasquatch appeared in the *Daily Columnist,* a newspaper in British Columbia. According to the story, the creature had been spotted by a train crew traveling between the towns of Lytton and Yale. The trainmen had stopped the train and chased the "gorilla-like" thing with coarse black hair. Upon catching it, they placed it safely in the guard's van. "Jacko," as he came to be called, was subsequently sold to Barnum and Bailey's circus.[134]

But wait a minute. If one of these things was captured and put on display back before the turn of the century, what's the mystery? Wouldn't some scientist or government official have required old P.T. to turn him over for a thorough examination? Apparently not. The record is silent about what happened to Jacko! And so far as we could determine, he spent the rest of his life traveling from town to town as part of "The Greatest Show on Earth." The speculation is that since no government or scientific agency had any interest in Jacko, he may have been more a product of P. T. Barnum than of the great Northwest.

The story did rekindle interest in the creatures once again, however, and suddenly other stories of a great, hairy "Sasquatch" began to pop up all over Canada.

[134] *Ibid.*

Apparently the early versions of Sasquatch were alarmingly malevolent. Reports began to come in accusing the creatures of everything from mayhem to murder. Two prospectors, the MacLeod brothers, were found in the Nahanni Valley in the northwest territories of Canada with their heads cut off. The blame was immediately assigned to Sasquatches reportedly seen in the area. The place has been known ever since as "Headless Valley."[135]

Reports of these monsters continued to come in at an ever increasing pace. A prospector's shack was attacked near Mount St. Lawrence in Washington. The assailants were reported to be eight feet tall and half-human, half-monster. Eventually, it was reported, the monsters had tired of the attack and left. So did the prospectors, never to return.

Sasquatch and/or Bigfoot sightings were reported in British Columbia and northern California as well as in the state of Washington. A lumberjack named Albert Ostman told an incredible tale of being kidnapped by a "family" of four of the Bigfoot monsters. He was, he said, kept a prisoner for more than a week before he was able to escape and make his way back to civilization. This event, Ostman said, took place in 1924, but, fearing people would think him "crazy" or worse, he kept the story to himself for thirty-three years. He described the events of that week in astonishing detail.

Professionals who interviewed Ostman said his story was consistent with what could be expected from someone who had suffered that kind of dramatic ordeal, and just before his death, Ostman swore to the truthfulness of his story in an affidavit.

Tales about the Sasquatch are many and varied, and

[135] *Ibid.*

over the years the monsters seem to have lost much of their ferociousness. One seldom hears today of a Bigfoot attack on campers or hunters or anyone else for that matter. But in the early part of the century a visitor to the Northwest might have thought a full-scale war had been declared between the Sasquatch and residents.

In 1924, the same year as the Ostman "kidnapping," a group of coal miners were reportedly attacked by a "gang" of monsters, enraged when one of the miners shot a Sasquatch in the back, killing him. According to the miner's account (the Bigfoot "gang" didn't hold a press conference), it was a running battle, with the panic-stricken miners holing up in their cabin throughout a long and terrifying night. Once again, the miners were the clear losers. They gave up the area, known as "Ape Canyon," forever.[136]

But where did Bigfoot come from? If it exists at all (a circumstance scientists are not willing to accept just yet), is it just a mistake in the evolutionary cycle, or is there some positive connection between these creatures and other life-forms we know about, or think we know about?

In spite of all the sightings and an ever increasing level of interest, North America is still in its infancy when it comes to trying to identify creatures such as this. To find real expertise in this area it is necessary to travel to Asia. The search for what many believe is an ancient relative there has been actively pursued for nearly three quarters of a century. This creature, Yeti, the Abominable Snowman, has been part of the lives and culture of the people in and around the mountains of Tibet for hundreds of years. In the Caucasus Moun-

[136] *Napier*, Bigfoot.

tains of Russia scientists claim to have found proof of such a Bigfoot creature. But it is the Himalayas that the Yeti is associated with in the minds of modern man.

Europeans first began a serious assault on these mountains in the latter part of the nineteenth century, and in 1925 a veteran Greek explorer, Nikolaus Tombazi, saw an astonishing sight. High up on a windswept slope he spotted a huge, hairy creature, which, he said, appeared to be digging for roots with a stick. Tombazi and his party were barely three hundred yards away, across an open stretch of snow against which the dark brown color of the creature's hair or fur stood out quite plainly. Still, and in spite of the corroboration of several in his party, Tombazi's story was thought to be more imagination than imagery and it was summarily discounted.

But in 1951 the first actual evidence of the Yeti was discovered. British explorer and mountain climber, Eric Shipton, seeking a new route up Mount Everest, stumbled upon a set of fresh tracks in the snow at the eighteen-thousand-foot level. Shipton was standing where no man had ever stood before, and he was looking at unmistakable evidence of some kind of bipedal creature preceding him up the mountainside. Describing himself as "a bit of an agnostic" where the Abominable Snowman was concerned, Shipton had an immediate change of heart. In an interview from his hospital bed years later, he recalled that the tracks were obviously fresh and clear, and "there seemed to be no doubt about it at all. Here one was in the presence of something quite unknown."

Another expedition in 1958 discovered a cave that they believed to be the "lair" of the Yeti, and in 1961 one expedition returned with what they believed to be a Yeti "hide." Another expedition discovered a mummified hand with a huge, clawlike finger in place of the index and ring fingers, and various monasteries claim to have in their possession Yeti "scalps." These scalps appear to come from virtually the entire top of the head from the ears up.

One thing appears certain, as Major L. A. Waddel of the Indian Army Medical Corps reported in his book, *Among the Himalayas,* "The belief in these creatures is universal among Tibetans." Waddel himself came to a more interesting conclusion about the Yeti, however, which he arrived at largely because none of the Tibetans he interviewed could give him a first-hand account of actually having seen one. He decided that the "so-called hairy wild men," were simply vicious, meat-eating yellow snow-bears that frequently preyed upon yaks. But that was in 1889. Tombazi wouldn't see his "Yeti" for another thirty-six years.

Some anthropologists seem to think these creatures are just some primitive species of man, lost somehow on the evolutionary ladder. Others suspect it might be a giant anthropoid that has taken a different evolutionary road. In either case, those who are convinced there is something to the Yeti legends, tend to believe also that they migrated to North America hundreds, perhaps thousands of years ago, over the Bering Strait land bridge which linked Russia to Alaska. Bolstering this theory is the hundreds of years of Alaskan and North American Indian folklore that includes the Sasquatch in paintings, on totems, and in stories handed down from generation to generation.

In all of these legends and stories, the names change, but the characteristics are unmistakably the same.

There is, then, at least a theoretical genealogy for

the North American Bigfoot, who can now engage our attention with a little bit more substance.

And engage our attention he certainly has. No less a luminary than Theodore Roosevelt, in a book he wrote about his days out West, talks about Bigfoot. This "true" story concerns two trappers on the Salmon River in 1852. The trappers encountered Bigfoot, and a fight broke out between the trappers and the creature. One of the men was killed. It was a common story in the Northwest by the time the future president got there, and Roosevelt wrote that, based upon what he had been told, he believed it.

But all of these stories from the past, colorful though they may be, are not quite enough to prove that Bigfoot exists. What is needed are accounts that have some currency—those recent enough that we can check on them first-hand. And, indeed, they exist.

Mary Lou Bowman was a teenager from a small town in western Michigan on October 6, 1974. The seventeen-year-old high school senior was waiting for her father to pick her up after baby-sitting for a family who lived some distance away, on the edge of town. John Bowman, Mary Lou's father, was a former high school football coach and respectable businessman, and he had never even heard of the creature that he and his daughter were about to encounter.

Bowman picked his daughter up, and they began the drive back to their own home. The couple Mary Lou had been sitting for had taken longer to return home than she had anticipated, and she was complaining to her father that the evening's chore would keep her working on homework through the entire weekend.

But Mary Lou's complaints were quickly forgotten when there suddenly appeared in the headlights of the car a huge, manlike shape standing in the middle of the road. Mary Lou screamed, and her father swerved just in time to miss the startled creature.

Whatever it was seemed confused by the lights of the automobile, and only John Bowman's quick reaction kept the car from slamming into the huge, dark hulk. Instead, his car skidded off to the side of the road, around the strange, beastlike form and back onto the road again.

Bowman slammed on the brakes and turned to look back at what his unbelieving eyes had just seen. There was nothing there but the empty darkness. Trying desperately to keep his own fear under control, John Bowman put his arm around his daughter and tried to calm her. A few moments later, his hands still trembling, he put the car in gear and continued on home.

Bowman notified authorities of his strange encounter, and the next day he returned to point out the exact spot where the near-collision had taken place. The skid marks of Bowman's car were clearly discernible. On the other side of the road, near where Bowman's car had skidded off the pavement and back on again, authorities found huge footprints in the dirt leading away from the road.

A long-time resident of the community, and widely regarded as an honest and sober man, John Bowman has never been doubted as to what he and his daughter saw on that night. And everyone who went to investigate the incident with him agreed that whatever the creature was, it had left very large footprints.

These footprints and eyewitnesses are, in fact, the most compelling evidence in the search for Bigfoot. There are hundreds of them, and each eyewitness description carries its own unique imprint, like this account from a former sheriff, Oliver Potter.

The sheriff, his wife, and another couple were driving through the Cascade Mountains when something caught his eye—something that made him bring the car to a sudden stop. At first he thought it was a bear, and he wanted the others in the car to see it. But even though it appeared to be the right color, there was something about it that wasn't quite right.

"I was born in the woods of the Cascade Mountains," Sheriff Potter told us. "I know the animals that are here, but I saw something different that day, something that I had never seen before. It was a large creature, about seven and a half to eight feet tall. It was a brownish-black in color, and as it went away from me, I could see the back side of it, walking as a man would walk. There were four of us in the car, and I was the first to spot it. We stopped and turned around and watched as it made its way up the mountain. I couldn't see its face because it was going away from me, but like I say, I've lived here a long time. This thing moved more like a man. And besides, bears just don't walk on their hind legs that long." The others in the car confirmed the sheriff's story.

It's easy for those of us who haven't had the experience to just write these reports off as the product of overactive imaginations. For some silly reason I haven't yet been able to identify, most people simply reject out of hand anything they don't understand. Some few of us, however, actually suspend judgment and take another look. Such is the case with this next eyewitness.

Shirley Adams was a teacher and school-bus driver in a small town on the coast of northern Washington. A long-time resident of the area, the young schoolteacher had heard stories about the giant, hairy apelike monsters called "Bigfoot," but she never expected to see one. Then, one afternoon, driving down the coast highway after dropping off the last of her student passengers, she spotted someone, or some "thing," on the beach near the ocean. The easy course of action would have been to just write it off as an animal of some sort that had made its way down to the ocean and keep on driving. It could very easily have been a bear looking for a fish dinner.

But it didn't look like a bear, and Shirley didn't keep on going. Instead she immediately stopped the bus and got out to take a closer look. Much to her surprise, as she drew closer it appeared to be one of the Bigfoot creatures she had only read about before.

Most of us, I daresay, would have experienced at least some small twinges of fright at seeing something so unusual and so large wandering about so close to a public road. But Shirley said that what she saw didn't frighten her. Rather, she said she experienced an unusual pleasure in seeing a creature at peace with nature. She observed the giant for several moments, not in a state of fear, but one of wonder.

The circumstances of Shirley Adam's eyewitness report are almost as unique as the creature itself. Few of us could have watched such a creature with such a sense of calm.

But calm or not, eyewitness testimony has little effect on the scientific community. "Eyewitness reports," we are told, "are unreliable. People can think they see things, but their mind can play tricks on them." Even when faced with the number and, for lack of a better term, "quality" of the eyewitness reports, scientists still want to see, touch, feel, and preferably put things under a microscope before accepting them as real. They point to the fact that hunters or campers, for example, have never found the remains of any dead Bigfoot in the forest.

Not all scientists share that view, I am happy to report. Dr. Lawrence Bradley, an anthropologist, points out that the forest has its own disposal system as far as dead animals are concerned, in the form of scavengers. He also points out that hunters seldom if ever come across the carcasses of dead bears or mountain lions either, though they exist in those areas in great abundance. The good doctor makes a good point. I have spent the better part of my life wandering around the mountains of Oregon, Idaho, Utah, and Wyoming. I cannot remember ever coming across the carcass of a bear, mountain lion, or any other animal that likes to keep to itself and avoid man. I would be hard-pressed to suggest that because I have never seen the carcass of one of these animals, they cannot exist!

Still, it is the lack of "hard" evidence that has kept Bigfoot in the shadows of scientific examination. Many people feel that the footprints themselves constitute "hard" evidence. After all, there are plaster molds of footprints twenty-one inches long, eight inches wide, and two inches deep, a full inch and a half deeper than even a big man is likely to make. But the fact is, a number of these footprints have been faked—admittedly faked. Then, too, experts point out that snow, and ice particularly, can play tricks with footprints. As the print melts, it tends to grow, then freeze, melt, and grow some more, making even small animal footprints appear large. And some have even suggested that bears, in walking on all fours, place their rear feet in the footprint of their front foot, creating the appearance of a larger footprint.

These are all possible explanations, so let's examine each of them.

We needed an expert tracker to tell us about footprints, so we turned to Peter Burns, formerly a big-game hunter in the Himalayas, and asked him about the theory of distorted footprints.

"Footprints of animals do appear larger as they melt," he told us, "but they do not melt with any uniformity, so that the melted footprints of a small animal come out . . . in different shapes, squares, circles, oblongs, and so on. I think it's ridiculous to suggest that a small animal making footprints in the melting snow could make a big foottrack."

Since the Bigfoot prints are usually very clearly defined, right down to such intricacies as heel and toe pressure, that would seem to rule out the "melting" explanation. We also asked Burns about the bear-footprint theory.

"I don't think it's possible," he said. "The footprints that I've seen [of Bigfoot] are very definite. They are definitely the footprint of a large, bipedal hominid. A humanoid creature with five toes. When you have an overlap you get a confusion of toes and heels and so on. The [Bigfoot] prints are clear-cut footprints, and in my mind there's no mistake."

The double footprint of bears as an explanation for the Bigfoot tracks, then, is also out. But what about the hoaxers, those who purposely carve oversize "feet," strap them to their boots, and run around the mountains leaving tracks in the snow. Could this explain all the Bigfoot prints that have been found and made into plaster molds?

We'd have to admit that hoaxers probably could get away with phony footprints once in a while, but at least one anthropologist, Grover Crantz of Washington State University, doesn't think they could be responsible for all of the footprints that have been found.

"There are a number of footprints I've seen that couldn't have been faked," Crantz said. "For example, one such footprint appears to be of a crippled individual. A couple of bulges have extended out between adjacent bone and are clearly visible in the print. They're shifted forward, making the heel longer and the front of the foot shorter. This is exactly what is required for a foot that is going to carry, perhaps, an eight-hundred-pound body. Now I don't think any faker could have thought of it and figured this out."

Apparently fake footprints can be detected by careful examination. And it's comforting to know that not all scientists find the Sasquatch such a tall tale that they are unwilling to examine the evidence carefully. It's comforting because in the past few decades even more hard evidence has begun to come forth that is subject to careful scientific examination.

With the help of computers and the digital analysis of which they are capable, scientists are finding new ways to test for the presence of Sasquatch. For example, in 1972 three men hiking in the high sierras, Allen Berry, Rick Murphy, and Vince Sawyer, came across footprints some twenty inches long. They had heard about Bigfoot but never imagined they'd run into him. So while the footprints were curiosities, the three men didn't spend much time worrying about them.

But that evening around the campfire they were startled by a series of strange grunts and groans. Berry had brought along a tape recorder, and luckily he went for that instead of his rifle. For fifteen minutes he recorded the guttural growls and snorts that seemed to come from everywhere around them in the dark woods. It's fair to say they were more than just a little uneasy, but being experienced woodsmen they were content to just listen, and let the tape run. Eventually the sounds stopped and the three men managed to get a good night's sleep in spite of the strange events of the evening.

During the production of the movie *Mysterious Monsters,* we obtained a copy of this tape and took it to Dr. Robert Sheldon, who subjected the tape recordings to a rigorous computer analysis. By digitizing the sounds and putting them into a computer they were able to isolate specific sounds and analyze them in comparison to known sounds. Peter Graves may be the only movie star in history to have had his voice compared digitally to the voice of Bigfoot.

The analysis did, however, yield some specific conclusions. Specifically, it was determined that the sounds recorded by Berry were made by someone or something with a vocal track at least fifty percent larger than Peter's. That meant that the person or animal making the sounds was also fifty percent larger than Peter. Since Peter Graves is just over six feet tall, that meant the creature Berry recorded that night in the high sierras was something in the neighborhood of nine feet tall.

There was one other interesting conclusion that came from the analysis of the tape. When asked if he knew what type of "animal" that had made the sounds, Dr. Sheldon's answer was a cryptic "No, I don't." In view of the fact that Dr. Sheldon has analyzed hundreds, perhaps thousands of sounds over the years, his answer is significant.

Allen Berry may or may not have recorded Bigfoot's sounds, but he definitely recorded the sounds of an "unknown" creature that, according to the analysis, was close to ten feet tall and more man than ape in appearance.

Which brings us to the film of Bigfoot that is probably the most widely circulated of all Bigfoot images.

Footage from this film has been seen as still photographs, shown in theaters, and is currently being used in a television commercial. Anyone with even a passing interest in the Bigfoot phenomenon has undoubtedly seen portions of this film.

In 1962 Roger Patterson and René Dahinden, a Swiss-Canadian Sasquatch investigator, claimed to have taken approximately twenty feet of color movie film of a female Bigfoot wandering through a California forest. The film was shown commercially to wide audiences in both the United States and Canada, who seemed to find the footage convincing. But Dr. Napier of the Smithsonian was an early detractor. Based on a private screening in 1967 Dr. Napier concluded that "the creature in the film does not stand up well to functional analysis. There is little doubt that the scientific evidence taken collectively points to a hoax of some kind."

Dr. Napier didn't say precisely what "functional analysis" the creature on the film didn't "stand up" to, and he did concede that "it was a brilliantly executed hoax, and the unknown perpetrator will take his place with the great hoaxers of the world."

Again the mystery remains. The film may be a hoax, but if it is, someone (we suppose the two men who made the film) went to an awful lot of trouble to produce it. Functional analysis notwithstanding, the film does appear to show a large, hairy mammal of some kind, hurrying to get away from whoever is holding the camera. It is obviously female and obviously not a bear. It does seem to have some "human" characteristics that match up rather closely with other descriptions provided by people who have seen Bigfoot. But even if it is a hoax, does it mean Bigfoot doesn't exist?

Dr. Napier doesn't think so. He is not, by the way,

one of those scientists who clings stubbornly to the "if I haven't seen it, it doesn't exist" idea. To the contrary, Dr. Napier has said that, "The North American Bigfoot has a lot going for it. . . . Too many people claim to have seen it, or at least seen footprints, to dismiss its reality out of hand. To suggest that hundreds of people at worst are lying or, at best, deluding themselves is neither proper nor realistic."[137]

Perhaps if there were a few more scientists like Dr. Napier, these mysteries would get cleared up a lot faster. Unfortunately, the mystery of Bigfoot remains. The hard evidence notwithstanding, the official, scientific consensus (which is different than a scholarly consensus in that it requires at least some hard evidence) seems to come down solidly against the existence of real Bigfoot creatures roaming the Earth. I, for one, however, intend to keep my eyes open and a camera close at hand when enjoying the splendor of our mountains and forests. It would be very uplifting, I think, to share a similar experience to that of Shirley Adams.

From the tops of the mountains, we turn our attention now to the depths of the sea, or at least to the depths of Loch Ness, or Lake Okanagan (yes, there is such a place), where hundreds, perhaps even thousands of people have seen and photographed "monsters from the deep." These monsters however, have taken on the persona of a lovable pet. In England and Scotland, it is simply "Nessy." In Lake Okanagan, near the town of Kowlona on the southern border of British Columbia, a similar sea beast has been given the unlikely but lovable name of "Ogopogo."

---

[137] *Angus Hall, "North American Monsters" in* Monsters & Mythic Beasts.

But one monster at a time.

Among monsters of the deep, Nessy seems to have found a special place. It's almost as if she has generated a full-time, worldwide, adoring fan club. She, if indeed it is a "she," has been photographed as often as Marilyn Monroe, and in fact Nessy has been featured in movies. She has also been on the front page of newspapers around the world, stared at in the dark recesses of her watery home, and sought after by kings and princes.

Eighty to ninety million years ago Nessy might have been just another pretty face. Back then, scientists tell us, huge reptiles roamed the earth and scoured the depths in search of food. But today Nessy is something out of sync with the rest of the world, and no one knows quite what to make of her.

For years, perhaps centuries, stories of the Loch Ness monster were consigned to the trash heap of myth and fable. But as with anything else that keeps on popping its head up to look around, she finally caught the attention of the scientific community. It was a long time coming. After all, monsters of the deep were the stuff of Jules Verne novels. They really couldn't exist. They were extinct. (So was the huge fish, the coelacanth. It had been extinct for probably sixty million years. Then, in 1938 one was netted live in the Indian Ocean. The fish was found near the Comoro Islands, where the locals had been drying and salting them for years.)

But let's get back to Scotland and Lake, or Loch, Ness. Many of the Scottish lakes are extremely deep, but Loch Ness is one of the deepest (over seven hundred feet at the deepest measured point to date), which might serve to give it some reputation in and of itself, but Nessy's popularity goes far beyond that.

In July of 1933 a Mr. and Mrs. George Spicer were driving home to London along the south shore of Loch Ness when they saw a strange creature "emerging from the 'bracken'" (a clump of coarse, hardy ferns with long fronds). The Spicers reported that it had a long, undulating neck a little thicker than an elephant's trunk, a tiny head, a thick ponderous body, and four feet, or more precisely, flippers. "Kind of like a huge snail," said George, "with a long neck—maybe twenty-five to thirty feet long." And it was carrying a lamb in its mouth. It sort of lurched along on its flippers, slipped down the bank, and dropped out of sight beneath the waters of the still placid lake.[138]

The Spicers, of course, were roundly ridiculed when they told their story, but they could not be persuaded that it was only their imagination.

This was not the first sighting of Nessy, not by at least fifty years. Ever since 1880 there had been more or less regular sightings of Nessy and for some inexplicable reason the Loch Ness "monster" was always referred to as female. Be that as it may, 1933 seems to be the year that Nessy became an international "pet," partly due to the Spicers' story and partly due to a road that was built along the north shore of her watery home between Fort William and Inverness.

By 1934 the excitement over the Loch Ness monster had grown to such proportions that *The Illustrated London News* devoted almost all of one issue to the beast.[139]

---

[138] Angus Hall, *"The Loch Ness Monster"* in Monsters and Mythic Beasts.
[139] *Ibid.*

It was also in 1934 that Kenneth Wilson, a London doctor, took the photograph that, along with one other successful shot, has been the focus of discussion and debate for nearly sixty years.

Aside from the aforementioned lamb, Nessy has never been known to harm anything or anyone. There are those who theorize, however, that it was Nessy's wake that disturbed the water and caused John Cobb's boat to disintegrate at high speed, causing his death.

Cobb, an internationally known racer, who held the land-speed record at the time was now going for the water-speed record on Loch Ness in his jet-powered speedboat. It was September 29, 1952, and Cobb, who had failed to get the record ten days earlier, decided to try again. An absolutely smooth surface is essential for such a run, and the lake was perfect. Cobb powered the boat to a new record, and seconds later the boat exploded, throwing him to his death. Some witnesses said they saw the wake of the Loch Ness monster suddenly appear in the path of the boat. More experienced racers believe that when Cobb began to slow down after setting the record, the pressure on the boat at such high speeds caused it to disintegrate. But, then, nothing of note can take place in Loch Ness, it seems, without Nessy being involved in some way.

In more recent years, modern high-tech methods have been employed to try to find Nessy. In 1969 an American by the name of Dan Taylor took a British crew in a homemade mini-submarine to search the depths of Loch Ness in hopes of finding the monster. Taylor was working under the sponsorship of an American encyclopedia company. And in 1973 a Japanese team went to Loch Ness to hunt for Nessy.

Nessy didn't show.

It may have been a team from the Department of

Electronic Engineering of Birmingham University that spawned some of this high-tech activity with rather spectacular findings the year before. In August of 1968 the Birmingham team mounted a sonar system on one of the piers, and according to author and journalist F. W. Holiday, "The scientists achieved dramatic success." At 4:30 P.M., August 28, and until 4:43 P.M., the sonar, which was being photographed every ten seconds by a movie camera, recorded the following sequence: "A large object rose rapidly from the floor of the loch at a range of .8 kilometer, its speed of ascent being about 100 feet a minute. This object then changed direction to move toward the pier at about 9 knots, keeping a constant depth. Finally, it plunged to the bottom at about 100 feet a minute before rising again at .6 kilometer range, when it apparently moved out of the sonar beam and was lost to record. Meanwhile, a second large object had been detected at .5 kilometer from the pier, which finally dived at the astonishing velocity of 450 feet a minute. Both objects remained many feet below the surface."[140]

One of the team leaders, Dr. H. Braithwaite, commented, "It is a temptation to suppose they must be the fabulous Loch Ness monsters, now observed for the first time in their underwater activities." Indeed it is a temptation, and no one has suggested any other explanation for what was recorded on the sonar screen and filmed by the cameras. But then no one has yielded to that temptation either. Descriptions of the event always stop just short of saying the Loch Ness monster has at last been electronically "seen."

Scientists have reconstructed the long extinct *Macroplata*, a prehistoric plesiosaur, and, interestingly,

[140] *Ibid.*

it bears an amazing resemblance to a model of Nessy created by Tim Dindsdale, a former electronics engineer. Dindsdale's model was based on his own sightings in 1960 and has since been modified from other information and sightings. Dinsdale's model now gives Nessy a substance and form. Amazingly, that form corresponds very closely to the most "technical" sighting so far: a strobe photograph, taken underwater. The photograph appears to show a flipper on some kind of thirty-foot creature swimming around in Loch Ness. And Dr. Robert Rines, of the Academy of Applied Science, took an underwater photograph that looks even more like the long extinct plesiosaur. But this time the image of virtually the whole creature was captured.

Still, traditional scientists are reluctant to put their stamp of approval on the fact of Nessy's existence. Like Bigfoot, Nessy hasn't been brought out of the realm of mystery where she can be probed and measured. The studied hesitation of scientists notwithstanding, Nessy, it seems to me, has indeed been found. Science may not be satisfied, but if I ever go to Loch Ness it will be with the full intention of getting a few pictures of Nessy on my own.

But we can't leave it there. We promised to tell you about Ogopogo in Lake Okanagan. I know, it sounds like the names themselves were contrived for a children's story, but Ogopogo carries all the credentials of a genuine deep-lake monster. His story (note that he is a "he") has been carried on the syndicated television news program "Inside Edition," and a team of Japanese scientists have been given a grant by their government to try to find him.

Reports of Ogopogo sightings are more recent by comparison, but are every bit as firm as those of Nessy. Certainly one of the more graphic accounts appeared in *The Vernon Advertiser* of July 20, 1959. The writer of the article was R. H. Millar, owner-publisher of the paper, and he tells the story as if he were reporting the visit of an old friend. "Returning from a cruise down Okanagan Lake [it is ninety miles long], "traveling at ten miles an hour, I noticed, about 250 feet in our wake, what appeared to be the serpent. On picking up the field glasses, my thought was verified. It was Ogopogo."[141]

Just like that. No ifs, ands, or buts. It was Ogopogo. And that seems to be the attitude of most of the residents of Kowlona. Most of them have never seen Ogopogo, but few of them would be surprised if he popped up in the wake of their own boats. Ogopogo, to the people of the area, is very real. The fact that they have never seen him is irrelevant.

The publicity given to Ogopogo is far less than that afforded Nessy, but given the descriptions of the two creatures, it is not difficult to think that maybe nature has preserved more than meets the everyday eye. Both are described as having long necks, both are apparently very large, and both are obviously capable of extended underwater habitation. Could it be that some of these amphibious dinosaurs found refuge in the deep-water lakes of the world and escaped extinction? If the coelacanth, believed extinct for sixty million years, can suddenly turn up on East Indian dinner plates, why not a plesiosaur or two in some of the world's deepest lakes?

---

[141] *Angus Hall, "Monsters of the Deep" in* Monsters & Mythic Beasts.

16

MEDICAL MYSTERIES

"The pain just seemed to flow out of my body; it was like magic."

Lorne Greene, TV star

NOSTRADAMUS WAS, IN ADDITION TO HIS PSYCHIC abilities, a first-rate physician in his day. But long before Nostradamus insisted on doing away with the practice of "bleeding" patients, ancient physicians were using techniques today's "modern" medicine men thought they had invented.

In the third century B.C., Etruscan dentists were using gold in Etruscan mouths. About the same time, a Roman doctor in Capua created a realistically modeled prosthetic leg of wood and gleaming bronze. Pre-Columbian surgeons in Peru, using copper or bronze implements, performed brain surgery on hundreds of injured warriors. The process was common in Europe as well. Cataract surgery was successfully performed in ancient times. A passage in the Code of Hammurabi hints that even Babylonian surgeons were familiar with the operation thousands of years ago. And Hindus, at least twenty-six hundred years ago, invented a method of rebuilding noses that is still used in the twentieth century.

The amazing human body is so complex we are only now beginning to understand how it works. Yet the ancients, it seems, knew how to fix it. Are there still undiscovered secrets they can whisper in our ear across the centuries? Perhaps! But only if we are willing to listen.

Ours is often described as the "age of specialization" when it comes to the practice of medicine. But today's clinics, filled with specialists of all kinds, are real pikers compared to the facilities of the ancient pharaohs. The kings of Egypt really knew what specialization was. They had, for example, a different doctor for each eye.[142] Taken to these extremes, an entire wing of the palace would have had to be reserved just for physicians of various kinds. But, then, they could afford it. And the Egyptians didn't let all that skill go to waste. They also had what amounts to a "national health service," with doctors being required to provide free medical service for travelers or during times of war. They were paid by the state.

According to medical papyri of 1500 B.C., even though doctors recognized and treated many maladies, their practices were more a matter of religion than medicine.[143] Some of their medications, however, are still with us today.

Probably somewhere in the neighborhood of four thousand years ago, Egyptian physicians used whatever was at hand that seemed to work. We're not entirely sure how they arrived at their conclusions, but some system of trial and error seems likely. One of the concoctions they used came from parts of the willow tree. Later on, Greeks and Romans also relied on the extract of willow trees for a wide variety of simple ailments such as earaches, inflammations, and eye infections. American Indians used a brew made from willow bark to alleviate colds and asthma. Then, in the nineteenth

---

[142] *Readers Digest,* The Last Two Million Years.
[143] *Ibid.*

century, chemists discovered that this ancient remedy was due to a bitter-tasting compound in the willow tree that they dubbed *salicin.* Once the secret was out, others went to work trying to improve on nature. One of the creations arising from that research we buy in stores today under the name of *aspirin.*[144]

What is commonly described as "folk medicine" is brimming with remedies like that. People regarded as "primitive" by Western standards have contributed to our general well-being in rather significant ways. The Jivaro tribesmen of the Amazon neither read nor write, but their knowledge of the curative properties of plants has given us quinine, for years the only known cure for malaria, and curare, a paralyzing poison that paradoxically works as a muscle relaxant.

In ancient India, the "moonshine plant," or *rauwolfia,* was treasured by holy men for its curative properties. It was particularly useful in giving relief to people suffering from mental illness, or what the ancients called "moon disease." Basically, it was used as a sedative in such cases, but it was also used for snakebite, fever, diarrhea, and dysentery. The holy men chewed its root during meditation, and a mild extract calmed cranky babies.

Rauwolfia remained in the realm of "folk medicine" until 1931, when Indian scientists announced that a drug extracted from the plant not only worked as a tranquilizer but lowered blood pressure as well. Here was a truly remarkable discovery, but Western scientists ignored their Indian counterparts until 1952. When rauwolfia was finally tested, the effects of the extract of this plant helped bring about a revolution in

---

[144] *Time-Life Books, "Ancient Pharmaceuticals,"* Feats and Wisdom of the Ancients.

drug use. Within two years this age-old tranquilizer was a part of drug therapy in the Western world for mental illness.[145]

From India to Egypt: During this same period, (1600 to 1500 B.C.), an Egyptian papyrus lists something in the neighborhood of a thousand remedies and, surprisingly, honey is listed as an important ingredient in over half of them. But what possible medical benefits could come from honey? Surely it wasn't anything more than an ancient substitute for the "spoonful of sugar that helps the medicine go down."

In fact, it is much more than that. Experiments have shown, much to the disappointment of some Western skeptics, that honey has a peculiar and very complex chemistry that effectively combats infections and speeds healing. It can also keep a bandage from sticking, a point worth remembering if you're a mother with small children.

Honey, as the Egyptian and Sumerian doctors of thirty-six hundred years ago somehow knew, is a potent killer of harmful bacteria. It contains an enzyme that combines with glucose and oxygen to form hydrogen peroxide, a powerful disinfectant. Honey also readily absorbs water and thus promotes the growth of healthy tissue. And since it can kill bacteria, honey defies decay. Archaeologists have unearthed honey that is still golden and sticky after twenty-five hundred years in a tomb.[146]

Next time you add honey to your breakfast toast, give a little tip of the hat to the lowly honey bee and some ancient apothecary who discovered that the bee's

[145] *Ibid.*
[146] *Time-Life Books, "The Healing Power of Honey,"* Feats and Wisdom of the Ancients.

product not only tastes good but can help you feel good as well.

In India, around 1500 B.C., a certain Lady Surpunakha had her nose amputated by order of a prince of the realm. At this time amputation of various body parts was considered just punishment for any number of offenses. The chronicles are silent as to the lady's indiscretion, but they do relate that the king took pity on her and ordered his physicians to rebuild the lady's nose.

Perhaps it was fear of what the king might do to their own noses if they failed, or perhaps it was a matter of not knowing that it couldn't be done. In any case, they went ahead with the project, and much to the surprise of the lady, they did it. Whatever their motivation, the ancient Hindu plastic surgeons achieved what is perhaps the most astounding medical accomplishment in the annals of ancient healing. They not only reconstructed the nose (and later other disfigurements as well), but the techniques they developed are still in use today.

According to the *Sushruta Samhita,* an ancient Hindu surgical "manual," the operation was performed in the following manner: Using a vine leaf as a template the size of the severed nose, a piece of skin was cut from the middle of the forehead, leaving a narrow, stem-shaped end attached to the bridge of the nose. Shallow cuts were then made in the flap to facilitate shaping, then the flap of skin was rotated to keep the skin side out and pulled down over the nasal area and stitched in place. To make sure the organ would be functional, two small pipes, probably bamboo or clay, were inserted at the lower end of the new nose to help mold the nostrils. A cotton bandage was placed over the area and sprinkled with sesame oil.[147] Rhinoplasty, the art of reconstructive surgery, had been born. Amazingly, the same basic techniques remain with us today.

We don't know whether or not the lady was pleased with the result, but in addition to having a nose once again, her reputation was also restored. In those days, having the nose removed meant you were also removed from virtually all social functions. Presumably the lady could once again hope to be on the king's invitation list. (We are not told how the prince felt about it.) Certainly it would have been worth whatever pain she had to endure.

The year 1890 was a banner one for endocrinology, the study of hormone-producing glands. That year Western doctors trumpeted a revolutionary treatment for thyroid hormone deficiency. But the breakthrough, so proudly hailed in the West, was ancient history in China, where, for more than two thousand years, doctors had routinely been curing goiters. A goiter usually manifests itself as a huge growth on the neck and results when the thyroid gland cannot manufacture enough thyroxin to facilitate the body's metabolism. The goiter itself is caused by a lack of iodine. The Chinese treatment was simple: They converted seaweed, which they must have known was a rich source of iodine, into pills and a wine-based tincture. It worked.

A more sophisticated treatment, called organotherapy, required chopped-up thyroid glands from sheep to be mixed with fruit and administered in pill form. This treatment supplied both iodine and thyroxin itself. Amazingly, all of this was written up in ancient Chinese

---

[147] *Time-Life Books, "Building New Noses,"* Feats and Wisdom of the Ancients.

medical literature and was there for the reading.[148] But Western scientists, either out of arrogance or ignorance, decided they would rather figure it out themselves. As a result, many Americans and Europeans, well into the twentieth century, were still trying to hide the unsightly and unhealthy goiters with high collars and ample scarves.

An ancient Chinese proverb states, "A wise man learns from experience. A wiser man learns from the experience of others." Why is it, do you suppose, we are so reluctant to learn from the past?

Speaking of ancient proverbs, here's one that typified the first approach to rational medicine nearly twenty-five hundred years ago: "One man's meat is another man's poison." It is a piece of wisdom that originated in 500 B.C. with the man generally considered to be the father of Western medicine, the great Hippocrates.[149]

The ancient Greeks were the first to divorce medicine from religion and mere speculation by observing that certain common symptoms always appeared together and that certain drugs brought relief. Hippocrates, who was the leader of this revolutionary new concept, was hampered by a lack of knowledge of basic anatomy and physiology, but his emphasis on the healing powers of nature, based on the value of personal hygiene and correct diet, gave him a head start on all other medical thinking of his day. Hippocrates insisted that the physician's role was to assist nature in the fight against disease. He also stressed a doctor's duties to his patient. These concepts, reaffirmed today in the doc-

[148] *Time-Life Books, "Healers,"* Feats and Wisdom of the Ancients.
[149] *Reader's Digest, "Man under the Microscope,"* The Last Two Million Years.

tor's "Hippocratic Oath," are still the foundation of medical ethics.[150]

Once again, it is ancient wisdom that provides the underpinning for modern thought.

There exists a certain cultural arrogance that suggests if we (our culture) didn't discover it, it hasn't been discovered. This attitude helped perpetuate the monumental errors of the Greek physician Galen for centuries. Following in the footsteps of Hippocrates, Galen became the personal physician to five Roman emperors. But Galen avoided clinical observation of his patients, preferring instead to use analogies based on animals. This led him into many serious errors, but it was fourteen hundred years before any of his misleading ideas were seriously challenged.

On the other hand, Louis Pasteur demonstrated the value of vaccines in the prevention of disease, but since the ideas were so radical, many members of the French medical establishment ridiculed him unmercifully. One wonders how they would have responded had they known that a form of inoculation had been in use in China since the eleventh century.

The record of this amazing fact is found in a mid-sixteenth-century text on China's imperial medical tradition. A Taoist hermit living on a mountain in the province of Sichuan heard that the prime minister had sent an urgent plea throughout the empire seeking anyone who could cure or prevent smallpox. The prime minister's son had just died of the disease, and he was afraid others of his family would suffer the same fate. The hermit, according to the story, journeyed to the capital, bringing with her a number of smallpox scabs.

Upon arrival in the capital, she was brought before

[150] *Ibid.*

the prime minister, whose hopes, we can imagine, were not encouraged by the sight of the ragged old woman who was ushered into his presence. Nevertheless, the Chinese were taught to respect these religious ascetics, and she had come a long way to help him.

"Can you protect my family from this dread affliction?" the prime minister asked.

"Indeed, I can, sir," was the immediate reply. "Bring your wife and your children to me at once, and bid them do exactly as I say."

Servants were sent out to gather the children while the prime minister himself went to get his wife. When they returned they found the old woman standing next to the table. Neatly arranged on a clean cloth were a dozen or more of the hideous smallpox scabs that she had retrieved from some unfortunate sufferer of the disease and a small quantity of cotton.

"Come," she cackled to the children. "You mustn't be afraid. Look, your father will go first."

The prime minister gulped, but stepped forward and bowed.

The hermit pinched off two small pieces of cotton and, placing a scab on each of them, inserted them into the prime minister's nostrils.

The process was repeated with each of the children and the wife, none of whom thereafter contracted the dreaded disease. The Taoist monk had just demonstrated the esoteric practice of inoculation.[151]

By the late sixteenth century Chinese physicians were routinely practicing this form of inoculation, having discovered that some smallpox strains are less virulent than others. They recognized that different symp-

[151] *Time-Life Books, "Ancient Inoculations,"* Feats and Wisdom of the Ancients.

toms accompanied the different strains, and they were able to use scabs from the less virulent strain, which did precisely what today's inoculations do: present the body with a virus too weak to cause the disease but strong enough to trigger the body's own protective antibodies.

No one knows how this particular bodily reaction was first discovered, but it is the basic theory behind all vaccines, up to and including the famous Salk polio vaccine. Perhaps the world owes its greatest debt of gratitude not to Salk or Pasteur but to some nameless Chinese hermit who lived over a thousand years ago.

The fact is that many of the cures we take for granted today have their origins in ancient science. The ancient Chinese, for example, treated eye ailments with bat dung. At least some of their patients probably showed improvement. Modern analysis shows that bat dung contains a high level of vitamin A, the active ingredient in an extract of liver prescribed by today's ophthalmologists for night blindness.[152]

The ancient Egyptians might have come even closer to the modern mark for the same problem. They placed "ox-liver . . . over a fire of grain or barley stems. Suffused with the vapors emitted in this process, the resulting liquids that were generated were then pressed on the eyes."[153] The Egyptian physicians had, in effect, created their own liver extract.

Another Egyptian discovery, a salve of "rotten bread" for wounds, has raised speculation that the bread had antibacterial molds similar to penicillin.[154]

But before we get too far removed from problems

---

[152] *Time-Life Books,* Feats and Wisdom of the Ancients.
[153] *Ibid.*
[154] *Ibid.*

with the eye, you may be surprised to know that in India, over three thousand years ago, surgeons with little knowledge of eye structure and only the crudest instruments performed one of the most complex and delicate operations in the modern physician's handbook. These ancient healers actually performed cataract surgery, the only known cure even today for those growths that lead to partial or total blindness. Not only are these operations known to have been performed in India sometime around 1000 B.C., but ancient Babylonians performed the operations as well. Records indicate that Babylonia even set rigid fees for the surgery. Apparently it was not an operation to be taken lightly. If the Babylonian surgeon botched the job on a freeman, he paid a frightful penalty—his hand was cut off.[155] An indication perhaps of the value placed on human sight in the ancient world.

Most of the ancient cures, even though they seemed to have worked, have long since disappeared from the scene. Bat dung is probably not an acceptable prescription to most of us, nor would we be likely to submit our children to having scabs placed up their nostrils. We have become adjusted to "shots," or, in the case of the Salk polio vaccine, a sugar cube containing a few drops of the weakened virus.

There are, however, two disciplines that have come down through the ages virtually untouched—one from ancient India, the other from ancient China, and they are gaining even greater currency today.

For centuries the yogis of India have practiced a rigid form of self-control that some feel may be the answer to complaints the medical doctors haven't

[155] *Reader's Digest, "The Astonishing Human Body,"* Strange Stories, Amazing Facts.

found a means to address. In its modern incarnation it's called *biofeedback*, but to the ancient and even modern yogis, it's simply a matter of "Patient, heal thyself."

This ancient practice, resulting in the ability of the practitioner to control many bodily functions previously thought to be beyond the individual's control is now seen as a possible answer to some illnesses connected with the heart, brain, circulatory system, and muscle groups. For years practitioners of yoga have demonstrated an ability to slow their heartbeat and control their respiration and their metabolism. In modern terminology, this means that EEG waves (or electroencephalogram waves) that are normally fast and irregular can be changed into slower, regular "alpha" rhythms promoting a deep relaxation.[156] It is basically a function of mind over matter.

The yogis who have practiced this discipline over the centuries were likely unaware of this kind of electrical activity in the brain, but their ongoing demonstrations of the power of the mind to control virtually all functions of the body has been the catalyst for modern research into biofeedback techniques. These techniques can eventually lead, it is hoped, to individual control of the autonomic system, the system that operates without conscious control. These applications have already been extended to treatment of insomnia, anxiety, high blood pressure, and asthma. Experiments are under way for relief of epilepsy, stroke paralysis, pains in the back, and migraine and tension headaches. Should these experiments prove conclusive, a great many of us who are currently trapped in debilitating situations over which we thought we had no control

[156] *Ibid.*

(asthma sufferers, for example) might find ourselves leading fuller, more enjoyable lives.[157]

Keep in mind, this is only theoretical healing in Western circles. But these are techniques that have been used in India for hundreds of years. The question seems to be, are we—that is, those of us who are a product of a Western heritage—willing or able to pay the disciplinary price to make the Eastern techniques work for us?

The other ancient healing art that has come down to modern times virtually untouched is *acupuncture,* a healing method that involves sticking needles into specific points of the body along certain lines, or *meridians.* Acupuncture has been practiced in China for over five thousand years. Its origins can be traced to the Stone Age.

The question that immediately leaps to mind is, why does something that seems to be a patently barbaric and archaic method of healing draw so much attention in our modern and sophisticated world?

The answer comes quickly: because it works.

The late Lorne Greene, star of the popular "Bonanza" television series, appearing on one of the late-night talk shows while still at the height of his popularity, enthusiastically explained to the host that after years of living with the pain of a back injury, he had found relief with a single acupuncture treatment.[158] I happened to be watching that particular show and I remember his words, almost verbatim. "The pain just seemed to flow out of my body," he said. "It was *like magic*" [emphasis added].

[157] *Ibid.*
[158] *Jeremy Kingston, "Borderland of Medicine,"* Healing without Medicine.

Many others who have had the courage to face a Chinese doctor with a fistful of long silvery needles have told similar stories.

But how can that be? How can putting a needle in your upper lip cure, say, an allergy?

No one knows for sure, but centuries of experimentation have undoubtedly created the complex application of acupuncture that is practiced today. The meridians that are traced along the body are very precise, as are all of the hundreds of acupuncture points.

Basically, acupuncture proceeds from the Taoist philosophy that suggests everything in the universe is comprised of two forces, the yin and yang. While these forces are opposites (*yang* is positive and active while *yin* is negative and passive) they are nevertheless complementary. Both are equally essential and together make up the life force known as *ch'i*. When yang and yin are balanced, the result is harmony, but excess of one or the other leads to illness. The purpose of acupuncture is to restore the balance of yin and yang in the life force, ch'i.[159]

This is where the meridians come in. This life force is believed to flow along twelve specific meridians in the body. Roughly nine hundred and fifty points along these meridians have been identified, and centuries of experience have shown some of them to be especially influential. Each of the twelve meridians has its own pulse, and the skilled acupuncturist will assess each one very carefully. The assessment of these pulses contains much more than just a pulse rate; it is the basis for the entire patient diagnosis. According to some reports, the skill of the acupuncturist is so finely tuned he can not only describe the patient's present condition

[159] *Ibid.*

but also determine past illnesses and predict future ones.[160]

The principal authority on the practice of acupuncture is a two-thousand-year-old book called *The Yellow Emperor's Book of Internal Medicine,* written in the form of a dialogue between the physician Ch'i Po and the emperor Huang Ti. In the book, Ch'i Po tells the emperor: "The pulse of the liver should sound like the strings of a musical instrument; the pulse of the heart should sound like the blows of a hammer; the pulse of the spleen should be intermittent and irregular; the pulse of the lungs should be soft like hair and feathers; the pulse of the kidneys should sound like a stone. . . ."

Perhaps not too surprisingly, Western physicians find it difficult to believe that pulses in the body can be that many or that distinctive, but the facts are that in many monitored cases acupuncturists have successfully treated asthma, bronchitis, convulsions, dysentery, emphysema, fevers, gastritis, and scores of other ailments.[161]

The gulf between East and West has been bridged, however, on a number of occasions, with the acupuncturists' needles being employed in place of a traditional anesthetic. In 1971 Dr. E. Gray Dimond, then chairman of the Health Sciences Department at the University of Missouri Medical School, visited medical facilities in cities large and small throughout China, where only acupuncture was used as an anesthetic. In one of these Dr. Dimond was able to observe an operation for the removal of a lung. A single needle was inserted in the patient's left arm and twirled; then the operation

[160] *Ibid.*
[161] *Ibid.*

began. The October 1971 issue of the *AMA News* published the following description written by Dr. Dimonds:

> The patient's chest was wide open. I could see his heart beating, and all this time the man continued to talk to us cheerfully with total coherence. Halfway through the operation he said he was hungry, so the doctors stopped working and gave him a can of fruit to eat.[162]

Western doctors (those who even acknowledge acupuncture as a treatment) readily admit that they don't know why acupuncture works, but with experiences like the one noted above, it is becoming more and more difficult to deny that it does. Many theories have been advanced, but none of them can be said to be definitive.

For their part, the Chinese seem to be quite content with the simple fact that the treatment works. Few Chinese acupuncturists are likely to look beyond the yin-and-yang theory to explain what takes place. They appear to be happy in the knowledge that they can cure infirmities with their long, slender needles, and they are more than willing to share that knowledge.

Incidentally, in case you're wondering, in the hands of a skilled practitioner acupuncture is virtually painless, even when the needles are inserted in normally sensitive areas of the body.

Let's move on now to another part of the world. "Pre-Columbian" is a term that is used to refer to the various cultures of the Americas anytime prior to the arrival of Columbus. Before that event it is generally believed that societies in this part of the world devel-

[162] *Ibid.*

oped without any European or Asian influence. But given the choice, some pre-Columbian citizens of ancient Peru might have opted for acupuncture rather than the brain surgery we now know was performed on a great many adult Peruvian males.

The discovery that the rectangular holes found cut in the skulls of these ancient Peruvians were actually put there while the patient was still alive came in the early 1860s. Anthropologists had long assumed that these holes, made by a process called *trephination*, were made after the person was dead. But Paul Broca, a prominent physician and anatomist, discovered that the hole he was examining could not have been cut after death because an infection had left characteristic pockmarks in the surrounding bone. The patient must have survived, he said, for at least a week after the "operation."[163]

A number of late Stone Age tombs in France had yielded skulls with similar holes, and following Broca's discovery, anthropologists began to review their earlier assumptions. They discovered that many of the neolithic French finds had also been operated on while they lived. Evidence of the same surgical procedure turned up in other European countries as well, but it is the ancient Peruvians who hold the record. More than a thousand trephinated skulls have been found in Peru, more than in all the rest of the world combined, suggesting perhaps that the operation was almost routine.

Most of the Peruvian skulls are adult males, and most bear the marks of terrible blows to the head. This suggests they were warriors, injured in battle and the surgeons "operated" not for ritualistic reasons but as

[163] *Time-Life Books, "Ancient Brain Surgery,"* Feats and Wisdom of the Ancients.

therapy to remove bone fragments perhaps, or relieve swelling caused by the blows of war. The Peruvians, it seems, "were practicing medicine, not magic." And judging from the degree to which the skulls had healed, the ancient surgeons had a pretty good track record. About fifty percent of their patients survived.[164]

Somehow the ancient physicians figured out how to deal with the human body long before so-called "modern medicine" came along. They performed complex surgical procedures, used vaccines, and practiced drug therapy, all of which worked. They were dentists, cosmetic surgeons, eye surgeons, and brain surgeons, and in a couple of areas they practiced a form of healing art we are only beginning to understand today.

We can, from our perspective in time, look back on their accomplishments with wonder at what they did. If they could look down the centuries at us they would probably wonder what took us so long to figure these things out.

It seems evident from even this cursory examination of the ancient healing arts that disease is as old as the body itself, and even today there is much we are just beginning to learn, and much more we simply don't know. Some cynics even suggest that doctors have never cured anything. At best, they treat the symptoms until the body heals itself. While that idea is completely compatible with the teachings of Hippocrates, most of us want to believe there's more to it than that. Like the emperors of Rome relying on Galen's errant concepts, we go to the doctor expecting—no, demanding—to be cured. And we are disappointed,

[164] *Ibid.*

even angry, if everything doesn't happen to turn out according to our expectations.

Western medicine has obviously made a great deal of progress. Modern surgeons have a much higher survival rate than fifty percent when it comes to brain operations, and certainly they do a neater job. But it could be that we still have much to learn from the ancients. No modern doctor, for example, has ever told me I could ease the pain and anxiety of removing a bandage from a frightened child with just a little bit of honey.

17

THE PSYCHIC IN SOCIETY

". . . this young man, a Democrat, to be seated as President in 1960, would be assassinated while in office."

Jeane Dixon, Psychic

THIS CHAPTER WAS THE SUBJECT OF MUCH DISCUSsion between myself and some of the editors and researchers. The basic question was, does "psychic phenomena" have a valid place in our consideration of the mysteries of the world? Obviously, the answer is yes. In fact, upon careful consideration it might even be said the answer is a "resounding" yes. But before we delve too deeply into the reasons for including this chapter, some definitions are in order.

Psychic phenomena generally fall into three rather broad categories: telepathy, clairvoyance, and ESP, or extrasensory perception. *Telepathy* is described as psychic awareness of what is going on in someone else's mind without the benefit of sight, hearing, or other sensory channels.

Clairvoyance is the ability to "see" or have a knowledge of people, objects, or events that are beyond the reach of the normal senses.

ESP, or *extrasensory perception,* is a term coined by Dr. J. B. Rhine of the Parapsychology Laboratory at Duke University. ESP is an all-inclusive term embracing telepathy, clairvoyance, and precognition (a form of clairvoyance), and it came about as a result of the modern study of all of these phenomena. In fact the term *parapsychology* is itself an attempt to come to grips with psychic events in some scientific way.

A *parapsychologist,* then, is one who attempts a scientific study of psychic phenomena.[165] There are, in fact, several major universities that offer a Ph.D program in parapsychology.

There is another area of psychic phenomena that has earned its own definition in recent years; it is called *psychokinesis.* Simply put, psychokinesis is the ability to control or manipulate matter with only the mind. This ability seems to be more rare than other psychic phenomena, but it is far more spectacular.

For purposes of this chapter, we'll accept Dr. Rhine's term as all-encompassing and refer to all of the phenomena discussed as ESP events.

Taken as a whole, ESP is arguably the greatest and most pervasive of all of the world's mysteries. No one, not even those who exhibit ESP skills, seems to know what or how it comes about. Furthermore, psychic ability crosses all barriers of time, race, sex, social status, or religion. Anyone, it seems, can have an ESP experience. I have had my own experiences in this regard,[166] and I can assure you that while the events were very real, how they came about completely eludes me. Interestingly enough, *why* these things happen is often self-evident.

Several years ago I produced a motion picture called *The Amazing World of Psychic Phenomena,* starring the late Raymond Burr as host and narrator. In it we told the story of Diana Rider, a legal secretary and amateur pilot whose one-time psychic experience is

---

[165] *Herbert Greenhouse,* Psychic Knowledge.
[166] *Charles Sellier,* Miracles and Other Wonders.

fairly typical of the kind of phenomenon that has a singular and immediate purpose.

Diana was an accomplished pilot but still took lessons on a regular basis to enhance her skills. One Saturday morning, as she lifted her small single-engine plane into the sky, strange thoughts seemed to block her concentration. She was preparing to do some rather difficult spin maneuvers that would require her full attention, but something kept drawing her mind away.

Alone in a small aircraft several thousand feet above the ground is not the best place to be daydreaming, so when repeated calls on the radio failed to get a response, Diana's instructor thought seriously of canceling the lesson for the day.

"Yes," he finally heard her say, "I hear you."

"Diana, if you're not up to this we can postpone it until another time."

"No," Diana responded, "I'm fine. I was just . . . thinking about something else for a moment. Let's go ahead."

The instructor positioned the earphones more firmly on his head, looked up to make sure he could see her plane, and started her on the maneuver.

"There'll be some G-force as you come out of the spin," he warned her. "It won't be much, and if you're expecting it you'll be all right. Are you ready?"

"I'm ready," crackled into his headphones.

"All right then, give it a hard right rudder."

As the instructor relayed his commands, he watched the aircraft carefully, poised to get back to Diana instantly if anything appeared to be going wrong. But the plane turned into a tight bank, headed downward in a smooth spiral, and a thousand feet or so down pulled out and leveled off.

"That looked great, Diana, just great. Come on back in."

The instructor expected to see the aircraft come around and start a slow descent toward the runway, but instead it lifted back into sky and headed northwest.

"Diana, are you all right?" the instructor shouted into the microphone. "Diana?"

What the instructor on the ground couldn't know was that coming out of the spin Diana had heard a voice crying for help. It was a telepathic communication that was so specific she could not disregard it. And something, not a voice, but something, compelled her to turn the plane to the northwest. Nothing the instructor said into his microphone after the spin, even though she may have heard it, registered on her consciousness.

Locked into a heading that was beyond her ability to change, Diana gave the engine full throttle and tried to overcome a growing feeling of anxiety. She knew the direction she was flying; she just didn't know why.

Seventy miles later that same something that had prompted her to fly to the northwest now prompted her to land in an open field. Without hesitation, she brought the plane down, bouncing to a stop in a field next to a secondary highway.

Shortly before Diana landed, a car on the highway had lost control trying to veer out of the way of an oncoming drunk driver. The car left the road and careened into a piece of heavy equipment, turning over and pinning the driver inside. Diana's airplane was rolling to a stop just as the car hit the back end of a road grader and flipped over. A wisp of smoke turned into flame, but the occupant of the car made no move to get out.

Diana rushed to the overturned vehicle and with

great effort was able to pull the driver from the wreckage. Pulling and stumbling, she dragged the half-unconscious driver to safety just moments before the car exploded.

The driver that Diana pulled from the burning wreck was Mrs. Cynthia Rider, Diana's mother. Somehow she had called out telepathically for help and Diana had heard the message. So far as we know it was Diana's first and only experience with ESP. Neither she nor her mother has any idea how it could have happened, but they are both grateful that it did.

History is full of these events. Some of them are religious in nature, such as the voices that guided Joan of Arc. Others are profane, such as the occult power said to be invested in the spear of Longinus, the spear belonging to the Roman centurion who pierced the side of Christ. An entire book has been written[167] on how Hitler attempted to pervert the power supposedly invested in that spear in his attempt to rule the world.

Ancient *shamans* guided whole societies by powers of divination. Great kingdoms were administered according to the insights provided the king by his astrologers and soothsayers, and at least one modern ruler was chosen solely by signs and portents. The fourteenth Dalai Lama, spiritual and political leader of Tibet, now in exile, was selected by temple priests in accordance with ancient traditions that go back thousands of years.

The Tibetans believe that the incarnation of "Buddha's Wisdom," which resides always in the Dalai Lama, never changes. The living body changes from time to time, but when the body of the Dalai Lama dies, the incarnation of Buddha's wisdom simply finds a

[167] *Trevor Ravenscroft,* The Spear of Destiny.

new home. It is up to the priests to find him through the oracles and bring him to Lhasa, the capital of Tibet.

In 1937, four years after the death of the thirteenth Dalai Lama, the Tibetan monks, through a series of mystical manifestations and signs, were led to the village of Amdo, a thousand miles northeast of Lhasa. Here the signs indicated that a small boy might be the subject of their search. But if this boy was in fact to be accepted as the incarnation of Buddha's wisdom, he would have to pass some very rigid tests.

Several items that had been personal favorites of the thirteenth Dalai Lama had been brought along, each with its perfectly matched counterfeit. The boy would have to pick the right one in every instance, and without hesitation. The child in question, by the way, was a two-and-a-half-year-old.

Solemnly, the monks placed four pairs of items in front of the boy: two black rosaries, two yellow rosaries, two identical walking sticks, and two small drums. One of the monks indicated the black rosaries and instantly the boy picked one up and placed it around his neck. Next came the walking sticks. The boy reached toward one, but quickly dropped his hand on the one next to it. The monk betrayed no sign of concern or approval and moved on to the yellow rosaries. The child smiled as he put one of them around his neck and looked up at the monk expectantly. At last came the drums. The boy not only selected one but immediately began to beat out the age-old tantric ritual. Silently, the monk conducting the test withdrew to confer with his colleagues.

It seems the walking sticks, the only item upon which the boy hesitated, were both used by the thirteenth Dalai Lama, but the one ultimately picked by the boy was the one he used most often. In each of the other instances the boy had chosen the favorite of the

Dalai Lama instantly. And what two-and-a-half-year-old can beat the tantric ritual, even in Tibet?

There were other tests, and finally this young boy, now barely three years of age, was brought to Lhasa and proclaimed the fourteenth Dalai Lama. If any of the monks had doubted their selection, those doubts quickly vanished when the boy was brought to his sleeping quarters in the thousand-room palace. Upon entering the room, the boy turned to the monks and, pointing to a small porcelain box on a bedside table, said, "My teeth are in there." Indeed, a set of dentures belonging to the previous Dalai Lama was found, still in the box.

If they were surprised, the Tibetan Buddhists didn't show it. So far as they were concerned, the Dalai Lama had been chosen in the "usual" manner.

This same young boy, grown to manhood, won the Nobel Peace Prize in 1989. He continues to be the spiritual leader of the Tibetan people, even though forced into exile by the Chinese.

Serious study of the various forms of ESP did not begin until well into this century. (Some studies were attempted in the late 1800s but did little more than add to the growing speculation.) And it is safe to say that parapsychologists are no closer to answering the question of how these remarkable events take place than they were when they started. That it happens, and that some people seem to be more skillful than others in controlling various ESP events, is about all that can be said for certain. Attempts to quantify ESP experiences in terms of controllable mental or nonphysical means have all failed to provide concrete and repeatable answers. Just one man, a young Israeli, is known to have performed incredible feats of psychokinesis virtually on demand. His name is Uri Geller.

I know Uri personally and have worked with him on several occasions. He has probably been tested more rigorously than all other psychics combined. His first international notoriety came in 1973 when he demonstrated remarkable feats of telepathy and psychokinesis, particularly an ability to bend metal objects with nothing more than the power of his mind. A year later, a well-known parapsychologist, Dr. Andrija Puharich, published a book in both Britain and the United States that brought the young Israeli even greater fame . . . and broader criticism.

The book was titled *Uri: A Journal of the Mystery of Uri Geller.* Unfortunately for Uri, the book, which was expected to be a bestseller, did his reputation more harm than good. Puharich, for some reason, chose this book to try to explain certain experiences he claimed to have had with extraterrestrials over a period of twenty years. Previously known for solid scholarship and scientific tough-mindedness, he now found himself the subject of scathing criticism, and by extension, so did Uri Geller.[168]

Geller became aware of his special gifts while still a child of six. His father had given him a watch, and when he tried to wear it, it would gain time excessively. He decided the watch was faulty and left it home. But at home on the dresser the watch worked flawlessly. He tried again, but when he could actually see the hands moving much faster than they were supposed to, he persuaded his parents to buy him another one. This time the hands of the new watch were somehow bent upward, against the crystal. The watch was ruined.

Then the spoon-bending began. One day while he was eating soup, the bowl of the spoon fell off. Later,

[168] *"The Making of a Mystic,"* The Geller Phenomenon.

in a coffee shop he sometimes went to with his mother, the spoons began bending even though he wasn't touching them. Needless to say this caused a great deal of concern, not only to Uri and his parents but to the shop owner as well. Still, all of this was as much of a puzzle to Uri as it was to everyone else. He was only dimly aware that he had anything to do with these strange occurrences, but as the realization slowly came upon him, he began to wonder just exactly what else he could do.

The first intentional use of his powers came some time later. In the family garage was a bicycle his stepfather had promised him as a bar mitzvah present. Uri was anxious to try the bicycle but it was secured with a large padlock. One day he decided to see if he could get the lock to open. Concentrating on it, he willed the lock to open. It took several attempts, but finally the hasp gave way.[169] His skepticism also gave way at the same time. He was now aware that he had some special power; he just didn't know why, or for that matter, what to do with it.

Like all Israeli youth, Uri spent time in the military. He chose the paratroopers and participated in the Six Day War in 1967. He was wounded (as he had foreseen he would be), but not seriously. After leaving the military, Geller went to work in a children's holiday camp near Tel Aviv. While there he met a young man, Shipi Shtrang, who would figure prominently in his life from that time forward. It was Shipi who saw the potential in Uri's special gift and persuaded him to put on a demonstration of his powers for a fee (Uri's first public performance). Shipi became Geller's best friend and business manager.

[169] *Ibid.*

Shortly thereafter Geller's career as a performer was launched. Even his sternest critics admit he is a gifted entertainer as well as a gifted psychic. The combination has proven to be rewarding for Geller but may have contributed to a general lack of acceptance for his psychic gifts. Entertainers, after all, are not meant to be taken seriously. But Puharich, in spite of the theme of his book, did take Uri seriously and conducted a number of tests that apparently convinced him that Geller's powers were real. In addition to bending spoons or letter openers or keys, and demonstrating amazing telepathic skills, Geller raised the level of the mercury in a thermometer about eight degrees on command while a nearby thermometer remained unaffected.[170] A number of critics have advanced theories as to how Geller bends objects, but no one has yet advanced a theory as to how he could have faked the rising mercury in the thermometer.

Geller's willingness to try just about anything with his powers made him a darling of the press and the public but seemed to polarize the skeptics. For better or worse, it also brought him to the attention of mainstream science. Following Geller's smashing tour of Britain, two mathematicians, Professor John Taylor and Dr. Ted Bastin, both wanted to test him in their own laboratories. It is not clear whether any such tests took place, but Geller at the urging of Edgar Mitchell, one of the astronauts to walk on the moon, had already been tested in America by the Stanford Institute, (not a part of Stanford University), a highly reputable scientific study group. The British did, however, finally get in on Geller's act. When the Stanford Institute's report finally appeared, it was published in the British journal,

[170] *Ibid.*

Nature, one of the world's foremost scientific compendiums.

Other scientists who started out skeptical but became convinced of Geller's special powers include Werner von Braun and Dr. Gerald Feinberg of the Physics Department of Columbia University. But even though many credible people seem to accept the fact of *what* he does, no one knows *how* he does it.

There are critics, to be sure. The "Amazing Randi" has written a book of his own that purports to demonstrate that all of Uri Geller's amazing ESP feats are simple magician's tricks, which not only he but many other magicians can perform. (There is no report that any of them have done the "mercury trick," however.) And like Geller, he has taken his version of the show "on the road." Randi has appeared on television and made many personal appearances, doing what are essentially duplications of Uri Geller's "tricks."

My own experience with Uri leads me to believe he does, in fact, possess powers most of us do not. A few years ago, Uri called to tell me was flying in to Salt Lake City and asked if I could meet him at the airport. It had been some time since our last meeting and I was anxious to see him again. I quickly agreed to be there, then hung up the phone and went back to work.

Spending time with Uri Geller is always an exciting experience, so I found myself looking forward to his arrival with great anticipation. Then I remembered I had told a writer friend of mine that if I ever had the opportunity to do so, I would introduce him to Uri. I picked up the phone and called my friend, and told him that if he wanted to make the trip to the airport with me in a couple of days I would make good on my promise.

Two days later we were waiting at the gate when

Uri's plane arrived. We spotted each other almost simultaneously, and, as always, he seemed genuinely glad to see me. After the usual greetings I introduced my friend and told Uri he was a big fan who had waited a long time for the opportunity to meet him in person. Uri is always gracious and never forward about his talents, so I was a bit surprised when he said to my friend, "You would like me to do something for you?" My friend, who had been trying to work up the courage to ask him to do just that, was shocked that his intentions were so transparent, but nodded and replied that, indeed, he would like a personal demonstration.

Without hesitation Uri asked him if he had a key. My friend produced a ring of keys and handed them all over. Uri selected the smallest key on the ring, held it between his thumb and forefinger, rubbed it gently, and handed it back. The key was bent awkwardly to one side. It never left the key ring and was never out of sight of either me or my friend.

As it turned out, the key was to my friend's post office box. When he tried to get a new one and was asked how the old one got so badly bent (destroying post office property is a serious offense), his explanation was not well received. Not everyone, it seems, has heard of Uri Geller.

But if there are so many examples of ESP and its many and varied manifestations, why is it that they, or it, cannot be proven?

In spite of all the testing, ESP powers fail most scientific evaluations for one principal reason: They are not repeatable. Scientists like to do the same thing over and over under identical conditions and get identical results. To them it is this repeatability that confirms the fact. Unfortunately, the mind is difficult to capture and pigeonhole in that manner. The fact is, as we pointed out earlier, nonphysical events are not subject to the same rules and regulations as physical events. It is quite possible to quantify the movement of mercury under specified temperature variations. You cannot necessarily quantify the variations of mind that create the same movement.

The truth is, ESP may never be proven to the satisfaction of the scientific community. To the person that experiences any kind of ESP event, however, that fact is irrelevant. If you ask Cynthia Rider if she can prove her daughter heard her telepathic cry for help, the answer is likely to be, I don't know and I don't care. It happened.

That seems to be the answer to all the questions and all the critics: It happens! Of that there can be no doubt. Jeane Dixon did try to get John F. Kennedy to cancel his trip to Dallas. As we have seen, her attempts to do so actually fulfilled a 450-year-old prophecy by Nostradamus. In fact, the story of Jeane Dixon's now famous psychic vision of the Kennedy assassination is one of incredible detail and is worth repeating.

It all began on a drizzly Sunday morning in 1952. Ms. Dixon, according to her own account, was standing reverently before the statue of the Virgin Mary, in St. Matthew's Cathedral in Washington, D.C.

"Suddenly the White House appeared before me in dazzling brightness," she writes. "Coming out of a haze, the numerals 1-9-6-0 formed above the roof. An ominous dark cloud appeared, covering the numbers, and dripped slowly onto the White House. . . . Then I looked down and saw a young man, tall and blue-eyed, crowned with a shock of thick brown hair, quietly standing in front of the main door.

"I was still staring at him when a voice came out of nowhere, telling me softly that this young man, a Democrat, to be seated as president in 1960, would be assassinated while in office."[171]

Eleven years later, John F. Kennedy was gunned down in Dallas, Texas, while still serving his first term as president. His funeral mass was said in the very church in which Jeane Dixon had seen her vision. Later, while at the Ambassador Hotel in Los Angeles, Ms. Dixon predicted that Robert Kennedy would also be assassinated. He was . . . and in the very same Ambassador Hotel.

Nor is this the only example of ESP affecting the leaders of the nation. Abraham Lincoln recorded in his own hand the strange dream that foretold of his death at an assassin's hands. In that dream, which he had just a few days prior to his excursion to Ford's Theater, Lincoln saw himself descending the stairs in the White House. He had a sense of foreboding, as if the entire world were in mourning. Upon entering the East Room he saw a casket, closed and draped, with one of the staff standing nearby. Lincoln asked who had died. The servant replied, "The president, cut down by an assassin's bullet."

What might the world be like if Lincoln had taken precautions against such an eventuality? We will never know, but all of this does suggest that there is some reason for these events that occur. That being the case, wouldn't we be better off if we dropped our shield of skepticism and accepted the "gifts" as being in our best interest? When did you hear of a psychic event that occurred in order to further evil designs? Invariably the

[171] *"The Moderns,"* Signs of Things to Come.

psychic sees or hears things that will accrue to someone's benefit if the warnings or visions are heeded.

"The Sleeping Prophet," Edgar Cayce, was a gentle and soft-spoken man who earned his greatest reputation as a "healer." His amazing insight into various medical problems and their cures seems to have been unbounded. He required nothing more than a name and address. Most of the time he had never even met the people who were asking his help, nor did he require them to give him an account of their illness. Cayce would lie comfortably on a couch, and with a stenographer close by to record what he said, he would slip into a deep, sleeplike trance. With amazing accuracy he would then diagnose the problem of the person who had sent him their name and prescribe a remedy. Records indicate he made virtually no errors. Some of his prescriptions actually predated a later discovery of the same cure by medical science.

Always sensitive to the plight of those who petitioned him for help, he swore that if he ever caused anyone any harm, he would cease providing his special kind of help. No claim of injury was ever made, and thousands of people praised him for giving them new health and life. One wonders how many others he might have helped had they not thrown up a barrier of skepticism.

There is another group of people that probably didn't care whether or not science could prove the existence of ESP. These were people who held tickets for the maiden voyage of the *Titanic*. Each of them canceled the reservation due to a premonition that the huge ship would strike an iceberg and sink. One man, J. Connon Middleton, dreamed twice that as the ship went down, he was floating a little above it. One member of the crew, convinced the ship would go down, deserted at Queenstown before it sailed into the open sea.[172]

But one of the most astonishing aspects of the sinking of the *Titanic* is that it all took place fourteen years earlier in the pages of a book called *The Wreck of the Titan*. Published in 1898, this story of a seventy-thousand-ton ship carrying twenty-five hundred passengers, most of whom were lost when the giant ship struck an iceberg and sank, caused little stir when it came out. But in 1912, after the loss of the *Titanic*, it became a sensation. People began to notice the amazing similarities between the fictitious story and the actual tragedy. The SS *Titan* was "the largest, most luxurious and, above all, the safest ocean liner in the world, setting out on her maiden voyage." The *Titanic* was indeed all of that, displacing sixty-six thousand tons. Both ships carried far too few lifeboats to accommodate the crew and passengers. The fictitious *Titan* had only twenty-four. The real *Titanic* had only twenty. Both ships were triple-screw vessels with a top speed of twenty-five knots, and finally, both ships were said to be unsinkable. Both sank with great loss of life.

The author of the *Titan* story was a little-known Englishman by the name of Morgan Robertson. It is not known whether he ever claimed any precognitive knowledge of the upcoming *Titanic* disaster, but his book is now regarded as "a most astounding instance of prophecy."[173]

And then there are always those who fail to heed the warnings. The British journalist, W. T. Stead, was warned by a seer that he would sail to America within a year. She saw him, she said, among a great throng of

---

[172] *Herbert Greenhouse*, Psychic Knowledge, *p. 44.*
[173] Signs of Things to Come.

people struggling in the water. He was told his struggles would do him no good.

Stead himself had warnings. He wrote a magazine article in which he described a catastrophe of a ship colliding with an iceberg. And, incredibly, Stead had a dream in which he saw himself standing on the deck of the sinking *Titanic* without a lifebelt, watching the last lifeboat disappear into the night. Stead ignored all the warnings and was among those lost when the *Titanic* went down.[174]

Is there, then, some worthwhile purpose for psychic phenomena?

Surely ESP in all of its manifestations is one of the great mysteries of the world, but perhaps it is more important that we recognize its reality than that we solve the puzzle it presents.

This is not to suggest that we should accept everything out of hand. Calling a 900 number to discover whether or not you should visit Aunt Maud or go to Schenectady in search of a lover strikes me as a bit ludicrous. And it is true that every day there are demonstrable acts of charlatans who will always take advantage of the gullible for their own gain. A cautious approach is certainly recommended. Unfortunately, the charlatans in large measure prevent us from accepting the benefits of the real psychic phenomena. After all, no one wants to look foolish.

But the reality of psychic phenomena is now beyond a reasonable doubt. It does happen. There is a power, whether from within or without the human condition, that permits some among us to see with the mind things that are not evident to the physical senses.

This power permits those so gifted to see events

[174] *Ibid.*

that even they don't understand: to peer far into the future and know the fate of all mankind, or just look around some brief corner of time to avoid a bump on the nose. It brings other voices into waking moments and visions of joy or sadness into the world of dreams.

The person who is psychically gifted may or may not be caught up in the mystery of it, but that person will almost certainly *believe!*

18

LIFE AFTER LIFE—THE FUTURE BEYOND

"I saw my soul, or something, come out of my body, like you would pull a silk handkerchief out of a pocket, by one corner."

Ernest Hemingway in
A Farewell to Arms

PERHAPS THE MOST ENDURING OF ALL OF LIFE'S mysteries is the final mystery: Death!

What is it? Is it, as some suggest, simply the end? As a modern bumper sticker so cryptically puts it, "Life's a bitch . . . and then you die."

Or is it a transition from one state of existence to another, as taught, in one form or another, by most of the world's religions?

These are simple questions that millions of people have discovered the answer to. Unfortunately, by the time they do, it's too late for them to tell anybody else. Without meaning to be facetious, it is nevertheless true that the only way to solve this mystery is to die.

At least that is what has been thought till recently.

If there is not absolute proof that there is life after death, there certainly is a large body of impressive evidence. Dr. Karlis Osis, director of research for the American Society for Psychical Research, conducted a study of doctors and nurses who stated that patients had reported seeing the spirits of dead relatives and friends at their bedside. Ten thousand questionnaires were sent out, and the results were most enlightening. Among the more interesting aspects of the study was the fact that those who saw these spirits were calm and

clear-headed at the time, and, as a group, better edu-
cated than terminal patients not having the experience.
Many of the spirits reported to have been seen were of
persons who, unknown to the patients, had themselves
recently died.[175]

One famous case of this kind occurred in the early
1900s and was recorded by the Reverend Mr. Minot
Savage. Two eight-year-old girls, Edith and Jennie,
were inseparable friends. They both became ill during
an epidemic, and Jennie quickly died. The passing of
her friend was kept from Edith, but as she herself lay
dying she suddenly brightened. "Papa," she said, "why
did you not tell me Jennie had gone? Here is Jennie
come to meet me."[176]

These visions are usually dismissed as nothing more
than deathbed hallucinations by skeptics and critics
who find little comfort in what they themselves cannot
see. And, indeed, a compelling case can be made for
some sort of mind trick taking place. Even collective
sightings of a ghost or spirit can be easily dismissed as
some sort of group hallucination. There are, however,
numerous reports that are not so easily explained.
What kind of hallucination, for example, permits several different persons, all at different times, to see and
describe the same "apparition," and each of them with
no knowledge of any of the others' experiences?

Some investigators have taken a more practical approach than others. Assuming a person's soul to be of
some substance, and all substances by definition having
weight and mass, a doctor named Duncan MacDou-
gall, in 1906, decided to weigh a soul. His method was
simplicity itself. He simply devised an extremely sensi-

[175] *Herbert Greenhouse,* Psychic Knowledge, *p. 196.*
[176] *Ibid.*

tive scale and placed it around the beds of dying patients. He made careful observations and weighed
them at the very moment of death. The difference, he
surmised, between their living weight and their weight
at the moment the spirit departed would be the weight
of the soul. At the instant of death one body lost three-
quarters of an ounce. In other cases the loss varied
from less than an ounce to slightly over an ounce.[177] To
this day there is no medical or scientific explanation for
this sudden and relatively uniform loss of weight.

Photography has also been used to try to record the
"migration of souls." In some cases spiritlike images
have appeared on finished photographs when nothing
in the room suggested any such presence. A Dr.
Baraduc, a nineteenth-century photographer, claimed
to have snapped a picture of his wife's spirit leaving her
body at the time of death and exhibited the photograph
broadly. But the problem with photographic "evidence" is, it is all too easy for skillful photographers to
produce fake images on film.[178]

Photographs of spirits are almost uniformly rejected as being at best unreliable and at worst pure
fakery.

There are, however, other methods of determining
whether or not there is a life after this one. In recent
years a phenomenon called *near-death experience* has
received wide attention. Perhaps due to improved
medical techniques that permit doctors to resuscitate
patients that might have been lost only a few short
years ago, reports of these kinds of experiences are
definitely increasing.

Interestingly, the reports are all amazingly similar.

[177] *Ibid., p. 201.*
[178] *Ibid.*

In broad strokes, they go like this: The patients (or accident victims) die and immediately find themselves in a long tunnel or passageway with a bright light at the far end. They are inexplicably drawn to that light, and when they reach it they are welcomed by either family members that have gone on before, or by a Being emanating love and compassion. Details vary, of course, and in some cases explicit information is given to the people to bring back with them to their living state.

The uniformity of the experience has prompted some to suggest that there may be some kind of physical response to dying that triggers a mechanism in the brain that, in turn, produces an image of what the person has always expected to experience after death. Others find that the similarity of the reports is an excellent reason to look closer at these experiences. After all, as we have just seen, the wellspring of scientific investigation is being able to repeat an experience time after time and get the same results.

In 1980 Dr. Raymond Moody wrote a book that challenged medical and laypeople alike to reexamine their attitudes toward these experiences. *Life After Life* has become something of a classic of the genre, but for a time, critics still insisted these experiences were the result of cultural training rather than spiritual reality.[179]

Then, in 1990 Dr. Melvin Morse, a pediatrician with a long-standing reputation as a NDE (near-death experience) researcher, published his book, *Closer to the Light*, a collection of the NDEs of children too young to have absorbed the cultural attitudes of adults about death. Amazingly, these children are also uniform in their reports and seem to be telling us that

[179] *Raymond Moody*, Life After Life.

death is something to be welcomed rather than feared.[180]

According to one reviewer, *Closer to the Light* describes what it feels like to die, yet it makes a convincing case that the same "something" that gives us life survives bodily death.[181] Be that as it may, the work of both Doctors Moody and Morse are proof that the modern medical community is beginning to look at *light* and *life* in new and exciting ways.

My first serious involvement with this subject came, once again, with the production of a movie. Called *Beyond and Back,* based on a book by Dr. Ralph Wilkerson, our film was an attempt to assemble some of these same experiences and put them into a format with which the public was generally familiar. That is, we put the NDEs we had researched in the context of stories, dramatized in and around a hospital setting. The research that was done for this picture yielded some very interesting information. For example, Mozart, probably the greatest music prodigy that ever lived, believed he had lived in another life. Beethoven, stone-deaf in his later years, maintained that his "other self" heard every note clearly and distinctly. Moussorgsky, composer of the haunting *Night on Bald Mountain,* insisted that he actually witnessed the "Witches' Sabbath" during an out-of-body experience. His description of that event is instructive.

According to Moussorgsky, "[T]he witches used to gather on this mountain, gossip, play tricks and await their chief—Satan. On his arrival they . . . formed a circle round the throne on which he sat in the form of a goat and sang his praise. When Satan was worked up

---

[180] *Melvin Morse with Paul Perry,* Closer to the Light.
[181] *Ibid.*

into sufficient passion by the witches' praises, he gave the command for the Sabbath in which he chose for himself the witches which caught his fancy. . . . My *St. John's Night on Bald Mountain* . . . I wrote [it] quickly . . . without any preliminary rough drafts, in twelve days. It seethed within me."

Other famous people have recorded their experiences as well. In the case of Ernest Hemingway the incident was recreated with all the skill of the great novelist.

Hemingway was a nineteen-year-old reporter during World War I, when he believed he was killed by a mortar shell on July 8, 1918. Hemingway wrote of his experience, but he gave it to one of the characters in his famous novel *A Farewell to Arms*. Those who have read the book may remember this dramatic passage:

> I saw my soul, or something, come out of my body, like you would pull a silk handkerchief out of a pocket, by one corner. It flew around and then it came back in again and I wasn't dead anymore.

Few readers knew that Hemingway was describing an event he had personally experienced.

But not everyone in the world sees death, or the transition from one level of existence to another, in the same way. There are those who believe the soul simply migrates to another life, or in the case of reincarnation, to some other life *form*. Still others suggest a departed spirit can continue its work or existence by using a still living host. There is, for example, the case of a lawsuit being brought against a man who was alleged to be using the talents of another man, long since dead.

Chico Xavier, a Brazilian writer, made no bones about the fact that he wrote while in a trance, "channeling" the works of not one but several very well-known, and very dead, authors. Xavier was sued in 1944 by the wife of one of these dead writers. The wife didn't want him to stop using her dead husband's talent —she wanted a share in the royalties. The sum was not insignificant. Humberto de Campos was the famous Brazilian author whose wife wanted the royalties from five books she claimed were actually written by her husband though the pen was in the hand of Xavier.

Xavier, for his part, did not contest the claim that the books were the dead man's creations. In fact, he offered to go into a trance and produce more of de Campos's work right there in the courtroom. Critics were put on the stand to evaluate the works, and they all agreed the books were typical of de Campos's style and composition.

People around the world followed the trial with keen interest, waiting to see if the courts could determine whether or not death was legal and binding upon the deceased, or whether he could continue to earn a livelihood for his heirs through someone else. Unfortunately, that question was never resolved. The suit was dismissed. The judge sidestepped the whole issue by ruling that the dead have no standing in a court of law.[182] Which means, I guess, that if I want to continue writing after I die it will have to be for love of the written word. My heirs will be unable to benefit from my post-departure work, no matter how it is accomplished.

Then there is the famous case of Bridey Murphy. In perhaps one of the most celebrated events of a past

[182] *"Possession and Multiple Personality,"* Psychic Voyages.

life ever reported, a Colorado housewife by the name of Virginia Tighe, claimed to have previously lived in Ireland as a woman named Bridey Murphy. Under hypnosis she was able to recall minute details of her entire life, up to and including her own funeral in Belfast. Investigation in Ireland confirmed the accuracy of the terms she used as well as many of the places mentioned.

A book and a motion picture were both created from the fascinating details of Bridey's very ordinary life. At the time (1956), the very fact that Bridey was so ordinary tended to give credence to the experience. Most people who claim to be reincarnated somehow always turn out to be kings or queens, or at the very least famous artists. Bridey Murphy was just an ordinary woman. After a brief but splashy affair with the media, Bridey Murphy faded once again into oblivion. In the final analysis, no conclusive evidence that she really existed was ever uncovered.[183]

Her case does serve to bring up the concept of reincarnation, however. Reincarnation is an entire belief system separate and apart from the world of psychic studies. Many Islamic sects accept the concept of reincarnation as easily and with as much fervor as Christians accept the concept of the Resurrection. And they have done so for hundreds, even thousands of years.

A friend tells the story, in all seriousness, of being roundly chastised by a cab driver in India for squashing a mosquito that landed on his neck. The mosquito might well have been his great-aunt, he was told, and he was unceremoniously invited to take another taxi.

In 1966 an American professor, Dr. Ian Stevenson,

[183] *Ibid.*

published a book entitled *Twenty Cases Suggestive of Reincarnation,* based on his own research and study of the subject. One of Stevenson's case studies, of a young boy named Imad Elawar, gives some insight into the depth of his investigations and the reasons why reincarnation is so easily embraced by so many people the world over.

Imad was born in the village of Kornayel. As soon as he could talk he began using the names of "Jamile" and "Mahmoud." His family was puzzled; no one in the family had such names. He also made much of the village of Khriby, about thirty kilometers across the mountains from Kornayel. When Stevenson met Imad, the boy was just five years old. He had never left the village in which he was born, but he had been talking about a former life in Khriby for almost three years. Stevenson gathered all the information Imad could give him, including a detailed description of the house he had lived in, then he trekked the thirty miles of rough mountain road to the village of Khriby.

On his first visit Stevenson confirmed forty-four out of forty-seven facts given to him by Imad, including the source of the names Jamile and Mahmoud. Based on the information from Imad and his own investigations, Stevenson concluded that Imad "had been" one Ibrahim Bouhamzy who had died at the age of twenty-five of tuberculosis.[184]

Stevenson returned to Kornayel and picked up Imad and returned with him to Khriby. Imad provided an additional sixteen facts about the life of Ibrahim, fourteen of which Stevenson ultimately confirmed. For example, the boy said that in his former life as Ibrahim he owned two rifles, one of them a double-barreled

[184] *Ibid., pp. 127–128.*

one. This Stevenson was able to confirm. Furthermore, when they entered the house, Imad was able to go directly to where Ibrahim had hidden one of the rifles.[185]

How could a five-year-old boy imagine such things? Unlike the Colorado housewife who had access to information about Ireland and might have invented Bridey Murphy, Imad had no way of "learning" about his former life or his former home. Yet he seemed to know names, places, and events. Is the migration of souls possible?

Tibetans believe the soul undergoes several transitions before rebirth, and, as we noted earlier, Buddhist monks accept it as a natural obligation to read the signs and oracles in order to discover where the incarnation of Buddha's wisdom has gone when the Dalai Lama dies. Nor does time seem to be of any importance. It was several years following the death of the thirteenth Dalai Lama before the new incarnation of Buddha's wisdom was discovered in a two-and-a-half-year-old boy a thousand miles from the palace in Lhasa.

A belief in reincarnation is by no means limited to Asian religions. Pythagoras, the great Greek philosopher and mathematician, taught the doctrine of the "transmigration" of souls and believed himself to have been a Trojan warrior, a prophet, a Thracian, peasant and a Phoenician prostitute in previous incarnations.

Those who support reincarnation point to some of the great thinkers and prodigies as proof of the theory. The idea seems to be that people like Mozart, who was already composing music at the age of five, bring their previous knowledge and life experience with them. Christian Henry Heinecken, born in 1721 in Lübeck, is

[185] *Ibid.*

a case in point. The "Infant of Lübeck" began speaking fluently shortly after his birth. By his first birthday he could recite all of the Bible; by the age of four he had learned Latin and French. Before the age of five, he was dead.

No one knows, of course, what brilliant light claimed this small body for so short a time, but if reincarnation is a fact of life—and death—that marvelous intellect is quite likely still with us, somewhere.

The concept of "life after life," to borrow Dr. Moody's phrase, brings with it a host of questions and suppositions. Some societies, like the Japanese, have long traditions of venerating, even worshipping, their ancestors, who, they frequently believe, still look after their well-being. This idea is not terribly far removed from the concept of *guardian angels*—those benign but loving spirits, often believed to be departed family members or friends, who watch over the living, protecting them from harm and worldly temptations.

Then there is the phenomenon of *poltergeists*. One of the most widely investigated of all psychic phenomena, these "restless spirits" can be anything, it seems, from a noisy nuisance to a malevolent threat. *Poltergeist,* by the way, is a German word meaning "noisy spirit." These bothersome spirits, thought by many to be miserable souls trapped somehow between their life on earth and what should be the life hereafter, are left with nothing to do but vent their frustration on the unfortunate living people who happen to wind up in what the "spirits" apparently consider to be their domain.

A more scholarly view, but one that still requires a certain acceptance of psychic phenomena, is that such things as levitation, moving objects, and strange noises are all caused by the psychic energy of the poltergeist *victim*.[186]

In any case, a belief that it is only the body that dies is essential for an acceptance of any of these ideas or philosophies. The humanist view that we are all strictly biological beings that simply come to an end when the body ceases to function will not support any notion of an afterlife.

Actually, the humanist view seems to be an idea that is getting tougher and tougher to sell. Evidence that there is something more to this life than just the physical is gaining greater acceptance. The books of Doctors Moody, Morse, and Wilkerson, referred to earlier, likewise suggest that the scientific community is finding greater opportunity to study the possibility, if not the probability, of an afterlife. Then, too, as people find greater acceptance in sharing their experiences, more and more detail is being brought to our attention.

Betty J. Eadie, a housewife turned author, has recorded one of the most comprehensive of all near-death experiences. She began by telling her family and a few friends about her NDE. The few friends suddenly swelled into packed auditoriums. She was then persuaded to let someone transcribe the description of her own "death" and return to life, and soon photocopies, dogeared from being passed around, began to show up wherever friends gathered to talk about the events of the day. Finally, someone suggested she put her story in book form. She did, and as of this writing, *Embraced by the Light* by Betty J. Eadie is a national bestseller.

Much of what Ms. Eadie tells us is familiar to all NDE stories. The principle difference in her book is

---

[186] *"The Poltergeists,"* Ghosts & Poltergeists.

the wealth of rich detail she shares with us, and the message she was given to bring back.

Betty Eadie was thirty-one years old when she died in a hospital after undergoing an operation. She has no idea how long she was "gone," since she was unattended at the time. What she shares with the reader may have been given to her in matter of minutes or over several hours. No one knows. It is however, a powerful story, unique in its detail and completeness. Anyone interested in this subject will find it both disturbing and fascinating reading.

One thing seems certain: Virtually everyone would like to know what happens when death draws the final curtain across the portal of our worldly existence. And even though a few, like Betty Eadie, tell us they do know, for most of us the questions remain. Is there a Heaven? Is there a Hell? Have some individuals really experienced death and lived to tell about it? Do we simply go from one dimension to another, leaving only the body behind? Do we reappear in another body and in another time?

However you choose to answer those questions, the evidence will likely support the belief system you already have in place. It is, therefore, a subject that is not only safe to explore but also difficult to ignore.

Life's greatest mystery is still . . . life's final mystery!

19
CONCLUSIONS

THE MAN WAS IN HIS LATE FORTIES, OF MEDIUM height and build, and except for a full moustache that he kept neatly trimmed, he was clean-shaven.

He looked out over the pile of rocks and sun-bleached stone that had undoubtedly been at least a village of some sort at one time or another in the nation's storied past, then glanced down at the book of poetry in his hands. This was it. It had to be.

The man shivered slightly against the early morning cold, slipped the book into a pocket of his jacket, and retrieved his pipe. He moved over to a large square stone that had become his favorite "chair" on these crisp mornings, struck a match, touched it to the tobacco in the pipe, and inhaled deeply. He was situated just below the highest point of a huge pile of rubble under the single, lonely tree that had somehow sprouted between the cracks. Around the base of this "citadel," as he called it, a stone wall snaked in and around the crevices. With a patience born of long, lonely hours of solitary work, he settled back to await the first, glorious splash of sunlight that would soon illuminate his "discovery." He had found what he was looking for at last—he was sure of it.

The scholars of the nineteenth century had been unremitting in their scorn. Surely he knew that the tales spun in his precious book of poetry were nothing more than folklore. He was wasting a fortune that had been dearly earned, and all for nothing. The press of the day had echoed that consensus, and publicly wondered why a man of such formidable means would let himself be taken in by a storyteller whose own reality was very much in doubt, and who, in any case, had been dead for hundreds of years.

But Heinrich Schliemann, a German by birth, scholar by honest intellectual pursuit, and self-made millionaire to boot, could not be disuaded. He didn't care if the entire academic world thought him nothing more than an eccentric fool, he was certain that the great classic poetry of Homer portrayed a real and vital history.

At some time in the distant past, mighty warriors in flashing armor, and wielding brass swords, had clashed with Titans in defense of their homes and women. But they had lost. A tide of violence had overwhelmed them and the magnificent walled citadels that had protected the richest cities in all of Europe were buried in the crushing onslaught. The magnificent art, exquisite knowledge of language, and glittering civilization that had grown and prospered for nearly four hundred years had slipped beneath the curtain of history and reemerged—as legend.

Schliemann's pursuit of the mystery of Mycenae had cost him a fortune and his reputation. But convinced that the scholarly portrayal of the Homeric epic as only a fanciful legend was pure poppycock, he set his business interests aside and went in search of the golden city of Greek legend. Now he was certain he was sitting right on top of it. The citadel of Mycenae was just beneath his feet.

It was 1876, and the world was astonished when

sensational finds in royal graves turned out to be the rulers of the citadel of Mycenae. Nineteen skeletons were found entombed with vast riches: jewelry, burial masks of hammered gold, magnificent weapons inlaid with ivory and precious stones, and gems of crystal and amber.

Schliemann had uncovered a vast treasure, and through his discovery the world was given great wealth, not just the gold and jewels and artifacts but the far greater "treasure" of a civilization restored. Literally resurrected from the scholarly graveyard of legend, a magnificent culture was again permitted to take its rightful place in the history of the inexorable march of humankind.

Until Schliemann's discoveries few believed that Greece had nurtured a culture of any real sophistication much before the age of Socrates and Plato. Now there was proof that the remarkable civilization glorified by Homer had indeed existed nearly three thousand years before these venerable philosophers were born. The world was richer by one magnificent, and formerly lost, society.

Was it worth it? Setting aside the vast fortune that was uncovered, and the triumph of discovery—was solving the mystery worth all of the effort and risk?

I believe it was. Even if there had not been a single amulet of amber found in any of those graves, if the discovery proved the existence of the citadel of Mycenae, it was worth it.

Schliemann certainly thought so. He had earlier discovered the lost city of Troy, home of the fabled Helen, whose great beauty put the fate of two powerful city-states in the balance. Many of his conclusions about this discovery proved to be erroneous, but that didn't stop him from continuing on to the even more significant unearthing of Mycenae.

Schliemann has his modern counterpart in Richard Hoagland and Joseph Davidovitz, and others who continue to seek answers to the mystery of the pyramids. His spirit of adventure in knowledge is present in the forty scientists who donated their time and enormous skills to solving the mystery of the shroud of Turin. Thor Heyerdahl's exhaustive and sometimes dangerous efforts to solve the puzzle of Polynesia and bring the human family closer together would undoubtedly bring praise from Schliemann and others like him, who brave the world's scorn to seek knowledge and truth.

Copernicus and Galileo turned their back on the wisdom of the world to seek answers among the stars. The result was disastrous for them, but succeeding generations have benefited beyond measure. Today many investigators, such as Erich von Daniken and Zecharia Sitchin, are belittled and berated for suggesting there may yet be answers among the stars—answers to questions most of us are too timid to ask. Will these and others like them at some future time be hailed as the courageous leaders who took twentieth-century thought out of the parochialism of Earth and opened it up to the treasure of the universe?

And let's not forget Columbus and those intrepid men who agreed to sail with him into the uncharted and the unknown. Who among us can imagine the courage it must have taken to embark on such a journey into a trackless sea? Scholars, priests, and princes were certain they were sailing into everlasting oblivion. Instead they sailed into undying fame.

Did it take less courage for Thor Heyerdahl and a

handful of scientists to launch themselves into the open Pacific Ocean in a boat made of reeds, just to solve the mystery of how people might have gotten from one place to another? Like Columbus and his crew, they deserve the world's gratitude.

The point of all of this, of course, is that mysteries have always been with us, and happily there have always been those who were willing to pay whatever price was necessary to solve them. The mysteries that remain today are no less intriguing than those of the past—indeed, in many cases they are the same. Every generation in recorded history has wondered at the mystery of the pyramids. They remain today as great an enigma as ever, and finding an answer to this mystery might enrich the world in ways yet undreamed of.

For over six hundred years the world generally has known of the shroud of Turin. Historians and biblical scholars trace its existence back to the time of the Roman crucifixions in Old Jerusalem. If modern scientists can somehow prove that it is in fact the burial shroud of Jesus Christ, the implications for this world—and the next—are enormous. Is it worth the effort to explore this mystery? I believe it is.

What do you think?

As I mentioned at the beginning of this book, the mysteries we have touched upon here are only the tip of the iceberg (or pyramid, if you prefer); there are literally hundreds more. All of them, in one way or another, bear upon the history of this planet and therefore upon our lives.

Over ten thousand years ago, ice-age hunters covered the walls and ceilings of caves all over Spain and France with lively paintings. Why? The Mycenaeans of

Greece apparently created enormous wealth in a very short span of time. How? The Etruscans of Italy, an apparently strong and civilized culture, were completely destroyed. What happened? In the village of Le Menec in Brittany, row upon row of towering rocks, twenty-five hundred of them, march across the landscape in detailed alignment. Who put them there? For what purpose? Huge stone pillars holding up the roof of a tomb on the island of Gavrinis, near Brittany, are literally covered with swirling lines, expertly carved by someone over five thousand years ago. Are they mere decoration? Do they contain a message? In Scotland a number of stone balls have been found, three inches in diameter and each one expertly carved with intricate patterns. What could they have possibly been used for?[187]

The list is endless. But, then, so is the joy of discovery. So long as there are mysteries to explore, there are opportunities to grow. Too often, I have found, people shy away from the unknown simply because it is unknown. I must confess I have never understood that attitude. Nothing engages my attention like finding out that there is still another strange mystery lurking in the shadows of our history. When I hear someone say that ninety-five percent of all UFO sightings have been proven to be false, easily explained, or a hoax, my attention is immediately drawn to that other five percent. What were they? Why can't we explain them? How many UFOs does it take to make up five percent of the total? And away we go down another mysterious road.

To me that is the "natural" response, and I'm always a little bit surprised at people who can look at the

[187] *National Geographic Society,* Mysteries of the Ancient World.

ninety-five percent and believe the mystery is solved. Not only do they miss the point, they miss the thrill of the unknown and the joy of discovery.

Which reminds me, at the beginning of this book I promised to take you on a journey into the mysterious and unknown with just a few stops along the way to kind of let you catch your breath and examine some of the evidence that has been uncovered. I hope you found the trip both enjoyable and enlightening. That was, after all, the purpose of writing the book.

One day, while working in his laboratory, Thomas Edison ignited a spark of electricity in a vacuum. How could that be, he wondered, and what would be the result if he could not only reproduce it but *sustain* it?

Completely absorbed in this mystery, Edison searched night and day for some filament that would burn, like Moses' burning bush, without being consumed. Element after element was tried, but nothing worked. But still he kept at it. He was reaching for no less a goal than the illumination of the world.

As everyone knows, after hundreds of hours and as many tries, he succeeded, and the incandescent light became a reality. It did, in fact, illuminate the world and, indeed, still does.

I hope that somewhere in these pages we lit a spark. I hope you have found at least some small measure of fascination with these mysteries and will continue to seek answers and perhaps even provide a few of your own. Schliemann, remember, was only a businessman who enjoyed Greek poetry when he felt the spark that led him to the discovery of Mycenae and Troy.

If your mind has been opened to the possibilities

that are represented by the strange and mysterious, you may find, as I have, that the richness of life is not in what you know, but in all the things you have yet to discover.

INDEX